W9-ANN-106

Mozambique: the Troubled Transition

Mozambique:
the Troubled Transition

FROM SOCIALIST CONSTRUCTION TO
FREE MARKET CAPITALISM

Hans Abrahamsson and
Anders Nilsson

Translated by
Mary Dally

Zed Books
LONDON AND NEW JERSEY

Mozambique: The Troubled Transition was first published by
Zed Books Ltd, 7 Cynthia Street, London N1 9JF, UK,
and 165 First Avenue, Atlantic Highlands, New Jersey
07716, USA, and in southern Africa (Angola, Botswana,
Lesotho, Malawi, Mozambique, Namibia, South Africa,
Swaziland, Zambia, Zimbabwe) by Southern Africa
Political Economy Series (SAPES), 50–53 van Riebeeck
House, 14 Loop Street, Cape Town, South Africa, in
1995.

Cover designed by Andrew Corbett.
Map of Mozambique reproduced from *Africa Recovery* by
kind permission of United Nations, Africa Recovery.

Set in Monotype Baskerville by Ewan Smith, London.
Printed and bound in the United Kingdom by
Biddles Ltd, Guildford and King's Lynn.

A catalogue record for this book is available from the
British Library.

US CIP data is available from the Library of Congress.

ISBN 1 85649 323 7 cased
ISBN 1 85649 324 5 limp

Contents

Figures

Tables

Abbreviations and Acronyms

ANC	African National Congress
CARE	Concerned Americans for the Reconstruction of Europe
CENE	Comissão Executiva Nacional de Emergência
CNE	Comissão Nacional das Eleições (National Elections Committee)
Comecon	Council for Mutual Economic Aid (Soviet-aligned communist countries)
CONSAS	Constellation of Southern African States
DPCCN	Departamento para a Prevenção e Combate às Calamidades Naturais
FFEM	Free Foreign Exchange Market
Frelimo	Frente de Libertação de Moçambique
IBRD	International Bank for Reconstruction and Development
IDA	International Development Association
IFI	international finance institutions
IMF	International Monetary Fund
ISRI	Instituto Superior de Relações Internacionais
MNR	Mozambique National Resistance
MPLA	Movimento Popular de Libertacão de Angola
NATO	North Atlantic Treaty Organization
NGO	non-governmental organisation
OECD	Organization for Economic Cooperation and Development
NIC	newly industrialising country
OPEC	Organisation of Petroleum Exporting Countries
PADRIGU	Peace and Development Research Institute, Gothemburg University
Renamo	Resistência Nacional Moçambicana
SADC	Southern Africa Development Community

SADCC	Southern Africa Development Coordination Conference
SADF	South African Defence Force
STAE	Technical Secretariat for Electoral Administration (Secretariado Técnico da Administração Eleitoral)
SWAPO	South-West Africa People's Organization
UDENAMO	União Democrática Nacional de Moçambique
UNDP	United Nations Development Programme
UNITA	União Nacional para a Independência Total de Angola
UNOMOZ	UN organisation monitoring the Mozambican peace process
ZANLA	Zimbabwe African National Liberation Army
ZANU	Zimbabwe African National Union
ZAPU	Zimbabwe African People's Union

Key Data 1993

Area	799,380 km²
Population	15.5 million
of which:	
rural	60%
urban	30%
Refugees within and	
outside the country	10%
Population growth	2.7%
Literacy	38%
Gross national product	$94/capita
of which:	
agriculture	26%
industry	14%
construction	11%
transport	15%
trade/other	34%
Growth in GDP	19.2%
Annual 1987–93	4.2%
Foreign trade	
Balance of trade	-$823 million
Exports	$132 million
Imports	$955 million
Leading exports	Shrimps 52%
	Cashew nuts 6%
	Cotton 8%

Export destinations (1992)   OECD 66%
                             Europe 44%
                             USA 13%
                             Japan 9%
                             South Africa 16%
                             Zimbabwe 6%

Leading imports (1990)   Food products 30%
                             Machinery and equipment 23%
                             Raw material and crude oil 29%
                             Spare parts 9%
                             Non-durable consumer goods 9%

Import sources (1989)   OECD 50%
                             Europe, West and East, 50%
                             South Africa 23%
                             USA 7%
                             Zimbabwe 3%

International debt burden $5 billion
In relation to GDP   300%
Contracted debt service   140%
Debt service paid   20%

Lenders   OECD 41%
                             non-OECD 11%
                             OPEC 9%
                             former Eastern bloc 27%
                             multilateral 20%

Aid (1992) $950 million
Important donors   Sweden 11%
                             EU 9%
                             Italy 8%

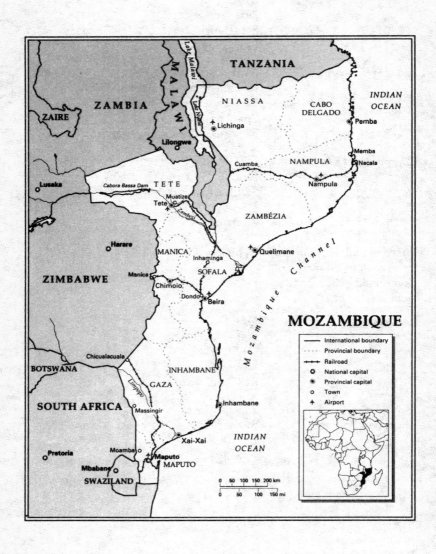

ZAIRE

ZAMBIA

MALAWI

Lake Malawi

Lake Niassa

TANZANIA

NIASSA

CABO
DELGADO

INDIAN
OCEAN

Lichinga

Pemba

Lilongwe

Lusaka

Cabora Bassa Dam

TETE

Muatize

Tete

Zambezi

Cuamba

NAMPULA

Nampula

Membа
Nacala

ZAMBÉZIA

Harare

MANICA

Inhaminga

Quelimane

Mozambique Channel

ZIMBABWE

Manica

Chimoio

Dondo

SOFALA

Beira

MOZAMBIQUE

International boundary
Provincial boundary
Railroad
National capital
Provincial capital
Town
Airport

Chicualacuala

BOTSWANA

INHAMBANE

GAZA

Limpopo

SOUTH AFRICA

Massingir

Inhambane

INDIAN
OCEAN

Pretoria

Moamba

Xai-Xai

Mbabane

Maputo

MAPUTO

SWAZILAND

0   50 100 150 200 km

0   50   100   150 mi

Foreword

New global geopolitical realities in the post-Cold War era, decreased regional tensions following the emergence of the majority-ruled South Africa and the peace accord in Mozambique, followed by the first multi-party elections, constitute the imperative force for publishing this book. The interdisciplinary and multi-level analysis of the Mozambican development history since independence presented in this volume aims at contributing to our understanding of some of the implications of these changes for the Mozambican people. The content of the book has been shaped by three different events during the last fifteen years.

The first was that throughout the 1980s the two of us were deeply engaged in Mozambique's development problematic as aid workers and researchers. The second was that the ten-year period during which we worked in Mozambique came to be a turning point in Southern African history, in the sense that the apartheid system in South Africa went through its most aggressive phase – a policy of destabilisation which was waged against the majority-ruled neighbouring countries – at the same time as the system's own development evolved closer to fundamental change. The third event was that during the same period a new research institution was built up at the University of Gothenburg, focusing on questions of peace and development . This research institution, PADRIGU, had a decisive influence on our methods of systemising our experiences from the field and analysing our empirical data, and on our attempt to describe the development history of a country by means of an interdisciplinary effort.

During our years in Mozambique we were able, in our roles as participants and actors in Mozambique's development, to observe at close quarters the political, economic and social changes the country was undergoing. At the beginning of the 1980s we shared Frelimo's vision of independent socialist development. We tried to the best of our ability to work within the public institutions and frameworks that were formed in order to implement this strategy. Today we know that Frelimo's development strategy could not be implemented. The reasons for this can be found in both internal and external factors, and our own perspective on this has changed over time. Until 1985 we were both ardent advocates of the external line of explanation, not least because the events we were able to observe at close quarters involved activities where there was a high international presence. Our view was affected by both the history and the course of the war, and the organisation of international disaster relief to Mozambique. Towards the end of the 1980s our perspective shifted so that internal factors came to occupy a more important position in the analysis.

In the problem-orientated, normative and interdisciplinary research tradition which Padrigu has since offered us, we have tried to develop a comprehensive view of why things happened as they did in the Mozambican development strategy and what could be done in order to initiate a sustainable peace and development process in the country. This comprehensive view involves all five research areas that constitute Padrigu's research programme.

The future role of Mozambique and Southern Africa in the globalised world market links up with Padrigu's theoretical work on international political economy. The growing problem of legitimacy for the nation state project, not only in Africa, together with the increasing globalisation of production and finance and counteracting tendencies to strengthen regionalisation in different parts of the world, raises the question of the relevancy of national development strategies for solving the problems which Third World countries will experience during the coming century. Unsuccessful development programmes and nation-building projects tend to generate ethnic or sub-national opposition, which in turn can develop into open conflicts. Deep-rooted ethnic or sub-national conflicts impose specific demands on alternative approaches to conflict resolutions, which are a growing part of Padrigu's field of research. Taken together this leads towards research where a holistic understanding of the problems of development is combined with an attempt to formulate alternative strategies and to find genuine social carriers of the development's long-term goals of development.

The fact that we have been active within Swedish aid cooperation with Mozambique has not only allowed collection of the empirical data for this study, but has also made large parts of the financing, not least the required translation to Portuguese patiently carried out by Dulce Leiria, possible. Many people in Mozambique and Sweden have contributed to our understanding of the development history of Mozambique. It would take too long to enumerate everybody. However, two people have made a particular contribution to our access to the different environments, where we acquired much of our knowledge: José Trindade and Carlos Cardoso.

Without Björn Hettne, there would be no Padrigu, whose colleagues patiently tried to help us, not just with elucidating our experiences, which our Mozambican fellow-workers shared with us, but also with improving our methods of description and our conceptual definitions.

Thanks to the reference group to which we linked ourselves, consisting of researchers and aid administrators in Sweden and in Mozambique, the quality of our work was continuously exposed to critical examination. Especially valuable has been our close cooperation with the Mozambique research institute ISRI (Instituto Superior de Relações Internacionais) and their ability to organise well-attended and very instructive seminar discussions concurrently with the results of the study being presented to a Mozambican readership. A final big thankyou to Eva Lannö and Gunilla Åkesson, who lived with our thoughts for several years and who, drawing on their own experiences, constantly questioned our findings and interpretations.

Through our study of why things happened as they did, we hope to be able to make a small contribution to the continuing discussion on the possibilities for formulating a future development strategy. Behind this hope lies our keen desire to contribute to reshaping social stability and long-term survival for a troubled rural population.

Gothenburg, December 1994

Hans Abrahamsson
Anders Nilsson

Introduction

The problem

Independence for Mozambique and the other Portuguese colonies in 1974–75 meant that the last colonial war in sub-Saharan Africa was ended. Portugal's resistance to the struggle for political and economic independence in Africa was the fundamental reason that the war of liberation broke out at the beginning of the 1960s; its energetic attempt to defeat the nationalist movements militarily prolonged the war and contributed to the radicalisation of the movements. In a struggle where the opponents were not willing to cede anything, a political will to take all developed.

The late decolonisation in Mozambique and Angola coincided with a growing domestic and international resistance to the apartheid system in South Africa. The trend of events during the period 1974–76 polarised Southern Africa around two questions: apartheid and the inclusion of the region's pattern of discord in the global East–West conflict. On the one hand there were the apartheid regime in South Africa and Ian Smith's illegal regime in Rhodesia; together these would witness how ever more countries in the region were changing over to black majority rule, which in many cases also represented radical development strategies that looked as though they could provide models for development in South Africa. On the other hand were the new governments in the region which, apart from their radicalism, also expressed an intention of providing support for the ZANU and ZAPU liberation movements in Rhodesia, for SWAPO in Namibia and for the ANC in South Africa.

This is a very rough outline of the political situation in the region of Southern Africa when the Frelimo government in Mozambique formulated its development strategy, its vision for the future. Through forced modernisation, in the form of a radical social transformation of the rural areas and rapid industrialisation, the pattern of under-development would be broken within ten years. This exceptionally ambitious goal was formulated in a regional environment that was characterised by a growing political and military polarisation.

1

Today, 20 years later, Mozambique is literally in ruins. At least a million people have died in war and famine disasters, a third of the population have recently resettled after years as refugees in neighbouring countries and the gross national product per capita has fallen below $100. Mozambique is today one of the world's poorest and most in-debted countries. Large parts of the physical, social and commercial infrastructure of the rural areas have been destroyed by the war. According to calculations made by the UN, the value of the destruction corresponds to 250 years of export revenues and is fifty times greater than annual aid to the country.

The focus of this study is the marked difference between vision and reality, between what the country's leaders said they wanted and the concrete result of their efforts. This broad definition of the problem area accommodates two different aspects, which are interwoven when considered in the study. One concerns our attempt to understand why and how this chasm between vision and reality formed. The other concerns how one investigates and describes such a process.

The aim

One of our starting points at the beginning of the 1980s was the then prevailing opinion that a national development strategy could be de-veloped and implemented in relative isolation from the world. It is important to stress *relative* isolation, because on Mozambique's part it was not a question of applying the Soviet strategy that it was possible to build 'socialism in a single country', although Mozambique's govern-ment saw the development strategy as a matter whose implementation would mainly be based on domestic resources, both material and human. However, this did not mean that the significance of international aid was minimised. On the contrary, it was regarded as essential to bring about the necessary investments for modernisation of agriculture, industrialisation and infrastructure. The relative isolation was evident mainly in that political and economic analysis, identification of needs and planning for implementation of the development policy were limited to the national level and to the central agencies of the state apparatus.

This view had two dimensions. One was a belief that a national development policy was mainly a national matter, which implied an underestimation of the aggravating circumstances which could be found in both the international and regional environments. The other was the central support surrounding a functional development principle. This meant that circumstances and conditions which at sub-national level made implementation of the development strategy more difficult were either not detected at all or were interpreted incorrectly.

It was obvious at an early stage to those who studied developments

in Southern Africa and Mozambique that many of the difficulties
encountered by development workers in Mozambique were of international origin. This led to a discussion on whether internal or external
influencing factors were the most important. Early studies on Mozambique tended towards the external line of explanation, not least because
the course of the war was so clearly linked to the South African policy
of destabilisation in the whole region. Towards the end of the 1980s,
studies were first presented that explained the sub-national limits which
had been and still were a serious obstacle to the implementation of the
development strategy. These later studies were often local field studies,
hence the possibility of making generalisations was limited.

During the ten-year period in which we have taken part in work on
Mozambique's development problem, our method of approaching questions of development has changed in at least two ways. The first change
means that previous conceptual limitations to the national perspective
were eliminated by including sub-national factors in the analysis of the
development problem. For this reason it became even more important
to discuss questions concerning political legitimacy, ethnicity and the
significance of traditional society in the development process.

The second change means that the definition of external factors
behind the development problem within a country was also broadened.
As a consequence of the continuing internationalisation process and
ever stronger global influence, a state has ever more limited opportunities at national level for economic management and development
planning.

It therefore became a question of trying to expand the analysis of
development history from prioritising the national anchoring of development strategies, to focusing on the tensions which arise through
reciprocal connections between local, national, regional and international levels. With reference to these tensions, it appears to be a
question of understanding the extent to which the national level can
resist and function as a filter, in order to absorb and render harmless
undesirable external influences at national and local levels.

Due to the intensification of internationalisation, the analysis of the
external factors behind Mozambique's problem can no longer be limited
to the region of Southern Africa and the relationship with South Africa.
It has become necessary to include the global political and economic
changes which have made themselves felt, directly or indirectly, at
national and sub-national levels. At the same time it has become ever
more necessary to find forms and a model in order to be able to
systematise the empirical material required for such an increasingly
broader effort. The aim of the present study is therefore to abandon
the discussion about the respective significance of external and internal
factors. It tries to map and analyse how the combined strength of

global changes over the period, in reciprocal interaction with both regional and sub-national factors, has affected both the formulation of Mozambique's development strategy and its implementation. Thus the study also aims to try and form a model within which a development history can be described in a way that takes into consideration the complex network of relationships between the internal and external factors that interacted over time.

Method and sources

This study is mainly an empirical study, whose concrete field experiences are based on field work in Mozambique during the period 1977–94. The field work which forms the basis of this study is of three different types.

The *first* type concerns technical assistance in the form of active participation in the Mozambican state's efforts to implement its development strategy. This involved, *inter alia*, participation in planning and implementation of activities in different sectors of society, which included analytical work regarding questions of policy. Hence many extensive journeys were undertaken within the country and formed an integral part of data collection for this study. Although the security situaton later became worse as the war spread and travel in rural areas became more difficult, it was possible to visit the majority of Mozambique's 131 districts. The purpose of these journeys can be summarised as the acquisition of knowledge of local conditions, follow-up and monitoring of the effects of central measures, and training of local employees. They thus played a role in the flow of information between local and central levels. This type of field work represents about a hundred such journeys out into the rural areas, each varying in duration between one week and one month.

The main 'work tool' was conversations with people of differing status and from different social classes: officials and representatives of local, provincial or central authorities, as well as different types of craftsmen, businessmen, larger farmers, entrepreneurs within fishing, small-scale industry and transport, soldiers and local journalists. A very large number were peasants, labourers, internal refugees and other groups from the rural population. The working language was usually Portuguese, with fellow workers interpreting from the local languages of the different provinces. Approximately 2,000 people contributed in this way to the collection of knowledge for this study. The results from such trips were most often reported in the form of lectures at the respective place of work. Occasionally shorter travel reports or other accounts were written, which were not kept systematically. As experience was added to experience, the knowledge to which this work gave rise was internalised by the present authors. Today this knowledge forms the basis for the description and analysis of development in Mozambique.

The *second* type of field study is more goal-directed investigative work into different aspects of Mozambique's development. The method mainly used was structured interviews, in combination with our own observations together with field visits and studies of project documents and earlier investigation material.

The *third* type of field study consists of as yet incomplete interview research into the development, progress and consequences of the war in the Homoíne district, in Inhambane province. This work has been carried out with the aid of structured interviews with internal refugees and former participants in Renamo's armed groups.

Literature

Few books or articles from the period before independence have dealt separately with Mozambique. Most of them had the main intention of shedding light on the Portuguese colonial system.[1]

Many of the standard works about Mozambique's economic and political development after 1975 have a basically positive attitude and express solidarity with Frelimo's vision of socialist development. The authors have most often concurred with the modernisation efforts of the Frelimo leadership. This fact, together with the South African military destabilisation so brutally and concretely destroying the conditions for implementation of the development strategy, meant that the majority of authors saw Mozambique's development problem as resulting from the great impact of external factors.[2]

Several standard works have held a discussion on the role of internal factors and the setbacks which the unilateral direction of the development strategy for modernisation and development entailed. However, these analyses are always based on Western perspectives and explanation models, which were also part of the Frelimo élite's intellectual luggage.

Few published books, papers or articles deal with principles of legitimacy, ethnicity or the role of traditional society and their impact on society's modern sphere.[3] Analyses of the characteristics of African cultural and rural realities in Mozambique have been few and far between. These questions became important only at the end of the 1980s, primarily through investigations carried out by Christian Geffray and Mogens Pedersen in Nampula province.[4]

Regarding the war, most descriptions have focused on the extreme violence and the external set-up behind Renamo. Renamo's history has been written by both its creators[5] and those who have been made morally and politically indignant by the nature of the war.[6] With a couple of exceptions there is no literature positively describing Renamo's activities in rural areas.[7]

Theoretical approach

In order to study a national development strategy one can choose to arrange the analysis at different levels of generalisation. The level of generalisation that we have chosen should be seen against the background of the methodological work which began to develop as a result of our experiences in the field. It can be characterised as a development history description, where the possibilities for generalisation are few and where the conclusions are valid only for the situation researched and only for the historical context in which the study took place. It is thus the specific times and places that determine the formulation, implementation and result of the research strategy as well as the outcome of the development strategy. Any comparison with other strategies or with similar strategies in other contexts must be made at a higher level of generalisation, by defining indicators and constructing typologies.

Such a higher level of generalisation can be composed of comparative studies of countries or development strategies. Comparative studies with the breadth of empirical material that we have used run the risk of becoming very unwieldy and complex. In order to make them more manageable, such studies probably require extensive work on typologising or designing comparative indicators. As regards the degree of generalisation, it should probably possess greater similarities with 'Middle Range' levels than with an empirical comparative study.

Another alternative would be the so-called 'Middle Range' level. Work on attempts to generalise, based on experiences from a country or a group of countries, falls within such a perspective. It may be relevant to take up certain components in one or more types of strategy or to classify different development strategies in typologies for analytical purposes. These can then be compared with regard to results or outcomes in accordance with certain indicators.[8]

A further level of method of generalisation would be to link up with some of the 'great theories' in the historical-sociological tradition. An approach that should present itself immediately is the question of whether it is possible at all for Western concepts of modernisation to root themselves in Africa or Mozambique. However, it would need far more extensive work than is represented by our limited empirical material in order to become relevant.

The choice of level of generalisation is connected with both the multiplicity of information relevant to an analysis of the complex reality in Southern Africa, and the method selected to systemise that information. For example, it would not be manageable to perform comparative analyses with such a large number of indicators as would be required in order to preserve the breadth of the empirical material. The more factors, dimensions and levels taken into consideration, the more a historical approach must be adopted. This work should therefore be seen as a development history description of a country's concrete experiences during the period and within the framework of a given historical context.

Our contribution to the discussion on the study about development strategies will therefore consist of our attempt to describe both horizontal and vertical connections between different factors which over the period affect the implementation of a nationally formulated development strategy. It is our hope that this 'model in the making' will come to be used for similar specific development history studies of other countries.

Points of departure and limitations of the study

The study takes as one of its three starting points the idea that a development strategy cannot be perceived as a free choice, in the sense that a government, for example at the time of a country's political independence, can freely choose between a number of different development alternatives.

In the case of Mozambique, the radical socialist-orientated strategy should rather be understood as a historical continuation process, characterised by both the colonial era and the forms of the war of liberation. The forms of organisation in the liberated areas built on a high degree of mobilisation and an active participation on the part of the peasants. At the same time Western democracies resisted the liberation of the country through their support for the Portuguese fascist regime and the apartheid regime in South Africa. Mozambique was therefore more or less forced into the arms of the Eastern bloc, which had provided the necessary military support for the liberation struggle.

The second starting point for the study is that the implementation of a development strategy is not a socially neutral process. It affects, and is affected by, the development of the social power structure at local level. A thorough modernisation strategy requires a breakdown not just of the institutions of the colonial state but also of the traditional social structure which characterised the rural areas. This proved difficult to implement in practice and it may be questioned later whether it was desirable.

The third starting point is that both the direction and implementation of a national development strategy are influenced to a high degree by international and macro-regional[9] conditions. At the time of Mozambique's independence the international political climate allowed some

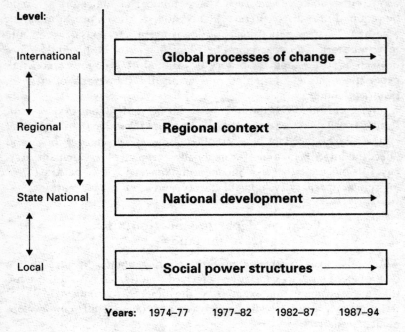

Figure 1 Starting points of the study

room for manoeuvre for the newly installed government, partly as a result of President Carter's policy of détente and the initial attitude of the apartheid regime under Prime Minister Vorster. Later on the international climates changed. During the first half of the 1980s the more liberal policy of détente was replaced by a more confrontational policy and an intensified East–West conflict.

In South Africa the 'total strategy' came to be fully applied in an attempt to maintain the country's regional dominance. Political developments in Eastern Europe during the second half of the 1980s further changed conditions for the individual countries in Southern Africa, their national policies and economic development.

In Figure 1 an attempt is made to illustrate our starting points. On each and every level of analysis (international, regional, national and local), that we describe, the political and economic situation changed over the period. This is illustrated by the horizontal arrows. At the same time the changes at each level interlock and affect each other, through constant interaction between the different levels. This is illustrated by the vertical arrows.

The development of the strategy itself and its implementation over the period is illustrated in the figure through the chronological interaction in the box at state/national level. In the study there is also an emphasis on describing the content of the boxes at national and local levels. As a background, the content and changes over the period in the boxes at international and regional levels will also be described, but in a considerably more general and summarised manner.

As is evident from the figure's vertical links, we also try to describe the connections between the different levels. We will thus show in what way the pattern of change formed over the period at international, regional and local levels contributed to changing the internal power base, the content of the strategy and the conditions for its implementation.

The present study restricts itself to indicating, on the basis of our empirical experiences, connections between the different levels and discussing the different channels and methods through which these connections operate. No attempt is made to measure the strength of the different connections or to deduce which factors have had the greatest influence on the trend of events. Therefore the arrows in the figures should be seen as symbols for the interaction between levels rather than illustrations of demonstrable causal connections. It is not possible clearly to distinguish external factors from internal ones. They interlock at different levels and interact with each other over the period.

The study further restricts itself to studying developments during the period 1974–94. Even if it is not meaningful to subdivide the presentation according to different time points, because developments at different levels interlock with each other at different times, for the sake of readability we have tried to divide our empirical material into two main periods. The first covers the period from independence in the middle of the 1970s and the following ten years. During this time the Mozambican development vision was formulated, the strategy was initiated and a series of external and internal factors combined to bring it down. The second covers the period thereafter, i.e. from the middle of the 1980s to the present. This period is characterised by the growth of a radically different development strategy and the initiation of an economic and political process of transition, on whose final destination it is still too early to comment.

The study's model and organisation

In the present development history analysis we make a gradual attempt to develop the model in Figure 1 and to weave a uniting web which can convey a picture of the interaction between the horizontal and vertical links. The guiding thread is composed of the course of events over the period at national level.

Against the background of the study's first and second starting points,

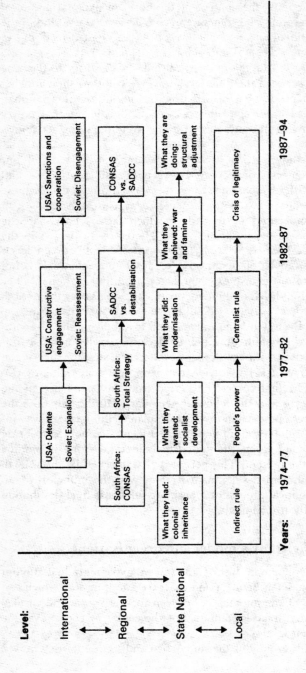

Figure 2 Model of the present study

Level:				
International	USA: Détente Soviet: Expansion	USA: Constructive engagement Soviet: Reassessment		USA: Sanctions and cooperation Soviet: Disengagement
Regional	South Africa: CONSAS	South Africa: Total Strategy	SADCC vs. destabilisation	CONSAS vs. SADCC
State National	What they had: colonial inheritance	What they wanted: socialist development	What they did: modernisation	What they achieved: war and famine	What they are doing: structural adjustment
Local	Indirect rule	People's power	Centralist rule		Crisis of legitimacy
Years:	1974–77	1977–82	1982–87	1987–94

Note: There are various reasons for describing the chain of developments in terms of what 'they' had, wanted, etc. 'They' in this context means primarily Frelimo's political leadership. In spite of the fact that Frelimo's decision-making, ever since the liberation struggle, has been guided by a principle of consensus, decisions 'they' took at central level were not necessarily implemented in reality at provincial or local level. There, 'they' had partly different interests and obligations, not least as a consequence of the actual power structure.

i.e. the colonial inheritance and the development and influences of the social power structure, the first chapters analyse the growth of the development strategy, its direction and change over the period.

As is clear from Figure 2, we will do this by first subdividing the horizontal box at national level into a number of different smaller boxes for different time periods and describe their horizontal interaction. Thereafter we will also subdivide the horizontal boxes at international and regional levels and describe their development as well as their horizontal and vertical mutual interaction.

Chapter 1 deals with the background to and formulation of the country's development strategy. Chapter 2 illustrates the fact that both the direction and the implementation of a national development strategy over the period was affected by international and regional conditions in a complex interaction. In Chapter 3 the economic results and social and political consequences, to which the development strategy gave rise, are then presented.

Chapters 4 and 5 provide a description of the interaction between horizontal and vertical development and analyses how different factors at international, regional, national and local level affected implementation of the Mozambican development strategy, as well as the current political and economic reorientation.

The subsequent chapters of the study discuss the measures taken in order to overcome the country's economic and political difficulties.

In Chapter 6, the formulation and direction of the economic recovery programme is discussed, as well as the visible results achieved up to the present. In Chapter 7, the role of aid in the formulation and implementation of the programme is analysed. Chapter 8 analyses the problems which the present economic and political development has created for the growth of a functioning state-market relationship, while Chapter 9 discusses the prerequisites for a Western-type democracy in an African context.

In the final chapters a normative discussion is initiated about the different scenarios for the future which may be perceived. Which of these scenarios may become reality, if any, it is naturally not possible to predict. The future will probably be characterised by a combination of the several scenarios outlined. As is clear from Figure 3, developments at international and regional level are of decisive significance for the country's future and for the ability of its government to meet new challenges such as will be entailed by socio-political and economic developments at local level.

In Chapter 10, the probable and desirable directions of the current transition process are analysed. Against this background Chapter 11 includes a normative discussion on which prerequisites and conditions exist for a long-term sustainable development in the country.

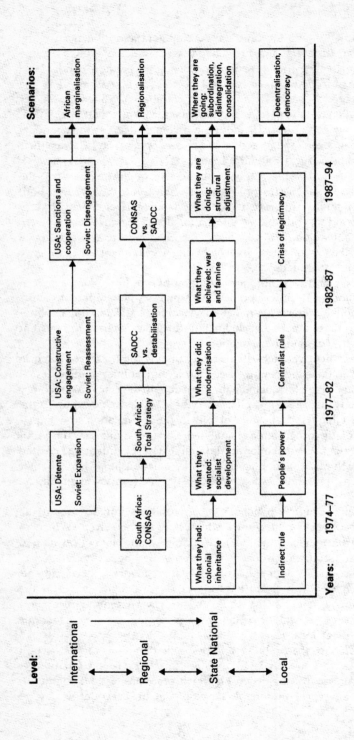

Figure 3 International and regional developments

Note: As Figure 2

Instead of a conclusion

The simplification of reality, which should mean simply entering all historical processes into boxes, even if at different levels, naturally has serious limitations. The result risks becoming a too static description of a historical development. In this work we have attempted to remedy this by also drawing attention to the connection between events and the historical processes described in the boxes at different levels.

In a final section we will attempt to elucidate parts of the pattern for this complex web of different factors in combination which grew from the different sections of the study and which reflect important fragments of the Mozambican history of development.

We will attempt to do this by briefly summarising several of the vertical and horizontal interactions discussed and enlarging earlier figures with the aid of a number of arrows which illustrate these inter-actions within and between different levels. The concluding text there-fore refers constantly to the numbering of the arrows in Figure 4. As indicated previously, it is not the intention of the work to demonstrate causality or to measure the strength of the different connections found. With the support of the figure, we wish rather to demonstrate the complexity and difficulty of trying to concretise and illustrate such interactions.

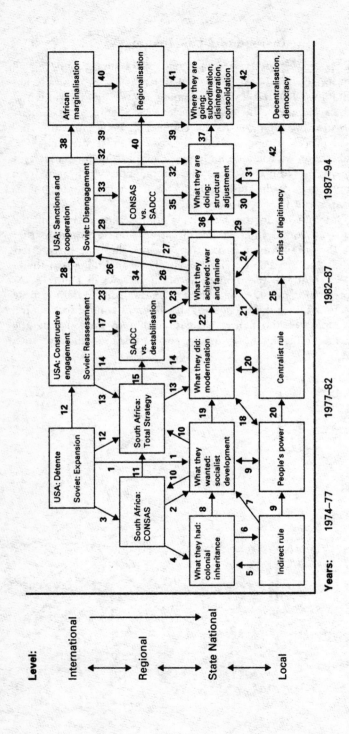

Figure 4 Interactions between different levels

Note: As Figure 2

Colonial Legacy: From Shopkeeper Colonialism to Nation-state Building

Colonialism and anti-colonial resistance

The arrival of the Portuguese on Mozambique Island in 1498 meant little or nothing to the Bantu people, who lived in the eastern African interior. For a long time, with few exceptions, the Portuguese presence was limited to a few strongholds along the coast. The main aim of this presence was to create bases for the growing maritime trade between Europe and Asia. East Africa's contribution to this trade consisted mainly of gold and ivory. A well-developed trading system linked the elephant hunters and gold producers of the interior with coastal buyers.[10]

During the period of the arrival of the Portuguese a political process for change took place in the area. The large state of Zimbabwe was well on the way to disintegration, at the same time as a new empire – Monomotapa – was growing, whose influence gradually came to stretch from the Zambezi river in the north to the Limpopo in the south, and from the Kalahari desert in the west to the Indian Ocean in the east. North of the Zambezi river the Marave empire developed in what is now Malawi.

From the end of the eighteenth-century, slaves became the dominant commodity in the region. The French sugar planters on the islands of Reunião and Bourbon in the Indian Ocean created a local demand for slaves. It is estimated that approximately one million slaves were shipped out from Mozambique during the nineteenth-century.[11] The slave trade continued until the end of the century. The slave trade also created cleavages within African society: between clans and tribes which engaged as intermediaries in hunting and trading, and those sold as slaves. These cleavages have been part and parcel of local and regional oral history and consciousness for centuries, in the north affecting the homo-geneity of the population and in the south contributing to the animosity created by the Nguni invasion and the subsequent creation of the Gaza empire of the nineteenth century.

The slave trade had devastating consequences. The hunt for slaves destroyed the existing village structure and forced the population out into new settlement patterns. In order to escape the slave hunters, the population dispersed over large areas, often far from the fertile river valleys and rainy high plateaus. At the end of the nineteenth century Portuguese influence in so-called Portuguese East Africa was still very limited. In practice the whole territory was controlled by a couple of African state formations, which had emerged strong from the slave trade period. The Portuguese were isolated in a few coastal locations.

In the north, Portuguese influence was outflanked by cooperation between local rulers of African or Swahili origin and international slave traders. The local kingdoms, which had converted to Islam, were able to organise armies, which proved superior to the Portuguese in several military confrontations.

During the nineteenth century the Gaza empire established a strong position for itself in the south. It had been formed by the Nguni-speaking people who, at the beginning of the century had moved from South Africa to southern Mozambique. From there they expanded northwards and quickly became a dominant power in large parts of the area that Portugal regarded as being its own. The expansion of the Gaza empire eventually reached the southern bank of the Zambezi river. Within the territory which today constitutes Mozambique, the Gaza empire came to rule mainly the same area as the former Mono-motapa.[12]

The centre of power moves southwards

Mozambique's modern history begins towards the end of the nineteenth-century, when the region's economic centre moved from northern Mozambique to the south. The slave trade period was over and Portu-gual had neither the political nor the economic capacity to control its colony territorially. The Portuguese officials and soldiers in the colony acted with great independence in relation to the government in Portu-gal, and mainly occupied themselves with building up their own private wealth.

Diamonds and gold were discovered in South Africa. The growing economic activity in Transvaal created a need for a harbour in the then Lourenço Marques (now Maputo), and the railway from Transvaal was completed in 1894.[13] The movement of the capital from Mozam-bique Island to Lourenço Marques at the turn of the century marked a decisive shift of power from the north to the south in the area that would become Mozambique. South Africa developed as a regional great power.

At the same time as these developments, there were negotiations between Europe's colonial powers on how Africa should be divided between them. One of the alternatives at the Berlin conference of 1884–85 was that Portuguese East Africa should be divided into three parts. The north would be allocated to Germany to be put together with Tanganyika, and the centre would be allocated to British interests to be coordinated with Rhodesia and Nyasaland (now Malawi). Southern Mozambique would be a South African area of interest. However, in this process Portugal managed to exploit antagonisms between the colonial powers and to carry through its 'historical right' to Mozambique.

It was actually more than 25 years after the Berlin conference that Portugal managed to assert political and military control over Mozambique. The main, but far from only, military resistance came from the Gaza empire. Its resistance was not just a spontaneous struggle with bows and spears, but was also built on international contacts and diplomacy. Mineral concessions, for example, were assigned to Cecil Rhodes, in the expectation of British support against Portugal.[14]

The Gaza empire's last emperor, Gungunhana, had an army which managed in several battles to defeat or withstand Portuguese troops. A large part of the army was made up of soldiers recruited in the occupied areas of the empire, in both southern and central Mozambique. The Gaza empire fell when Gungunhana was taken prisoner and deported to the Azores in 1895. In other parts of the country different local rulers kept up the resistance to Portuguese penetration, but they never managed to coordinate their actions.

A colonial service economy

Until the 1930s, as a consequence of Portugal's inadequate political and economic strength, economic exploitation of Mozambique was dominated by non-Portuguese companies. These established their own administration over the territories they were allocated through concessions, mainly in the central and northern parts of the country. Portugal seized some of the tax paid by the population to the companies.[15]

In southern Mozambique recruitment for migrant work in South Africa grew. As early as 1912 more than 90,000 miners had been recruited to South Africa. Annual recruitment came to vary between 80,000 and 118,000 right up until Mozambique's independence in 1975.[16]

With the fascist takeover of power in Portugal in 1926, Portuguese colonial strategy changed. Contracts with concessionary companies were not renewed. Growing Portuguese industry needed better use of the colonies, above all as producers of raw materials. Mozambique's most important role in this strategy was to produce cotton for Portugal's textile industry and to be a market for textiles and wine from Portugal.[17]

In the 1930s Mozambique's economy acquired a pattern that lasted, more or less unchanged, until 1975. This pattern rested upon two sets of foundations. One was Mozambique's service function for other countries in the region, which had traditionally contributed about half of Mozambique's foreign revenues. Approximately a quarter came from migrant work in South Africa's mines and an equally large amount came from railway and port charges for the use by neighbouring countries of Mozambique's transport links for their foreign trade. The second foundation was the export of goods, which corresponded to the other half of foreign revenues. These goods consisted mainly of agricultural products in the form of plantation crops, such as sugar, tea and copra, as well as groundnuts, timber and, during the 1970s, shrimps.[18] Export production was based mainly on forced labour, where farming families could choose between either cultivating a certain area with cotton or the man being sent to do plantation or construction work for three months of the year.[19]

The modern consumer goods industry

During the 1960s the build-up began of what for Africa was a relatively extensive industrial sector. Thus in 1973 Mozambique was responsible for 4 per cent of the continent's total industrial production, while the country only had 2 per cent of the continent's population. In total the industrial sector employed approximately 100,000 people.[20] A large number of these were white workers.

Two-thirds of production was sold on the domestic market, mainly in order to satisfy the demand from the Portuguese population in the colony, while one-third was intended for export. Nevertheless, the industrial structure meant that certain important links were established between industry and agriculture. About half of the industrial production was dependent on local material supplies (food industry 40 per cent and the textile industry 14 per cent). The remaining industry sector was totally dependent on imported raw materials. Spare parts and other consumable supplies were imported mainly from South Africa.

The location of industry was characterised by a strong regional imbalance. The major part of the manufacturing industry was located in Maputo, and a lesser part in Beira. The exception was the processing industry, which was dependent on domestically produced raw materials and was located close to agricultural plantations, cultivation and timber areas. There was a high degree of concentration. Five per cent of industrial enterprises were responsible for over 40 per cent of total industrial production.

Dominance of subsistence agriculture

The majority of the country's area under cultivation is rainfall-dependent and is therefore extremely sensitive to climatic changes. The cultivable area amounts to 36 million hectares, of which approximately 2 million are suitable for irrigation. About 95 per cent of the utilised area has been requisitioned by slash-and-burning.[21]

The settlement pattern is sparse, partly as a result of the slave trade and partly because of slash-and-burn's great need for areas which periodically have to lie fallow.

During the colonial era, agriculture consisted mainly of plantation cultivation of export crops, local food production for the urban Portuguese population and the majority of the population's 'subsistence agriculture'. The plantations were mainly situated in the central areas of the country and they were followers of the concessionary companies. Local food production was largely supported by immigrant Portuguese settlers, to whom land was allocated in particularly fertile areas. They received state assistance in the form of credits and mechanisation.[22]

Peasant slash-and-burn cultivation was characterised by extremely low productivity. It was nevertheless the dominant source of food supply for the Mozambican population. At the same time it was a precondition for export industry activity and profitability that the provision of the workforce was supported by their families living at home. This family-based link between town and country has also been an important 'supply line' after independence. Through migrant and forced labour the men were separated from their traditional agricultural tasks of felling and clearing, and the soil's ecological vulnerability increased as the women were forced to over-exploit already cleared land. The decreasing yield could be partially supplemented by the men's incomes, mainly from the mines.

The rural population's purchasing power was limited by a regulated price system, which when purchasing agricultural products gave higher prices to the Portuguese settlers than to the Mozambican family farmers. Through low productivity and the high degree of exploitation, the preconditions for the growth of the domestic market with sufficient demand to stimulate the development of a national economy were reduced.[23]

Chronic deficit in the current account

The pattern of the economy has led to a unique macro-economic imbalance, namely that Mozambique's economy has existed with a permanent negative current account. The period 1958–74 showed no year with a positive current account.[24] Only about 50 per cent of the costs for imports has been covered by exports.[25] A permanent deficit in the balance of trade has been compensated for to some degree by a positive balance of services in relation to South Africa (railway and port charges, miners' wage remittances). But the current account has still remained negative.

Before 1975 this chronic deficit in the current account was paid by transfers from Portugal. These transfers were based on the fact that the Portuguese state's share of miners' wages was paid in gold directly to Portugal. Portugal was able to sell the gold at a profit on the world market as the price of gold rose.[26] During the colonial period this 'surplus profit' on migrant workers covered the necessary transfers from Portugal to Mozambique and thus financed the Portuguese state's strategy of offering cheap raw materials to the Portuguese textile industry.

Unequal regional distribution

The three southernmost provinces, Inhambane, Gaza and Maputo, were, according to an agreement between South Africa and Portugal, a pool of labour where South Africa had complete freedom to recruit the necessary workforce, in exchange for maintaining a certain minimum level of use of the railway and ports in Maputo. The central areas of the country were dominated by plantations, which were controlled to a lesser extent by Portuguese interests. In the northern provinces colonial exploitation was undeveloped. The concessionary companies which were established concentrated mainly on peasants' cotton production.

The whole territory was infrastructurally neglected. This type of economy required few investments in the infrastructure or industrial development in order to function. Wages for farm labourers were kept extremely low and a large proportion of the recruitment for plantations and large-scale farming was based on forced labour, so-called *chibalo*, just as cotton production was based on forced cultivation. Both labour organisation and choice of technology and anticipated profit could also assume that wages could *de facto* be kept below a subsistence minimum because reproduction of the labour force was finally guaranteed by families remaining in the home villages.

Colonial modes of production and principles of legitimacy

When the Portuguese landed in Mozambique, they found a society that was characterised by subsistence agriculture, where different extra-economic rules for the distribution of production applied. Even if individual families were responsible for their own subsistence, i.e. the group which produced was also the one which consumed the result, there were also social mechanisms which redistributed the result within a larger group according to the fluctuating needs of the individual.

These principles for extra-economic distribution were never broken down completely during the colonial era. Portuguese colonialism neither contemplated nor could introduce a pure market economy where the labour force and goods were offered for sale and priced on the market. The Portuguese needs from the colony were linked to raw materials and the provision of a labour force and were organised with the aid of force. Reproduction of the labour forces was guaranteed by the redistribution principles applying in Mozambican society before the arrival of the Portuguese.

The plantation economies in the central areas of the country and the more extensive Portuguese penetration after the 1930s did not lead to any immediate growth of a market economy involving the majority of the population. The law on forced labour was not abolished until the 1960s. Only during the 1960s were more goal-directed efforts introduced on the part of the colonial state in order to integrate larger parts of the rural population into the market economy. However, a market economy, in the true sense, where the domestic market expands as a result of increased productivity by the rural population, never became a reality. The peasants marketed only what they themselves could spare from their own low production in order to gain access to coveted consumer goods.

With time Portuguese colonialism came to break apart some of the pre-colonial reciprocity. At the same time there was still a need to retain other parts of Mozambican society's traditional norms and principles of legitimacy. This duality came to characterise the formulation of the principles of legitimacy which the colonial power needed to exercise its power. Through the institution of local regents (*régulos*) and 'land guards' (*cabos de terra*), the Portuguese attempted to involve in their colonial project that type of nobility which had deep roots in Mozambican culture and history, and thereby to exploit Mozambican society's traditional principles of legitimacy for the exercise of power. In exchange for allegiance and subordination, domestic rulers were allowed to retain the right to some of their own culture, traditions and religious worship. This was not always successful. Frequently the traditional rulers did not accept this subordination, and as a rule the Portuguese then appointed other families or clans to these functions.

Internal colonial antagonisms

Portuguese economic policy was also shaped by Mozambique's role in the region. Heavy infrastructural investments that were made were most often subordinated and adapted to the region's needs, while the activities of the 'resident' Portuguese were concentrated in service economies and small-scale production, not least within agriculture. Many foreign enterprises in Mozambique also employed Portuguese officials at both management and intermediate level.

The Portuguese central power prioritised industrial development in Portugal and had formulated a development strategy that satisfied the centre's political power base. Close relations with the British–South African mining capital were a prerequisite for this strategy, as transfers from migrant workers and transport payments were a decisive component in the 'trade triangle' between Mozambique, Portugal and South Africa.

But over the years this strategy encountered opposition from the 'Mozambican' Portuguese (or white Mozambicans, as they were also called), who were struggling to develop their own economic dominance in Mozambique. Their struggle led them into an economic policy which almost completely excluded black Mozambicans from formal economic activity. Mozambicans could not even make progress within local trade and small-scale agriculture.[27]

Export production of cotton is one example of how the Portuguese accumulation requirement promoted a far-reaching vertical integration, where all opportunities for profit in the production chain could be utilised. Apart from direct manual labour in the cotton fields, no part of the production chain was left in the hands of the native population. Cotton production in Cabo Delgado at the end of the 1950s is a striking example. When enterprising Mozambican farmers organised themselves in order to increase production by employing a labour force, this was considered to be a political conspiracy. Although cotton production multiplied rapidly, the black initiators of this increase in production were imprisoned. Peaceful popular protests were put down using armed force, at the Mueda massacre in 1960, *inter alia*.[28]

Through rigid application of this strategy within all production sectors, opportunities to create a black Mozambican middle class, with which the resident Portuguese could have allied themselves before independence, were lost. When policy changes began to be made in this regard it was too late – anti-colonial opposition had already been radicalised and was virtually totally behind Frelimo.

This radicalisation was strengthened by cracks in the social structure, where health-care and education for the Mozambican population were neglected. Ninety-three per cent of the population were illiterate and only about 13 per cent of school-age children went to school in 1960.[29] The focus on improved education and health-care, which started after the start of the war of liberation in 1964, was concentrated in towns and larger communities. Due to the sparse settlement pattern in rural areas, the majority of the population were left without social services.

Frelimo takes power

During the period around 1960 there were three nationalist organisations, which tried to achieve independence for Mozambique by peaceful means. They were mostly based among Mozambican migrant workers in neighbouring countries and therefore had a clear regional profile.[30]

Members from the three movements came together in 1962 and founded Frelimo (Frente de Libertação de Moçambique). An armed liberation struggle began in 1964. During the first years liberated areas were quickly established in northern Mozambique. However, they were limited to the Niassa and Cabo Delgado provinces. In 1968 the war of liberation also began in Tete province.

At the same time anti-fascist resistance was growing in Portugal. In the rest of Europe and the USA, Portugal's non-democratic political system was also increasingly considered to be a relict of a bygone age. Democratisation was necessary in order for Portugal to be able to develop into a politically acceptable economic partner in Europe.

There was thus widespread criticism of Portugal's fascist rule and its colonial war. However, at the same time Portugal was of strategic value to NATO. An American military base on the Azores was an important link in the control of the South Atlantic. The Portuguese presence in Mozambique and Angola was a guarantee that the oil routes from the Persian Gulf to the USA and Europe would not be disrupted from the African continent. Together with South Africa, the Portuguese colonies constituted a 'Western bloc' in Southern Africa. For a long time the Portuguese state's leadership was able to balance demands for democratisation and NATO's strategic requirements.

Portugal thus obtained extensive material support for its colonial war, despite the fact that it was generally considered to be politically unjust, which angered the Frelimo leadership.[31] Thus Frelimo, like other liberation movements in Portuguese colonies, became completely dependent on the Eastern bloc states and on China for military support for their armed struggle.

Although it is said that the Lusaka Agreement of 1974 contains a secret section, in which the colonial army surrenders to Frelimo, Frelimo achieved no total military victory over the colonial army. Combined pressure from the liberation movements in Mozambique, Angola and Guinea-Bissau had actually completely altered political development in Portugal before that. In Mozambique alone there were at most 70,000 Portuguese soldiers. The social base in Portugal for recruiting officers loyal to fascism was not sufficient for the growing requirement, and an ever larger proportion of officers were recruited from working-class and liberal middle-class environments. These came to constitute the foundations of the 'captains' movement', which in April 1974 staged a military coup and overthrew the fascist regime. A route to political change for the Portuguese colonies was thus suddenly and unexpectedly left open.

The war of liberation therefore never covered more than 30 per cent of the area of Mozambique. At the end of the war probably less than 10 per cent of the population lived in Frelimo's liberated areas.[33] At the same time experiences from the liberated areas would come to have a great influence on the development of Frelimo's development vision and strategy.

Frelimo's two factions

Frelimo gathered within its ranks both revolutionary socialists and more moderate groups. These two political tendencies within Frelimo survived through the war of liberation of 1964–74 and into the independence period. In Frelimo's official language they were called the 'revolutionary' and 'reactionary' factions. The balance of power between both factions varied over the period, but the antagonisms within Frelimo remained.[34]

Very shortly after the start of the war of liberation, the question of what sort of society Frelimo would create in its liberated areas was brought to the fore. The common goal for everyone in the liberation front was independence. However, as soon as Frelimo was forced to take responsibility for administering liberated areas there arose different perceptions of the type of economic policy that should be operated and the sort of society that should be created.

The revolutionaries in Frelimo's leadership recommended a radical transformation of society. The victors' version of history is that a spontaneous organisational form was developed, where reciprocity between Frelimo and the peasants and their collective production constituted preconditions for both the soldiers' and the peasants' survival. According to the same victors' version, the reactionaries developed a completely different policy with regard to how the rural economy should be organised, whose mainstays were that Frelimo's members would themselves occupy the place of the Portuguese after independence, without undertaking any basic social changes.

A concrete question that came to be decisive in this matter concerned the way in which the population's surplus agricultural production would be managed and how consumer goods would be made available. The revolutionaries argued that food production, over and above what the farmers needed for their own use, should be collective. Surplus production would finance the war's requirements and would be distributed according to collective decision. Consumer goods would be introduced into the liberated areas by Frelimo. The moderate forces felt that there should be a private trading system in the liberated areas, which could purchase the farmers' surplus in exchange for consumer goods.[35] When some members of Frelimo began to build up a trade network in the liberated areas a conflict developed between Frelimo's revolutionaries and moderates; the revolutionary group won.

Some of the moderate wing left Frelimo and tried to return to non-liberated zones of Mozambique and to link up with the local Portuguese. The hope was that the opposition by local Portuguese interests to Portuguese central power would result in a different policy after independence than that which Frelimo was expected to offer. Others remained in exile in different countries in Africa, Europe and North America. Yet others remained within Frelimo and subordinated themselves to the decision of the majority.

Ethnic tensions

However, internal antagonisms in Frelimo during the war of liberation were not only economic and political. They also had regional, or ethnic, dimensions. One question concerned the way in which Frelimo defined its principal enemy during the war. One spontaneous feeling amongst black Mozambicans, who joined Frelimo, was that the white Portuguese were the principal enemy. They endeavoured in the first instance to increase political and economic power for black Mozambicans, at the cost of the whites. The revolutionaries within Frelimo argued that it was not individuals who were the enemy, but the colonial system. This question also applied to Frelimo itself. Should whites be allowed to be members at all?

Another question concerned the tensions between different parts of the country, which arose for different reasons during the war of liberation. The war's leadership structure is sometimes described as an alliance between the intellectual leadership from the south and the Makonde population in the north. This description implies ethnic and regional tensions, some of which have been directly related to the course of the war of liberation.

At the same time as the first period of successful drives against Portuguese outposts in Niassa and Cabo Delgado in 1964, Frelimo opened a front in Zambezia. After a very short time it was forced to withdraw, and it was not able to resume the war of liberation in the province until after the military coup in Portugal in 1974. The sudden halt in Zambezia was caused by inadequate preparations in the province on the part of Frelimo. The difficulties for Frelimo in establishing itself in Zambezia can be illustrated by the very high turnover amongst sympathisers. The late president Samora Machel has claimed that 2,000 guerrilla soldiers with roots in Zambezia deserted from Frelimo during the war of liberation.[36]

Another tension was that between the Makonde and Makua peoples in northern Mozambique. Frelimo's rapid advances in the northernmost Makonde-dominated areas were halted at the traditional border between the Makonde and Makua in southern Cabo Delgado. In military terms the border was never crossed throughout the whole of the war of liberation.

Several of the leading dissidents, who during the war advocated an anti-white line in policy-making, had their roots in central Mozambique. They had recruited many youths as guerrilla soldiers for Frelimo through underground work in boarding schools run by the Catholic Church. However, the Church was intimately allied with the colonial state, and this was reflected in the recruits' education. Many of Frelimo's leaders had acquired their education in Protestant mission schools. This meant that the Catholic-educated group, with roots in Beira, felt itself to be regarded with suspicion by the leadership.

UDENAMO, with many members from southern Mozambique, was the best organised and most experienced of the three nationalist movements. Frelimo came to have great similarities in policy and function with UDENAMO. The Mozambican intellectuals, who directly affiliated themselves from exile in Europe to Frelimo in Tanzania, had their main anchor in the capital, the then Lorenço Marques. This was determined not least by the fact that all higher education was concentrated there.

The conflict, which Frelimo in its own documents usually describes as the conflict between the 'two factions', was in reality very complex. Descriptions of economic and political antagonisms in the two factions conceal the fact that there were also disagreements on ethnic, regional and racial matters. The positions taken by members were not obviously 'revolutionary' or 'reactionary'. An economic 'revolutionary' could at the same time be 'reactionary' in the racial/ethnic/regional conflict, and vice versa. It is probable that a large proportion of Frelimo sympathisers, members and guerrilla soldiers drew on elements from all these different positions to shape their political perceptions. The internal conflicts during the war of liberation were consequently resolved only on the ideological plane and within the organisation. As to the rest, all the causes of conflict lived on in Mozambican society. After independence they were reproduced on a national scale, both within and outside Frelimo.

Black allies

The material basis for these conflicts had been strengthened during the ten-year war of liberation. During the period 1965–75 the Portuguese, mainly those who had settled for good in Mozambique, had realised that it had been a mistake to hold back the blacks' economic activity.

Certain social strata of Mozambican society were encouraged to develop and mechanise their agriculture and to start running businesses.

In the first instance support was given to allies of the colonial state found among black Mozambicans. They were families belonging to the traditional power structure in African society, or to other economically influential families and assimilated groups. Frelimo's leadership also had its social roots in this stratum. The material basis for the moderate group was thus greatly strengthened and its ambitions were a visible force in the Mozambican economy in the period before independence. However, its economic ambitions were concealed behind a wave of overwhelming political enthusiasm from the whole population, which saluted Frelimo and its revolutionary leadership on independence. The conflict, which was resolved internally and ideologically during the war, now came to dominate the whole social picture, but it was effectively concealed behind the rejoicing over independence.

Neither the dissidents from Frelimo nor the local Portuguese had sufficient strength, either on their own or together, to threaten Frelimo's hegemony after the military coup in Portugal on 25 April 1974. During the unstable period between April 1974 and Mozambique's independence in June 1975, many attempted to set up political parties with black Mozambicans as leaders.[37] However, none of them provided a viable alternative to Frelimo. The white groups in Mozambique, which at that time were looking for black allies for a unilateral declaration of independence (of the Rhodesian type), were not able to mobilise sufficient support for their project. The Mozambican anti-Frelimo forces were too weak to be able to organise themselves as a political opposition, and were not able to make themselves relevant externally as a credible alternative to Frelimo after the fall of Portuguese fascism. The government that took office in Portugal after the 1974 coup surrendered power in Mozambique to Frelimo.

White mass exodus

During the later years of the liberation struggle, a large proportion of the white colonisers began to leave Mozambique. It is estimated that over 185,000 of the total 200,000 Portuguese in the country had returned to Portugal or sought refuge in South Africa when independence came. Unclear messages of political reconciliation from Frelimo during the liberation struggle had made them susceptible to intensive propaganda from Rhodesia and South Africa regarding the dreadful fate that awaited the white population under a black majority regime. Through mass emigration the whole of the country's educated workforce largely disappeared. This would have a great effect on continued development.

The cornerstone of the Mozambican development strategy

Frelimo's development strategy was presented at the 1977 third congress. This was later made concrete in a ten-year perspective plan (PPI), whose explicit goal was to put an end to underdevelopment in ten years' time. The experiences of the war of liberation and the ideological struggle would now be extended to the economic sphere, and in a gigantic effort of will the whole society would be transformed.

Experiences from the colonial period were characterised by fascist and repressive colonial power. Forced labour in agriculture, as well as the unfair terms of exchange in trading of agricultural products, represented the same degrading system for the population and for Frelimo. The anti-colonial struggle became synonymous for Frelimo with the struggle against Western capitalism. At the time of independence a socialist vision was probably the only one psychologically acceptable to Frelimo's leadership. The failures of the colonial state would be compensated for by the independent state satisfying the needs of the population, and private exploitation would be eliminated.

The economic and social consequences of colonial repression would be set aside as quickly as possible. Apart from the material progress people hoped for, Frelimo's leadership talked a great deal about the population's restored dignity. Anti-racism, nation-building and a general modernisation policy were the cornerstones of these visions. The social sectors came to be considered as spearheads in Frelimo's strategy of transferring the collective experiences from the liberated zones to the whole population and creating a legitimacy for its own policy. In the same way as the liberation struggle, Frelimo's vision of modern society would be brought about based on popular mobilisation and popular power.

Introduction of the planned economy

Nationalisation was implemented in five[38] main areas: land, banking, rented housing, health-care and education. As to the rest, the state sector was created by taking over abandoned properties, so-called intervention, where foreign owners left the country. Railways, ports and power stations were already state-owned during the colonial period. At the same time institutions were established for economic planning and the state control of all economic activity. This had two cornerstones. The first was to take control of and administer abandoned property. The second was programmatic control of the development strategy, which was based on people seeing state intervention in the economy as a replacement for market forces which never existed and which the present government did not intend to develop.

The Ministry of Planning would theoretically control the development process. To establish and maintain a reasonably effective state administration required a political alliance between Frelimo and the remaining white functionaries with higher or intermediate education. Many of these were politically motivated to choose Mozambican citizenship. They often had their political history in the Portuguese Communist Party, and they came to have a great influence on the formulation and implementation of policy.

Within agriculture, state farms and agricultural projects were created which could vary between a few thousand hectares and 400,000 hectares. Investments in the state sector were given priority, to the detriment of the cooperatives, peasants and private farmers.

Socialisation of the countryside

With the coming of independence the rural population's expectations for rapidly improved material welfare were great. At the same time Mozambican development planners and decision-makers had very little idea of how the dispersed rural population could be supported and integrated into the development process.[39] There was also an acute need to take care of abandoned farms within the modern sector. This was more concrete and represented a project which foreign aid contributors could consider financing without difficulty.

The development strategy that emerged in connection with independence was thus based on the necessity of transforming the economic structure through rapid industrialisation based on the agricultural surplus. In order for this to be possible agriculture had to be modernised at a rapid pace, and its productivity grow explosively. Peasant production methods and productivity were not thought able to produce an economic surplus on a sufficient scale to provide adequate financing for long-term development. A transition from traditional slash-and-burn to some form of mechanised modern agriculture was seen as an absolute precondition for raising the productivity and purchasing power of the rural population. State farms would thus become the hub of the agricultural strategy, produce export goods and cover a large share of the country's total food requirements. They would be established from plantation properties and amalgamations of the Portuguese settlers' smaller holdings which had been abandoned. In total this involved slightly more than 4,000 agricultural enterprises. The motivation for their takeover was the destruction of capital which would otherwise have become a reality. Moreover, it was also necessary to provide the towns with food.[40]

Rapid mechanisation within agriculture was motivated in the first instance by the endeavour to increase production, but also by the need to replace forced labour with more modern farming. Mechanised agriculture would also be able to offer miners returning from South Africa work that corresponded to their technical skills. The anticipated export revenues from the plantations and large-scale agriculture would contribute to financing a full-scale transformation of the rural areas.

The majority of the population were peasants and in order to improve their living conditions and material standards, rural areas would be reorganised. By encouraging the scattered peasants to move together into communal villages it would be easier to provide education, healthcare and water. In order to improve purchasing power, a gradual relinquishment of traditional methods, permitting increased productivity, became paramount.

The route to such development was seen as being via producer cooperatives; these would be financed and supported by the state farms, which would provide extension services and access to mechanised agricultural equipment. The villages in their turn were a prerequisite for the organisation of producer cooperatives.

However, functionaries and development planners within the state administration in Maputo had insufficient knowledge of the realities of the rural areas. The planning process was further divorced from Mozambican reality by the presence of Soviet and East European state officials and planners. There was also the Mozambican–Nordic agricultural cooperation (MONAP), which initially also stressed the importance of the modern sector. The question of how the peasants' production methods would be improved was left to a future date.

Importance of the industrial sector

While agriculture would form the basis for development, industry would constitute the 'dynamising factor'. Because the building up of industry during the colonial period had gathered pace during the first half of the 1960s, the production technology was relatively modern. Knowledge about the maintenance and care of machinery had, however, been reserved for the owners and white workers. The need for foreign expertise for continued operation, as well as foreign currency for imports of spare parts and raw materials, became very great after independence. There was also a problem with the marketing because a large number of the Portuguese who constituted the customers left the country at the time of independence. However, few measures were proposed in order to correct the basic structural problem affecting industry's production trends.

Colonial prototypes

As the basis for the perspective plan and for development projects that international aid contributors showed interest in financing, the colonial development plans and investment projects from the years preceding the country's independence were used.[41]

These experiences, together with the positive signals coming from both the West and the East about the at least passive acceptance of the Third World's struggle for independent economic development, naturally influenced the formulation of the Mozambican development strategy. However, with the exception of the Nordic countries and Italy, it soon proved difficult for Mozambique to mobilise the granting of Western bilateral aid. In the same way as during the liberation struggle, Mozambique was forced to seek assistance from the Soviet Union and the Eastern bloc in order to realise its development plans. The utilisation of the colonial prototypes of development also reflects how deeply rooted the European conceptualisation of the development process within the Mozambican leadership really was. This applies to the economic strategy (economic growth through rapid modernisation) as well as to the political strategy to unify the country through a rapid process of nation-state building.

2

The International Setting and the Regional Constraints

Decolonisation – modernisation under conditions of East–West rivalry

At the final stage of the Second World War in 1944, 700 delegates from 44 countries got together in Bretton Woods, a small skiing town in New Hampshire, USA, in order to initiate discussions about the way in which post-war trade and international economic transactions should be organised. The previous world order (Pax Britannica) under Great Britain's hegemony was at an end, and a new world order should now develop under American leadership (Pax Americana).

The delegations came mainly from the industrialised world. The majority of the world's population was not represented. Asian and African colonies were still subordinate to Europe and had no independent voice. Socialist countries were represented by the Soviet Union.

The starting point was to create a world order that would contribute to national political stability and international security. The necessity for a strong and interventionist state and full employment in order for economic growth and material development to be able to take place was stressed. Such a development was considered possible only through a deregulated international trade, a free movement of capital and an international monetary system, based on the American dollar as a reserve currency, giving rise to the concept of embedded liberalism.

It was with some reluctance that the Americans took on the role of shouldering the British burden. Isolationist groups in the USA, who were opposed to the very last to Americans entering the Second World War, were even less interested in assuming any long-term responsibility for international security. But West European leaders were successful in getting the American administration to understand the importance of using American military, economic and cultural strengths for the purpose of international leadership, not least to prevent the spread of communism (the policy of containment). With the aid of massive transfers of resources (the Marshall Plan), Europe would be rebuilt.

In its endeavour to facilitate European reconstruction and in order to shape the cornerstones of the new world order, the conference in Bretton Woods took the initiative of establishing two international financial institutions, namely the International Monetary Fund (IMF) and the International Bank for Reconstruction and Development (IBRD), usually known as the World Bank. While the IMF would supply its members with short-term credits in order to correct occasional deficits in current accounts, the World Bank's task was to supply credits for member countries' more long-term development aspirations.

At the end of the 1950s the Marshall Plan had largely been implemented. By then the foundations were laid for the international trade and economic exchange on which the Bretton Woods institutions would be able to operate. The fact that this process took 15 years is explained by the need for the European countries first, under tariff protection, to carry out the structural building up of capacity of domestic industry required for international competitiveness, and second, the possibility of achieving a macro-economic balance. Thus it took over 15 years of massive transfers of resources, in combination with a national protectionist policy, for European production capacity to be able to compete in a liberalised world market.

Decolonisation and aid

The world order of the post-war period had yet another starting point, which the Americans were anxious about for economic reasons. It concerned the necessity for Europe to surrender its colonies.[42] Decolonisation, political independence and economic development would be facilitated through international aid, and would hereby support the implementation of the policy of containment.

The Americans' demand for decolonisation and European withdrawal had been preceded by an intensive debate in the US Congress. Several members had warned of the risk that the independence of the colonies would come to be used by the Soviet Union in order to strengthen its position in the Third World.

During the 1960s several African nationalist liberation movements had acquired a radical image, which was disquieting for Western countries. These movements saw colonialism as a result of capitalism and set goals for the social changes that the liberation struggle had intended.

Zbigniew Brzezinski,[43] later national security adviser to President Carter, played down the risks of an increase in the Soviet Union's influence in Africa. According to Brzezinski, the Soviet economy was still too weak to be able to provide any more extensive aid and the failure of its agricultural policy would be a particular deterrent for a continent so agriculture-dependent as Africa. The Soviet Union had no experience of cooperation with Africans either. The rigid analysis of antagonistic class conflicts, which was a cornerstone of Moscow's theory on the driving forces behind social change, would be less relevant on a continent characterised by little social differentiation, cultural loyalties, kinship relations and traditional customs. Brzezinski maintained that the West had acquired knowledge about all this during the colonial era. There was also the West's superior experience in trade and its developed diplomatic and commercial contact network.

Brzezinski saw peaceful decolonisation as being essential for continued development. According to Brzezinski, colonies which had hitherto become independent had been colonised by Western powers intelligent enough to hand over power to an élite which they themselves had created. The fact that this élite was:

> bitterly hostile to the departing colonists does not alter the fact that they had been conditioned, influenced and inspired by their former sovereigns. A highly symbolic and politically important aspect of this fact is that English and French have become the languages of the new élite, thereby making them susceptible to continuing European cultural influence and even imperceptibly shaping their thought patterns.[44]

Brzezinski saw a danger of increased Soviet influence in that the liberation struggle in colonies not yet independent would drag on and that the movements would thus be radicalised. This would imply an opportunity for the Soviet Union to politicise both the élite and the population to communism's advantage. Brzezinski's conclusion was that the West's aid cooperation with African countries was immensely important and that

> it makes little difference how the African leaders act *now*, whether they are friendly or hostile to the West; that what is considered decisive is that their societies reach the stage of 'take-off' in the processes of modernization, with the expectation that subsequently many of the tensions and hostilities to the West will inevitably subside.[45]

Demand for a new international economic order

Within the framework of the UN system, the first development decade was introduced in 1960. The gap between the rich and the poor world was then estimated at the ration of ten to one. Through global transfers of resources, in the form of international aid, the growth of a strong state and forced modernisation, the gap should be levelled out. The amount of aid decided on came close to one per cent of the rich world's gross national product.

Ten years later, in 1970, the gap between the richer industrial countries and the poorer developing countries had reached a ration of 14:1. The UN's second development decade was introduced. The role of the state and modernisation in development was emphasised once again.

Nearly five years later, in 1974, the non-aligned movement and a special session of the General Assembly at the UN demanded a new international economic order. The guidelines drawn up during the Bretton Woods conference 30 years previously were regarded as being formulated too unilaterally in the interests of the industrialised nations. In order to implement modernisation significantly larger transfers of resources and other preconditions for international trade were required.

The African roots of the Mozambican development strategy

During the second half of the 1960s and the first half of the 1970s large numbers of the élite within Frelimo were to be found in the liberated areas in northern parts of the country, in Tanzania or in military training in Algeria.[46] All these places offered an environment which came to play an important role in the formulation of Frelimo's political vision and economic development strategy.[47]

Experiences from the liberated areas acquired great political significance. Frelimo's guerrillas obtained strong support from the peasants and together built up the functioning collective production and supply system. This was regarded as clear evidence of the mobilising force of 'the people's power'.

In Tanzania and Algeria an intensive debate about development theory continued. The development optimism that characterised Africa during the first half of the 1960s disappeared as the results of modernisation failed to materialise. The decade did not turn out to be the decade of development proclaimed by the UN.

The Latin American dependency debate began to acquire ever increasing influence on the continent, especially in Tanzania.[48] According to the dependency school, the only way to bring about development was to de-link from the world market and the capitalist mode of production and *create demand* in rural areas, with the aid of collective self-reliance and socialist planning, which were required in order to bring about dynamic economic development.

Tanzania's president, Julius Nyerere, based parts of his vision for the Ujamaa villages on this analysis. For an agricultural country such as Tanzania, it involved not only modernising agricultural production as before, through concentrating on capital intensive large-scale agriculture. By means of the dispersed rural population moving together into villages, the peasants' production would also be mechanised through a cooperative and at the same time the provision of water and social services to the population would be made easier.[49] In this respect industrial development directed according to the needs of the rural population was important, not least in order for Tanzania to be able to reduce its dependence on the world market.[50]

A corresponding strategy had earlier been formulated and debated intensively in Algeria. However, through its raw materials (oil and natural gas), its contacts with the world market would initially play a big role in financing the industries required for increased domestic production of machinery for modernising agriculture. Also in Algeria the rural population would move together into villages and the rural areas would thus be urbanised.

Algerian planners, under the leadership of de Bernis,[51] the French economist, largely agreed with the dependency school's analysis of the causes of underdevelopment. At the same time they were critical of the practical implementation of the collective self-reliance policy and its possibilities for rapid industrialisation. Instead increased cooperation with the Eastern bloc and the Soviet Union, whose level of technology within several important sectors (for example the steel and mining industries) was considered to be more suitable for Algeria's level of development, was recommended. Through their strategy of forced modernisation, the Algerian development planners endeavoured to catch up with the Western level of development within 25 years.

When, ten years later, Mozambique presented a very similar development strategy, the goal was to overcome underdevelopment within ten years. The pace of the proposed modernisation had thus further increased. In order for this to be possible, Frelimo's party congress in 1977 considered that strong centralisation of decision-making was necessary. Frelimo was transformed into an avant-garde party, a measure also intended to convince Moscow of the seriousness of its socialist orientation and thus ensure future aid and financing. In this context Marxism ceases to be a foundation and a tool for social analysis. Instead it is used as an instrument in the implementation of the forced modernisation and nation-building project. So Marxism is given the dubious role of ensuring the course of history that the theory itself has determined, and hence loses all its analytical strength.

Soviet expansion in the Third World

During the Soviet Communist Party's 25th congress in 1976, Leonid Brezhnev declared that socialist currents were dominant in the countries of Asia, Africa and Latin America. One reason for this statement was obviously the Portuguese collapse in Africa and the new governments led by socialist-orientated liberation movements, Frelimo in Mozambique and the MPLA in Angola.

Brezhnev's speech should be interpreted as an appreciation of the new opportunities for political alliances in Southern Africa. At the same time the speech indicates a changed political view in Moscow about the Third World's preconditions for socialist development.

Based on a strictly orthodox Marxist analysis, these preconditions had previously been assessed as being very minor. Capitalist penetration of the Third World was perceived by both Marx and Engels as a necessary evil. Capitalism certainly implied a brutal exploitation of the populations of these countries, but it also broke down the feudal structures, which slowed down further development. Only by abandoning the old modes of production and introducing capitalism would it be possible to develop productive forces, which were necessary for a future conversion to socialism.

Lenin largely shared this view. For capitalism to be progressive in this historical context it was, however, necessary that countries in the Third World liberated themselves from the colonial yoke. Stalin developed this further and considered that preconditions for economic development in the Third World were based on the opportunities for the domestic bourgeoisie to bring about rapid industrialisation and the development of productive forces.

This analysis probably came to constitute the chief explanation for the Soviet Union's somewhat wary attitude towards, and in practice relatively limited cooperation with, African liberation movements during the decolonisation process that characterised the continent during the 1950s and 1960s.

Moscow's attitude changed during the 1960s as a consequence of de-Stalinisation and Khruschev's policy of peaceful coexistence. In Moscow optimistic assessments were made of the Soviet Union's future economic development and of its ability to become an ideological magnet for the Third World through limited support for national liberation movements. According to Moscow's new view of the social forces that would carry out national liberation, the bourgeoisie in the Third World would be isolated and the struggle for national independence would instead be based on a broader class alliance, mainly consisting of the lower middle class, workers and farmers. Socialism was still not on the agenda but the strategy went under the name of 'non-capitalist development'.[52]

As a consequence of the American defeat in Vietnam and the advances of socialist-inspired liberation movements during the first half of the 1970s, the Soviet Union's opportunities for new political alliances in the Third World increased. These opportunities also coincided with foreign policy requirements. It was perceived as important to exploit the ideological vacuum left behind by the USA, not least to stop it being filled by China. There was also a purely military strategic aim and the Soviet Union's need for political allies in order to build up naval bases that would provide global coverage for its nuclear weapons programme.

Under Brezhnev, the theory of non-capitalist development was reformulated into a theory of socialist-orientated countries which could thus be admitted as valid partners in cooperation in the Soviet economic community. This explains the Soviets' readiness, together with Cuba, to comply with the MPLA regime's request for military support during the South African invasion of Angola in 1975. The Soviet and Cuban presence in Angola would have enormous consequences for the future attitude of South Africa. The Soviet Union entered into an agreement with Mozambique on military support for similar reasons, even if it was considerably more limited.[53]

Waiting in the West

During the Carter administration, the international community reacted relatively passively to the attempts at independent socialist development introduced here and there in the Third World during the second half of the 1970s. Direct foreign intervention by the West was precluded as a consequence of the backlash from the Vietnam war.[54]

At the same time the socialist international took on an ever-increasing role in order to strengthen the bridge between North and South which was considered necessary for the world economy. Its demands for increased and international measures for progress towards black majority rule in South Africa and independence for Namibia and Zimbabwe were well known.[55]

These demands were also embraced by many in the Carter administration. For American transnational companies, stable peaceful development in Southern Africa was a condition for continued supplies of the region's strategic raw materials and metals. Such supplies were regarded as being far more important than propping up a conservative apartheid regime, with the obvious risks of increased Soviet influence in the region that this implied. This perception was formulated in the following way by the Carter administration's UN ambassador, Andrew Young, on his appointment:

> [T]he best thing the Communists have going for them is the presence of racist minority regimes in Southern Africa. If those were no longer there, there would no longer be any need for the weaponry which the Soviet Union supplies and the issue would be one of development. When it comes to development, I would say that our track record is as good as anybody's.[56]

Hence, as already mentioned, most signals, both from the West and from the Soviet Union during the second half of the 1970s, indicated increased international scope for radical development attempts in the

Third World. In fact, the debate on a new international economic order created expectations in the Third World of access to future international financing of its modernisation programmes. In Southern Africa optimism about rapid development was reinforced by the UN's recommendation of the international isolation of Rhodesia and the encouragement of South Africa's black majority.

The geopolitical realities of Southern Africa

Vorster's détente *policy*

At the time of Mozambique's independence in 1975, the military and political situation in Southern Africa was characterised by the South African Prime Minister John Vorster's *détente* policy, which developed as a result of internal and external reactions to the regime's apartheid policy during the 1960s.[58] The Sharpeville massacre in South Africa in 1960 meant paradoxically that the white minority was temporarily able to consolidate its power. The massacre was followed immediately by the declaration of a state of emergency and the political organisations working for majority rule, the ANC and PAC, were banned.[59]

Through international contacts, legislation extremely favourable to foreign investors and the exploitation of the West's increasing demand for strategic minerals for its industries, the South African political leadership was able to turn the outflow of capital after the Sharpeville massacre into an inflow. The regional context had also favoured the South African white minority's consolidation. Since the end of the Second World War, South Africa had been successful in surrounding itself with a number of dependent so-called buffer states that were inclined to be friendly to the government. In fact Botswana, Lesotho and Swaziland operated in practice as South African economic enclaves.

The South African strategy aimed to tie the buffer zones economically to the South African economy. Together with an active regional *détente* policy, this strategy had had great success in maintaining regional dominance. These experiences laid the foundation for the somewhat vague theory on the Constellation of Southern African States – CONSAS – which was developed during the second half of the 1970s as a stage in Prime Minister Vorster's 'outward policy'.

This relatively stable period of economic growth and consolidation of the apartheid policy was broken, however, during the middle of the 1970s. The successes of the liberation movements in the Portuguese colonies meant independence for Angola and Mozambique. With regard to domestic policy, the Soweto uprising in 1976 would have great significance for continued political development within South Africa. Thousands of young black South Africans left the country in protest against the apartheid regime's brutal action in order to join the ANC's armed wing in Tanzania, undergo military training and to take part in the armed struggle within South Africa.

The Vorster regime's *détente* policy was forced to a halt by the South African armed forces in the face of Angola's impending independence. The fear that the MPLA would come to power and, together with the Soviet Union, enable the Namibian liberation organisation SWAPO to operate from Angolan territory gained the upper hand. The South African government responded, despite protests from the country's Ministry for Foreign Affairs and the Bureau of State Security, to a request for military support from UNITA and invaded Angola several months before the country's independence.[60]

The South African government's attitude to political independence in Mozambique was different for several reasons. The invasion of Angola was motivated not only by unease at the possibility of an intensified struggle by SWAPO in Namibia but also by South Africa's interest in Angola's supplies of raw materials. Access to these would be obtained if UNITA, sympathetic to South Africa, came to power. It was considered inconceivable that the Marxist-inspired MPLA movement would be so cooperative.

South Africa had a corresponding economic strategic need for Mozambique; in particular it needed access to the country's transport corridors linking Transvaal to the Indian Ocean and to electricity from the Cabora Bassa dam. However, in contrast to Angola, there was no domestic political force in Mozambique that South Africa could sponsor which would be able seriously to hinder Frelimo's accession to power. The South African military's proposal to go in and sponsor Portuguese colonial interests that attempted a coup in Maputo was rejected by Vorster. There was too great a risk that the Frelimo leadership would be forced into the bush and from there continue the liberation struggle. Such a situation would pose a serious threat to the Mozambican infrastructure that South Africa needed.[61]

Instead, in 1974 a secret non-aggression treaty was drawn up between the South African government and the Frelimo leadership.[62] South Africa would not intervene in Mozambique in return for Mozambique not allowing the South African liberation movement, the ANC, to operate from Mozambican territory. South Africa would also not attack Mozambique in a situation involving Mozambique–Rhodesia relations. The treaty emphasised the importance of continued economic co-operation against the background of the countries' geopolitical realities and mutual economic dependence.

After some years, however, both parties began to breach this treaty. The South Africans wanted to get Mozambique to realise the economic importance of continued loyalty and economic cooperation with South

Africa and did this by, for example, reducing the number of miners recruited from around 100,000 to approximately 40,000 between 1975 and 1976.[63]

Over the following year Vorster was exposed to extensive criticism both from conservative forces in parliament and from the military. His regional *détente* policy was not regarded as being as resolute as his domestic policy of preserving and consolidating the apartheid system. His over-confidence in the ability of the South African economy to attract cooperation from neighbouring countries was questioned and demands increased for the implementation of the 'total strategy', developed several years previously by the country's defence minister P.W. Botha. The 'total strategy' was publicly presented in 1978. That year Prime Minister Vorster was removed from office and P.W. Botha took over the country's leadership. A new era in Southern Africa was thus introduced.

Carter and human rights

The USA's attitude *vis-à-vis* Southern Africa was more explicitly formulated by Henry Kissinger in 1976. The Southern Africa policy comprised three strands. First, the USA would work on a peaceful solution to the Rhodesia conflict. However, majority rule would imply respect and protection for the rights of minorities. Second, it advocated the UN being given an opportunity to supervise the transition to an independent Namibia. Third, it would work for a 'peaceful end to institutional inequality in South Africa'.

The fear of radicalisation of the liberation movements if the liberation struggle dragged on and the danger of a long-term increase in Soviet influence during the 1960s formed the basis of Brzezinski's position 15 years later when, as President Carter's national security adviser, he argued for increased pressure on more radical reform of the apartheid system in South Africa.

The Carter administration thus went further than its predecessors, and during a meeting between Prime Minister John Vorster and the USA's Foreign Minister Walter Mondale in Geneva in July 1977, the USA demanded the introduction of the principle of 'one man one vote'. President Carter's position on human rights made him a strong supporter of majority rule in South Africa. There was also his need for support from the political constituency represented by the black American population. Through this positive approach to black majority rule in Southern Africa, the USA's relations with the rest of black Africa were considerably improved. While Foreign Minister Henry Kissinger had been refused an entry permit to Nigeria in 1976, President Carter was warmly received two years later.

At the same time disquiet was expressed in conservative circles within the US Congress that the administration had underestimated the significance of the Soviet and Cuban presence in Southern Africa. The USA needed to show the black majority population in South Africa that it was serious about its demand for black majority rule at the same time as getting the white population to accept the possibility of remaining. The whites would not give way to what they saw as Soviet and Cuban attempts to exploit racism in order to clear the way for communism in Southern Africa.[64]

P.W. Botha and the 'total strategy'

Prime Minister Vorster appeared to be considerably more conservative where domestic policy rather than foreign policy was concerned. His 'outward policy' was regarded as being liberal and was praised in Washington. With Prime Minister P.W. Botha in power, the situation was virtually reversed. As former defence minister he saw the threat from the region in military terms and stressed the need for military intervention to avoid the effects of dissemination.[65]

At the same time Botha realised the need gradually to reformulate the policy of apartheid so that the change would not appear to be too provocative, regionally or internationally. The Americans had tried in vain to get Vorster to understand both the implications of Carter's human rights policy and the importance of political reforms in South Africa, and the lack of progress had increased dissatisfaction in the USA. For Prime Minister Botha it was a matter of quickly reducing the growing distance between Pretoria and Washington.

However, he wanted to bring about changes at a pace which South Africans themselves would be able to determine so that they did not feel that their security was threatened, either internally or from outside. Only through slow change, over which the whites themselves had control, would it be possible to maintain and even extend white dominance in South Africa and in the region.[66] Botha's emphasis on military means to defend the apartheid regime's interests in the region was also motivated by the Soviet and Cuban presence, which greatly troubled President Carter's closest advisers.

The goal of South Africa's regional strategy was to make possible the survival of the apartheid system by keeping the black liberation struggle in the region at as great a distance as possible. During the colonial era this was done through active – including military – assistance for the colonial powers, and after the period of independence through the 'outward policy' followed by CONSAS with the aim of increasing the economic dependence of neighbouring countries and thus their political loyalty to South Africa.

Political independence in the Portuguese colonies in 1975 would come to change the preconditions for this strategy. Through the support given by the newly installed Mozambican government to ZANU, the liberation struggle within the then Rhodesia could be intensified. The closing of the borders with Rhodesia at the request of the UN contributed to the isolation of the Ian Smith regime.[67] The protection that the buffer states had previously provided to the white minority regime in South Africa thus began to disintegrate.[68] The Namibian liberation movement's increasing struggle, now directed from liberated Angolan territory, was experienced as a direct threat to the apartheid system's long-term survival.

The P.W. Botha regime in South Africa attempted to apply different strategies at the same time. On the one hand the 'total strategy' for the survival of the apartheid system, developed during the Vorster regime by P.W. Botha in his capacity as defence minister, was now developed seriously and introduced at the domestic level, partly as a motivation of military intervention in Angola. According to the doctrine, economic methods were not enough to resist communist infiltration in Southern Africa. It was necessary to mobilise all resources – not least the military.

On the other hand in 1979 Prime Minister Botha revived Vorster's earlier work on CONSAS and re-launched it in the so-called Carlton Plan. In this way he attempted to satisfy economic interests in the country while at the same time playing down his militaristic, aggressive image *vis-à-vis* the region. The private enterprise sector, like the multinational companies located in South Africa, gave its continuing support to the plan and promised increased regional investments.

Constructive engagement

Under the Carter administration few attempts were made to analyse and relate to the Southern Africa problem from an East–West perspective. On Reagan's election in 1981, American foreign policy changed. The Carter administration's *détente* policy during the 1970s had meant that the Soviet Union was able to promote its international position, expressed not least by the invasion of Afghanistan. The Reagan administration demanded measures which would be able to halt and fight communism wherever it spread, and regional conflicts were analysed from an East–West perspective. This 'Reagan doctrine' came to acquire a pervasive force in Southern Africa.

Prime Minister Vorster's stubborn resistance to domestic policy reforms on the one hand, and his more liberal foreign policy on the other, meant that he not only prepared the way for P.W. Botha's takeover of power in 1978 but also influenced changes in the American Southern Africa policy. This found clear expression when immediately after his accession to power, President Reagan introduced the concept of 'constructive engagement'.[69]

For the American administration it became increasingly clear that the policy of apartheid in South Africa needed to be reformed in order to avoid too great a radicalisation of the black resistance movement. This would threaten the preconditions for continued market-oriented economic development and jeopardise future American supplies of raw materials. American support for such political reform had also been demanded for a long time by politically important black civil rights groups in the USA. The Soviet Union's increased presence in the region, together with South Africa's Marxist-orientated neighbours, imposed further demands for such political reforms.

Chester A. Crocker, newly appointed assistant secretary of state for African Affairs, criticised the Carter administration above all for promising that the blacks would gain more from political change in South Africa than the white minority were actually willing to give. This, according to Crocker, was also why the Carter administration got into an impasse in its Southern Africa policy. Through a more subtle and realistic approach the USA would, according to Crocker, be able to increase its role as mediator in the region of Southern Africa and in this way neutralise the Soviet Union's influence.[70]

Washington regarded its attitude as largely conforming with Prime Minister Botha's position. With regard to domestic policy he expressed a willingness to commence work on reforming the policy of apartheid at a rate which was politically feasible. This was regarded as being worthy of all support. P.W. Botha was perceived as being strong enough to be able to keep the extreme right at a distance and sharp enough to get domestic enterprises to understand the need for reforms.

Botha's significantly more conservative foreign policy position, as compared with Vorster's, was also praised by the USA. The 'total strategy' was perceived by Washington as a natural response to an increased threat from the Soviet Union. Prime Minister Botha was thus successful in getting both the Americans and the South African white opposition to concur with the analysis of the 'communist total onslaught' which he had developed several years previously within SADF in his capacity as defence minister, and in making the regional conflict in Southern Africa appear to be an East–West conflict.

At the beginning the Americans turned a blind eye to South Africa's destabilisation strategy. Washington was still uneasy over the Soviet presence and the fact that Frelimo had developed into a Marxist–Leninist avant-garde party. When the Mozambicans expelled several American diplomats, accused of being CIA agents, from Maputo in 1981, relations with Mozambique were radically worsened. Several demands were delivered from the opposition in the US Congress that the USA should begin to support Renamo. The compromise was that the USA cancelled aid to Mozambique for a number of years.

Mozambique's foreign policy

Mozambique's foreign policy was formulated in plain language during the third Frelimo party congress in 1977. The importance of non-alignment was emphasised.[71] The policy's clear anti-imperialist line placed the country amongst the more radical countries within the non-aligned movement. The congress also stressed the importance of regionally increased independence from South Africa. Support for the struggle for black majority rule in neighbouring countries was an important principle.[72]

Regional thinking and attempts at regional cooperation soon came to characterise the Frelimo leadership. For the development of majority rule in Southern Africa which would allow regional cooperation, both the region's free market capitalism and racism would have to be combated. The liberation of neighbouring countries was also perceived to be a precondition for future economic development in Mozambique.

The military threat to which the country was exposed came in the first instance from Rhodesia and South Africa in the form of retaliations, or the threat of retaliations, for Frelimo's support for the ZANU and ANC liberation movements. The national security policy formulated against this background was conventional and realistic in the sense that national security was mainly analysed in military terms.

Here the foreign and security policies diverged in one important respect from the experiences of the liberation struggle, namely by ignoring the role that low-intensity warfare in rural areas could play in economic destabilisation. Frelimo perceived itself as having full political support from the country's population, and no sub-national threats were perceived. Other threatening scenarios, in the form of economic, ecological or cultural obstacles to development, were thus not included in the security policy analysis. Instead Frelimo sought foreign assistance to build up a minimal military defence which, using conventional weapons, would be able to repel invasion attempts from racist neighbouring countries.

Regional cooperation

Together with the independence of the Portuguese colony in 1975, the political situation and balance of power in Southern Africa changed radically. With Zimbabwe's independence in 1980 another so-called buffer state, which the white minority regime in Pretoria felt it needed as protection against black Africa, disappeared.

In the same year the Frontline States formed SADCC, with the aim of also changing the region's economic realities. Political expectations for reducing dependence on the West in general, and on South Africa in particular, through strengthened regional cooperation would be made concrete. The basis for this was the Frontline States' endeavours to find an alternative to the South African dominance strategy represented by CONSAS.[73] Economic cooperation within the framework of SADCC was based on political resolutions agreed by the emerging nation-states, which in turn were characterised to a great extent by more or less radical and nation state-building development strategies.

The situation within the prevailing international political economy allowed the organisation to develop with the aid of extensive financial support, mainly from West European international aid donors.[74] Through economic support to the organisation Western Europe wished to maintain its influence in the region.[75] This support was perceived to be a precondition for reducing the dependence of the frontline states on South Africa and was expected to put increased pressure on the South African regime to reform the country's apartheid policy.[76] For the decision-makers in Southern Africa the organisation thus came to have a particularly important function as a mobiliser of aid and hence a source of financing for several urgent development projects (often national).

Especially disturbing for the South Africans was the initiative taken within SADCC to reduce the landlocked neighbouring countries' transport dependence on South Africa, with the help of extensive investments in the transport technology infrastructure, financed by aid from the West. In this way an important protection against the introduction of international sanctions would disappear. As long as the landlocked neighbouring countries were dependent on the South African transport network for their trade with the world and for their food supplies, international sanctions would rebound directly against those countries. With alternative transport routes now being offered via Mozambique, this situation would change.

The Frontline States' increasing international diplomatic mobilisation for sanctions against South Africa, together with the creation of SADCC, formed too strong a challenge to the Pretoria regime. The thinking behind CONSAS was abandoned and the total strategy's military component gained the upper hand. An extensive military and economic destabilisation campaign was begun, and Mozambique was particularly vulnerable.

Mozambique's foreign policy position, which held that only a black majority-ruled South Africa could lead to long-term stability in the region and provide the right conditions for peaceful development, provoked the South African regime. It also felt threatened by Mozambique's development strategy and ideological image. Through its broad concentration on the construction and modernisation of social sectors (e.g. education, health) Mozambique would become a source of inspiration for the blacks' struggle within South Africa. Frelimo's transformation into a Marxist avant-garde party was also perceived to be an ideological menace. By constantly calling attention to this and to the Soviet presence in the country, the white minority regime in Pretoria tried to find, for domestic consumption, a legitimate explanation for its destabilisation campaign.

3

The Turning Point: Vision and Reality

Initial successes

Between 1975 and 1981 falling production levels within both agriculture and industry were halted and replaced with an increase, which during 1981 reached the highest value after independence for most goods for domestic consumption and export crops. As is evident from Table 3.1, exports increased by 83 per cent between 1977 and 1981. The most important reason for this was that the euphoria of independence created fertile ground for the government's political mobilisation of the population in 'campaigns' and 'voluntary work' to get out of crisis situations and through bottlenecks.

Within the social sector the schools system expanded. The number of teachers doubled to 20,000 up to 1982. Illiteracy was reduced over five years from 93 per cent to about 70 per cent. The health-care system was extended, mainly in the rural areas where the number of health posts increased fourfold during the first seven years of independence and the number of inhabitants per local health-care institution sank from just over 26,000 to 10,000.[77] Within the framework of child and maternity health-care, the most highly praised vaccination programme in the world was implemented. Virtually all children were reached.

Political misgivings

At the same time as the economy's measurable indicators showed a positive development during the first years following independence, the political and social preconditions for peasant production in the longer term worsened. The gap between the development strategy's far-reaching goals and the social progress envisaged by its implementation was widening slowly but surely. In rural areas long-term production capacity was impaired by a politically and ideologically motivated structural transformation, whose scope and rhythm had no counterpart in economic development. Hence in practice the rural population was left ever more to its own resources. Within the state sector, in both agriculture and industry the possibilities for future increases in production were undermined by the shortage of skilled labour and difficulties with organisation, administration and levels of technology.

During this period Mozambique was also involved in extensive open warfare with Rhodesia. At the same time the first signs of South African destabilisation began to appear, mainly in economic relations with South Africa. Recruitment of mineworkers decreased after independence to about one-third of the previous level, which reduced revenues in convertible currency. The agreement with South Africa on payment of miners' wages in gold, which the Frelimo government had taken over from Portugal, was breached unilaterally by South Africa in 1978.[78] The use of Mozambique's railways and ports decreased dramatically when the main part of the region's inter-continental cargo flow for technical or political reasons was redirected to an ever-increasing extent to ports in South Africa. Hence international rail traffic through Mozambique was halved between 1975 and 1981.[79]

Economic setbacks

Quite soon after independence a public political rhetoric was developed, where the vision was described as though it had been largely brought about. This should have had a mobilising effect on the population, but over the years it became increasingly difficult for people to recognise their own reality in these official statements.

Agricultural policy under stress

The modernisation strategy for rural development that Mozambique chose on independence could never be brought to its conclusion. State farms, despite gigantic efforts, did not reach their targets but showed stagnating production. Hardly 50 per cent of the area that had been cultivated commercially during the colonial era had been put into use. Those areas that were cultivated gave rise to huge deficits. Farmers who lived around the state farms were not allowed to cultivate non-utilised land for themselves. No employees on a state farm had more than one hectare for the family's own farming. A lack of planning, leadership and administrative capacity in the newly established state farms meant that allocated resources were abused or misused.[80]

The state farms' economic failure also allowed no financial scope for supporting mechanisation of the agriculture cooperatives. Of the planned 15,000 cooperatives, by 1983 only 350 had been set up, most of them with huge administrative problems. Movement into communal villages came to a standstill. Of the 6 million planned, it was estimated that a maximum of 1.4 million people lived in communal villages in 1983, i.e. barely 20 per cent of the planned figure.[81]

The state farms have sometimes been criticised for being 'over-mechanised'. The problem was, however, more a political and social one. The rural policy was based on a number of assumptions, which were consistent with neither the material preconditions for food supplies for the rural areas of Mozambique nor the prevailing cultural pattern.

Domestic surplus agricultural production decreased as Portuguese and, to a lesser extent, Indian traders disappeared. The fact that the government, instead of rebuilding the trade network and stimulating family farmers to increase production for sale through increased access to consumer goods, concentrated much of its energy on modernisation of the newly formed state farms also had implications for an economy based on domestic production.

The reason for Frelimo's development strategy over-emphasising production without corresponding attention being devoted to effective trade should be understood against the background of the experiences of Portuguese colonial exploitation. On independence the trade concept itself became a symbol of unequal exchange and came to be replaced by a distribution concept, where transport and handling costs were neglected in the official setting of prices.

The policy implemented did not take into consideration the fact that motivation for the traders, and their ethic behaviour varies considerably among different types of traders. Retail traders operating at the district level are in more direct contact with their clients, thus forcing them to take into consideration the importance of contributing to the satisfaction of the social needs of the population. This is not a philanthropic issue; it is more an effect of both a certain kind of social control prevailing in the countryside and a certain understanding among traders of the need to increase their legitimacy through a certain care and credibility. This could be understood as a certain 'promotion cost' that local traders are willing to pay.

For traders acting as wholesalers at the provincial level (and temporarily penetrating the district level whenever commercially justified) the situation is different. They act on a far more commercial basis due to their anonymity amongst the rural population and the belief that the benefits of short-term business often outweigh the benefits of long-term confidence. Hence their preparedness to pay the extra 'promotion costs' of adopting the same social behaviour as the local traders is not so well developed. The Frelimo analysis never made this distinction.

The lack of hoes and other implements for sowing, etc., gradually reduced the ability of the peasants to produce for their own consumption. The shortage of consumer goods meant that peasants further reduced their production for sale or channelled it to the black market, where the general shortage of food created the scope for large price increases. In this way the basis for the traders' legal activity disappeared and the black market developed explosively.

The international interpretation of the dramatically reduced production for cash crops starts out from the fact that the producer prices were far too low. However, it can be strongly questioned whether sinking production was a result of too low producer prices. In several areas the elasticity of prices was itself negative as long as farmers did not have access to consumer goods to purchase with their own money. Often increased producer prices only entailed a further reduction in production because the supply of goods was not improved at the same time. The farmers' need for cash could quite simply be satisfied by lower production. In other cases increased production prices meant a corresponding increase in the prices of consumer goods. As long as the supply of consumer goods did not increase, higher producer prices tended to imply reduced production or increased inflation and not as expected increased production for sale. The scope for the traders' profit margins constituted a greater problem. As a consequence of the scattered population and small volumes available for sale, the costs for purchase and sale of food surpluses in rural areas were unusually high in Mozambique. During the colonial era Portuguese traders often compensated themselves for the high marketing costs by integrating activities as traders with their own activity as farmers. They were already compensated for the high costs of marketing by applying a price system which was negative for the farmers.

These high marketing costs increased further during the 1980s as a result of the security problem. The regulated price system frequently did not allow the traders to fully cover their costs. They were therefore often forced either to sell their purchased products on the black market or to compensate themselves by extracting a significantly higher price than stipulated for consumer goods. The extensive shortage of goods together with an insufficient number of traders and the lack of competition meant that the current liberalisation of trade still signified no improvement in the farmers' terms of exchange. The traders still extracted significantly higher prices for consumer goods in rural areas than in the towns and often purchases of agricultural products were made below the state stipulated minimum price. This fact naturally affected the peasants' motivation.

The reduction in the family farmers' production for sale after 1982 could not be compensated for by increased production on the state farms. On the contrary, their production sank even more. To these problems was added military destabilisation, which at the beginning of

the 1980s targeted the state farms. As a result the country's food production was greatly reduced.

The drought that struck southern Mozambique at the beginning of
the 1980s worsened the situation for the rural population. The government's preconditions for implementing its strategy, using agriculture as
an economic base, decreased rapidly.

It was not only the lack of rain that caused the famine. The region
has a climate with great variations in rainfall, but during the twentieth
century ecological vulnerability has increased markedly. The male
labour force was recruited to the mines in South Africa. Agriculture
was left to the women, and slash-and-burn cultivation's requirement for
land to lie fallow and continual clearing of new land had to give way.
The soil was impoverished, with a resulting decrease in production.
Famine was kept at bay with the incomes that the mine-workers sent
home to their families, who were able to compensate for their low
production by buying food in the markets. Each family in the Inhambane province, for example, was dependent to a great extent on incomes
from minework in the neighbouring country for its supplies. This also
required a functioning trade network.

As stated previously, the number of Mozambican mineworkers was
reduced from over 100,000 to 40,000 after the country's independence.
Together with the collapse of the trade network this created a vulnerability which Mozambique saw the effects of at the beginning of the
1980s. There was also the fact that the agricultural policy's failures
further reduced the rural population's defence against variations in
rainfall. Popular migrations and the new stratification in the rural areas
reduced production capacity. The changed settlement structure increased ecological vulnerability and quickly destroyed even more cultivable land.

Industrial bottleneck

However, the role of rural areas in the economic decline cannot be
seen separately from industry. Frelimo's failed agricultural policy is
usually held up as the main cause of many of the difficulties that developed during the 1980s. It should however be noted that agriculture's
share of GNP *rose* between the years 1981 and 1986 to 45 per cent,
while industry's share fell over the same period from 40 to 27 per cent.
Industry was based more than any other sector on a white labour force,
from top to bottom of the enterprises. Also a large proportion of
industrial workers were white Portuguese. Industry was thus dealt a
particularly severe blow by the flight of the Portuguese from Mozambique on independence.

This had two important effects. The first was that industry could no longer play a dynamic role in the development of the economy, which was a precondition of the development strategy, and the anticipated positive link effects between agriculture and industry failed to appear. The second effect was that the industrial sector became a heavy financial burden on the economy. For political and social reasons no employees were made redundant, and industries continued with a full staff complement and very low utilisation of capacity.

Difficulties in industry thus reinforced the difficulties within agriculture, as one of the most important income bases for the modern economy was considerably weakened. But this burden was unequally distributed. Workers who did not produce continued to collect wages, whilst the shortage of consumer goods and agricultural implements in rural areas became acute. The political problems that these economic difficulties could be expected to create consequently did not arise in the towns but in rural areas, where the instrument of destabilisation was later successful in taking root in marginalised peasantry.

Decreased revenues

The downward trend in economic development after 1981 also reveals itself in reduced service revenues from South Africa, falling exports and increased imports. Reduced export revenues and faulty prioritisation took the economy further downwards in a vicious circle. A large number of small imports of consumer goods to rural areas, which had actually been made previously, were now rendered completely impossible as a result of the enormous shortage of foreign currency. Currency that was available was mainly used to maintain the level of imports of crude oil, machinery and raw materials for the modern sector, which were judged essential. With time this policy proved to be mistaken because of the reduced surplus production for sale from the family sector. In this way the shortage of foreign currency was exacerbated. At the same time as export revenues were falling further, the country's import demand for food rose in order to maintain the urban population's food supplies.[82]

This situation meant that farmers continued to reduce their surplus agricultural production or sold their surplus on the black market, whose dealers often smuggled out the produce to neighbouring countries where the supply of consumer goods was greater.[83]

However, the problem was not only the lack of foreign currency and the large requirement for international borrowing. During 1983 the state's revenues had fallen rapidly, at the same time as expenditure on defence, subsidies to consumers and state enterprises and wages for public employees had risen sharply. For the first time since independence the state budget showed a large deficit. It was financed by printing banknotes.

Table 3.1 Development of production and foreign trade in selected years, 1973–86

	1973	1974	1975	1977	1981	1983	1985	1986
Production GSP (billion meticais, 1980 prices)	112	92	71	75	84	64	54	56
of which:								
Agriculture	37	32	25	31	31	24	25	25
Industry, fishing	42	35	28	28	34	23	15	15
Transport	12	11	9	7	9	6	4	4
Exports ($ million, current prices)	226	296	185	153	280	132	77	79
Imports ($ million, current prices)	465	460	395	336	801	636	424	543
Exports/imports (%)	49	64	47	45	35	21	18	15

Source: Ratilal, 1990; *Informação Estatística,* CNP, for various years.

In 1985 exports were only 27 per cent of 1981 figures. Thus imports were reduced by 47 per cent over the same period.

Necessary cuts in the country's imports of oil, raw materials, spare parts and consumer goods further aggravated the shortage of goods. The money supply and popular demand exceeded the supply of goods many times. Inflation rose sharply and the parallel market increased in extent.

Economic action programme

At Frelimo's fourth party congress in 1983 there was great dissatisfaction that so many resources had been concentrated on the state farms and so little had been allocated to the rural population. In the same year the government formulated an action programme to break the downward spiral.

It was established that the macro-economic balance had to be restored as quickly as possible. State expenditure and the size of the money supply had to be adjusted to the country's production capacity. Wage rises and subsidies had to be kept to a minimum. Also a number of more long-term changes would be initiated. According to the new guidelines for agriculture that were developed, large investments would be made in order for peasants to gain access to essential agricultural implements and consumer goods. The state sector would be consolidated and restructured, and state enterprises would be divided up into smaller units. Also peasants without land and private farmers with proven ability would be allocated land from the state sector. Thereafter the state farms would play a decisive role in advising and financing the growing cooperatives. Domestic industrial development would mainly be directed at producing consumer goods for the domestic market. The expectation was that the economic action programme, together with peace negotiations with South Africa and access to cheaper credits, would set the wheels in motion again.

Accumulation versus mobilisation

Many international intellectuals who largely supported the formulation of the country's development strategy commended the result of the Frelimo congress. As distinct from the Western aid donors, who mainly saw and lauded the fact that the market economic thinking was gaining ever-increasing influence, the former saw the congress as a victory for the forces within Frelimo who realised the importance of re-establishing the traditional political alliance between the party and the rural population to advance the socialist transitional process.

> [U]nder very real pressure from the peasantry itself the Party was also inching its way towards a greater acceptance of the 'economics of expanded socialist reproduction' as a key to defining other aspects of the industrial mix, in particular the balance between heavy industrial and infrastructural development on the one hand and consumer goods industries on the other ... These emphases bore the promise – other things being equal – of closing crucial gaps in Frelimo's post-independence economic policies. Moreover, this was a promise which built upon historic precedent: the precedent of Frelimo's close links with the peasantry, links which had premises in the movement's victory in the guerrilla war. For anyone in attendance at the Fourth Congress it was hard to escape the feeling that a fundamental aspect of Frelimo's practice was reasserting itself.[84]

For these commentators there was no contradiction between the party leadership's endeavours for modernisation, with appurtenant accumulation and long-term economic growth, and satisfying the peasants' short-term material needs required for their mobilisation. On the contrary, according to the theory on 'expanded socialist reproduction' the satisfaction of the peasants' basic needs was a precondition, even if an inadequate one, for long-term accumulation.[85]

This perception built upon the farmers forming a homogeneous group which in essential respects accorded with the government's socialist development plans.[86]

However, the peasantry was far from being homogenous, and this resulted in part from the economic policy pursued by the state ... The interests of both the rich peasantry and the larger private farmers were quite different from those of the poor peasantry, whose standard of living was eroded by the parallel economy.[87]

For large parts of the rural population the contradiction between accumulation and mobilisation was actually real, at least in the short term, until the country's economy was developed far enough for it to be able to satisfy the increased purchasing power to which accumulation would give rise through increased employment, with a corresponding supply of goods and services.

The congress avoided discussing the contradiction between party and state which began to develop as a result of the modernisation strategy and its planning and management structure. The state administration also began to live its own life and different decisions taken at the political level were blocked increasingly often at the executive level by functionaries with other interests. Several political decisions taken by the party were reformulated on implementation by the state administration's functionaries or were not implemented at all. One example of this is the decisions taken during the fourth party congress regarding the country's agricultural policy and a strategy for rural development, which in practice were implemented only to a very minimal extent.

In reality the implementation of a more capital-intensive and import-dependent agricultural policy continued, even if the main focus was gradually shifted from the state farms to what were perceived to be more production-inclined private farmers. Despite the increasing share of agricultural investment, few funds were allocated to the family sector. Investments continued to be concentrated on modernising rural areas, mainly in southern Mozambique. The fertile provinces in the north were constantly neglected.

Actual investments which were still made, not least in an attempt to increase the supply of consumer goods, never had a chance of achieving any concrete result.[88] The four-year drought which struck the whole of Southern Africa in 1982–85 had a marked impact during 1983. South African destabilisation was also increasing. In 1984 hundreds of thousands of people were to be found in rural areas, fleeing from violence and terror. In 1986 the number had risen to 3 million. Agricultural production collapsed and the marketed surplus fell dramatically from 86,000 tons of maize in 1982 to 21,000 tons in 1986, i.e. 75 per cent in total. Taken together, this implied a significant requirement for imported food.

Industry operated at 20–40 per cent of its installed capacity. The state budget deficit increased. Prices on the parallel market were 20–40 times higher than official prices. Between 1980 and 1986 the gross

Table 3.2 Marketing of domestically produced food (in 1,000 tons)

	1980	1982	1984	1986	1988	1989
Total	140	153	136	75	98	113
of which:						
maize	65	86	82	21	44	68
rice	44	42	19	19	32	16
cassava	9	10	7	6	12	14
other	22	15	28	29	10	15

Source: Eduards et al. (1990)

Note: The table shows the decline in agricultural products marketed via the official trade network. With regard to the growth of the black market, the figures do not give an exact picture of the development of either total food production or marketed production over the period. However, the reduced quantities sold on the official market are considered to be substantially higher than the growth of the black market.

national product fell by over 30 per cent. Consumption per person had been reduced to an even higher degree, because the population was increasing at the same time.

4

External and Internal Factors in Interaction

The regional security complex

Independent Mozambique did not enjoy many years of peace and social stability. A few years after Frelimo's takeover of power, the white minority-ruled neighbouring countries in the region initiated extensive economic and military destabilisation of the country, which would come to obstruct the implementation of the development strategy formulated during the third party congress in 1977. The security policy basis for the South African military destabilisation of Mozambique should be understood against the background of the specific situation that prevailed in Southern Africa at the end of the 1970s.

On the one hand the conflict between South Africa and Angola and Mozambique may be analysed as a regional conflict set in the global superpower pattern. South Africa can be seen as a white, Western bastion in black Africa and also the world's most important producer of gold and a range of the industrialised Western world's most important mineral raw materials. Angola and Mozambique can be portrayed as black Marxist-Leninist states which, after a Soviet- and Chinese-supported armed liberation struggle, now worked together with the Soviet-supported ANC to smash capitalism in Southern Africa. However, unequivocal and clear support from all Western countries for South Africa would be in line with all reasonable power political considerations, if the situation had been limited to this.

On the other hand there were antagonisms based on the apartheid system. These included both internal contradictions in South Africa, and relations with the black majority-ruled states in the region. The apartheid system was condemned, politically and morally, in all countries, which rendered impossible a simple interpretation of the conflicts in the region as a reflection of the superpower conflict. This was especially significant during the first years after 1975, which coincided with the first year of the Carter administration.

After 1980 and Reagan's appointment as president, however, the pattern of antagonisms at global and regional level came to coincide completely. South Africa's defence of the apartheid system divided the region with nearly razor-sharp borders in race terms. Also, the white South African establishment saw a double threat. This threat referred not only to the risk of losing its power to a majority-rule regime: black majority rule was also seen as resulting in a communist state. This picture coincided with the foreign policy orientation which the Reagan administration came to adopt. This meant that for most of the 1980s South Africa had international political scope to accomplish by military means both its own strategy for defending the apartheid system and the global American strategy to combat Marxist-Leninist regimes in the Third World.

The regional security complex that the states in Southern Africa lived with has thus in certain respects been a reflection of the global situation. At the same time it had and has a regional basis. However, these aspects have reinforced each other by the definition of friends and enemies in relation to the apartheid system in Southern Africa. Countries such as Mozambique and Angola were consequently successful in ending up 'wrong' (or right, depending on how one looks at it) both in the global and the regional pattern. Through their socialist development strategies they were perceived as being allies of the Soviets and communism, and through their militant support for the ANC they were the sworn enemies of the white regime in South Africa.

Growth of Renamo

The most important instrument employed by South Africa for its military destabilisation, Mozambique National Resistance (MNR), was formed by the Rhodesian security service at the end of the 1970s in an attempt to prevent Zimbabwe's independence.

During the 1970s cooperation between Frelimo and the Zimbabwean liberation organisation, ZANU, was initiated. ZANU's guerrillas had bases in Frelimo-controlled areas in Mozambique, in areas bordering what was then Rhodesia. As the inability of the Portuguese to combat Frelimo became clearer, the Rhodesian military and security service began to operate independently within Mozambique in their hunt for ZANU soldiers and their sympathisers. Rhodesia chose the same tactic, using groups of pseudo-terrorists, as had been successful against the Mau-Mau 20 years earlier.[89]

After Mozambique's independence in 1975, ZANU had full access to Mozambican territory in order to organise its guerrilla war against Ian Smith's Rhodesia. One of the Rhodesian security service's main countermeasures was to develop and coordinate its pseudo-terrorists into a larger unit, which was given the name Mozambique National Resistance (MNR). In this work they were helped by the Portuguese and by former commandos from the Portuguese army and security service. Many of these fled from Mozambique to Rhodesia on Frelimo's takeover of power.[90]

For historical and geographical reasons the black Mozambicans who were included in these special groups were recruited from the most central parts of Mozambique. When after 1971 Frelimo attempted to advance south of the Zambezi river, towards Beira, influential Portuguese in Beira began to organise their own special forces. These were recruited locally and came to be dominated by the N'dau ethnic group. When these groups then went into Rhodesian service after 1975, it was in precisely their home areas in central Mozambique that ZANLA had most of its guerrilla bases. At that time the N'dau dominance was established, and it is still evident today in the military cadres within MNR.

When in 1980 Rhodesia was transformed into independent Zimbabwe, the South African military security service was anxious to take over MNR. In an airlift some weeks before Zimbabwe's independence, the larger part of MNR's manpower, equipment and Rhodesian officers was transferred to South Africa. They were located on a military base in Phalaborwa, close to the border with Mozambique.[91]

When MNR was installed in South Africa, extensive development work commenced. This went in two directions. One involved the development of military destabilisation of Mozambique, while the other involved the psuedo-unit MNR being tranformed into an internationally credible organisation.

The Portuguese component

As Frelimo's war of liberation against the Portuguese developed, antagonisms between the central government in Lisbon and the Portuguese in Mozambique also grew.

The similarities between developments in Rhodesia and Mozambique were striking. In both countries there was a relatively large group of Europeans, who yearned increasingly for their 'own' independence, i.e. a release from the colonial power without any black majority rule being introduced. In Rhodesia unilateral independence was declared in 1965. Many Portuguese in Mozambique nurtured expectations of a similar development.[92]

Political development in Portugal, however, went faster than expected and the military coup on 25 April 1974 changed the preconditions for a unilateral declaration of independence by the Portuguese in Mozambique. There was great bitterness towards the old central government in Lisbon. It was even greater towards the new Portuguese government, which through a treaty of 7 September 1974 transferred all power in Mozambique to Frelimo. On the same day the treaty was signed a state coup was attempted, but failed.

To a great extent all the Portuguese living in Mozambique left the country on independence. A large group returned to Portugal, but many opted to remain in Africa and settled in neighbouring countries, mainly Rhodesia and South Africa. In South Africa there is today a population of Portuguese descent of 700,000.

There are three distinct groups of Portuguese origin, who participated in different ways in the destabilisation of Mozambique. One group has its roots in Portuguese financial capital. The two main representatives of this group are both businessmen, Manuel Bulhosa and António Champalimaud. Both were among the part-owners of Maputo's oil refinery[93] and Champalimaud had interests in the world of banking and insurance, a steelworks in Maputo and other industries.[94] Champalimaud was also linked to Lonrho, the British industrial conglomerate, via an aluminium project in the border areas between Mozambique and Malawi.[95] Financial support for MNR's activity came mainly from this type of source.[96] MNR's representatives in Portugal during the 1980s had positions in, *inter alia*, Bulhosa's publishing house in Lisbon.

A second group is those Portuguese who settled in South Africa after 1975. Many of them are employed within trade and service activities. This group was probably the one that lost most by leaving houses and other property in Mozambique. It contains many who are today returning to Mozambique in an effort to regain their old assets and perhaps re-establish themselves. People in this category have, for example, participated in the civilian contact network surrounding MNR's activities in South Africa. Their enterprises have sometimes been used as 'front organisations' to disguise the South African military's logistical support for MNR and in certain cases they have links with Mozambique through transport enterprises.

A third group is the Portuguese who served in the Portuguese army or the security police during the colonial period. Many of these are now to be found in the South African army, and some have leadership functions and other tasks in a military unit which has been deeply involved in MNR operations.[97]

In addition, with reference to the so-called Portuguese component, throughout the 1980s many politicians in Lisbon assumed an ambiguous attitude to relations with Mozambique. Also, within the Portuguese military apparatus there was active support for MNR.[98]

Political leadership

So long as MNR was only an internal name for a pseudo-terrorist unit within the Rhodesian security service there was no need to formulate a political line. But when MNR was transformed into a pseudo-guerrilla unit the need arose for a political guise. The post of general secretary was given to the Portuguese former agent in Portugal's security service (PIDE), Orlando Cristina.[99] His position as 'guerrilla leader' in Mozambique built, however, on sources other than popular support. In a letter to a guerrilla who defected from Frelimo,[100] he wrote from Rhodesia:

> It is the Rhodesians who pay my wages and my upkeep here, as well as costs for those taken inside Mozambique. Without this support we would all be sitting in cafés in Lisbon, dreaming of unrealistic battles. Neither in South Africa or in Malawi would we be able to organise such guerrillas. This is only possible through Rhodesia ...[101]

After moving to South Africa, Orlando Cristina, in his capacity as general secretary of MNR, was allocated an office in the South African army headquarters, ZANZA House, in Pretoria.[102] One of his first measures was to attempt to organise political leadership for MNR, which now began to be called Renamo, after its name in Portuguese, *Resistência Nacional Moçambicana*. He made a couple of worldwide journeys to seek out old dissidents from Frelimo. The hope was that amongst these would be suitable candidates for a political branch of Renamo.

There was no shortage of Mozambicans in exile hostile to Frelimo. Internal conflicts during the war of liberation had produced a considerable number of dissidents, who were now scattered in different countries. There had never been any political alternative for them. Most had been assimilated in their new home countries, had acquired some education, and had families and decent jobs. Very few of them wanted to make a move in order to involve themselves once more in Mozambican politics, now as representatives of the South African destabilisation policy. Only two names with any well-known anti-colonial past came up in the discussions concerning the composition of MNR's 'National Council' in exile: Artur Vilanculos and Fanual Gideon Mahluza.[103] Others were former Portuguese colonialists, PIDE agents or former soldiers in the colonial army.[104]

The formation of Renamo's national council created extensive turbulence amongst Mozambicans in exile. In Portugal, West Germany, France and the USA there were groups of Mozambicans who were involved in different ways in a closed, yet intense, discussion. Their common denominator was hostility to Frelimo. The most important difference seems to be between those who accepted the South African strategy and those who did not want to be a tool of the apartheid regime.

The greatest problem for everyone in exile was the difficulty in maintaining any contact with those who operated inside Mozambique. All such communications went via the South African military.[105] Not one of Renamo's official representatives had been able to maintain any independent contact with the organisation's leader, Afonso Dhlakama.[106] Several delegations from different groupings of Mozambicans in exile tried in different ways to make independent contact with the movement's leader, Afonso Dhlakama, in Mozambique. No one succeeded.

Destabilisation's underlying aim

Even if Renamo was developed to become South Africa's main instrument for the destabilisation of Mozambique, the South African government and its military apparatus were not the only ones to stand behind MNR[107] over the years. Points of support have been found in Portugal, West Germany and the USA.[108]

The different perceptions of Renamo found among Mozambicans in exile were in some ways reflections of alternative approaches to Mozambique's future found among different governments in Europe and the USA. In simplistic terms they may be described as the military and the economic alternatives.

The goals for the military alternative were to pursue military destabilisation until the Frelimo government fell and could be completely replaced. At worst, those who advocated this perception accepted that conservative members of Frelimo might enter an alliance with Renamo in order to form a government of national reconciliation, in which the possibilities for Frelimo's radical policies to assert themselves would be very limited.

The military alternative had its strongest support in the South African military apparatus, mainly among special troops and officers of Portuguese stock.[109] This alternative had also been dominant in ultra-conservative circles in the USA. Support for Renamo was mobilised among conservative foundations and within the military intelligence service, DIA. Within DIA they were very displeased that during the 1980s the former assistant secretary for African Affairs, Chester Crocker, was successful in convincing President Reagan to deviate from his own doctrine on support to anti-communist guerrilla organisations in the world, by maintaining good ties with Frelimo instead of Renamo.[110]

The economic alternative involved forcing Frelimo, via destabilisation, into transforming its socialist economic policy, leaving the Eastern bloc and adopting the principles of the market economy and democracy. When this transformation was regarded as irrevocable, a transformed Frelimo would be given responsibility for reconstructing Mozambique and functioning as a recipient of international aid for this purpose.

In Southern Africa this economic alternative was in principle a continuation of the South African *détente* policy of the middle 1970s. It was aimed at consolidating South Africa's dominance in the region through economic penetration. The South African economy needed rapid expansion and consolidation in order to emerge relatively 'unscathed' from the transformation to a post-apartheid South Africa. In this perspective Frelimo could well remain in power in Mozambique, provided that the government had no power to influence the outcome of the political process in South Africa. Continued destabilisation of Mozambique would be counterproductive, because it would frustrate attempts by the international community to 'admit' a Mozambique which had been changed through destabilisation. The thinking behind this alternative was probably that the economic changes that Frelimo implemented itself would upset the internal economic balance of power in a direction that would make it irrelevant which party or parties were in power.

Both these alternatives, military and economic, were not clearly visible when Renamo's first secretary-general, the Portuguese former security agent Orlando Cristina, made his recruiting journeys all over the world at the beginning of the 1980s. But they can still be traced in a series of dividing lines, found within different sections of Renamo, among Mozambican exile politicians and within the power apparatus in several different Western governments.

First, it is not the same players who have dominated Renamo's military activity inside Mozambique who have been visible in the international network. There has actually been a virtually watertight bulkhead between the reality of the war in Mozambique and exiled circles in Europe and North America. The military alternative has controlled operational activity, while for a long time the economic alternative's followers have had a better international standing.

Second, there has also been a dividing line between different groupings of Mozambicans in exile. On the one hand there are those who have a credible political history as anti-colonialists or former members of Frelimo. On the other hand there are those who were drawn into Renamo either through previous contacts with the South African or Portuguese security services or through different types of personal contacts. The first have tended to operate in a context which has closely supported the economic alternative.

Third, there has also been a dividing line between different factions of the government and security service agencies in South Africa and the USA. The economic alternative's followers have long attempted to wrest the whole of Renamo from the grip of the South African military, in order to halt destabilisation before it becomes counterproductive.[111]

These antagonisms, together with different perceptions of when the aims of destabilisation could be considered to have been achieved, were an important factor underlying the difficulties of the peace negotiations.

The effects of economic and military destabilisation

The destabilisation of Mozambique manifested itself in different ways. The most obvious economic consequences have been the reduced recruitment of Mozambican mineworkers to South Africa and the reduced volume of freight using Mozambique's transit railways and ports.

The military destabilisation of Mozambique has been directed at two main targets. The first are the heavy nationally and economically important infrastructural targets. Examples of military actions of this type are the sabotage of the oil port in Beira in 1982, the blowing-up of strategic bridge connections and the constant attacks on railway links with neighbouring countries.

The second type of goal is the social infrastructure in rural areas, mainly schools and health-care institutions. This type of destabilisation has also been directed against society's social network, by setting brother against brother, children against parents and town against country in a chain of abnormal violence, which extends beyond all norms for human behaviour.[112]

Overshadowing everything else has been South Africa's organisation and leadership of Renamo, whose terror campaign in rural areas has meant that it has not been possible to maintain regular food production. The supply of clothing and other primary consumer goods has ceased. Disruption of the infrastructure has been very extensive: countless roads, bridges, shops, stores, schools and health-care institutions will have to be rebuilt in order for the rural economy to be able to function again.

The destabilisation of Mozambique led to near total destruction of the rural infrastructure and economic flow. The costs of bringing about this massive destruction by conventional military means would have been a great deal higher. Both international opinion and the Mozambican population were kept in doubt about what the final goal of this activity was.

This indirectly influenced the population's view of the political system and its function. It was not a question in the first instance of Frelimo's legitimacy as a party increasing or diminishing. It was mainly a matter of the rural population's perception of the nature of the national political system, that allowed them to be exposed to this violence. Because of the war, the 'nation' (in the sense of the central government)[113] has demonstrated an ever smaller presence at local level, not least in that schools and health-care posts have ceased to function.

Frelimo's strategy for consolidating the legitimacy of state power in the whole country included a substantial expansion in education and health-care for those sections of the population that colonialism had neglected. Thus a capillary system was created, where legitimacy and political trust flowed in one direction in exchange for improvements in social sectors.

It was precisely against this exchange of political trust for social welfare that destabilisation was directed via the destruction of schools and health-care posts. In the same way as Frelimo was not always successful in protecting the population militarily and socially during the war of liberation, throughout the 1980s the Frelimo government was incapable of maintaining normal conditions for survival in the rural areas. The near-surgical precision in choice of targets for attacks meant that population groups who had *not* pulled out from Frelimo's modernisation project ran a greater risk of being attacked. Especially prominent in this respect were attacks against health-care institutions and boarding schools. Sending one's child to a boarding school or being admitted to a smaller maternity hospital in rural areas meant taking a higher risk than staying outside society's modern institutions. The destruction thus not only reduced the supply of social services, but also significantly reduced demand.

Instead the rural population has attempted a strengthened adherence to traditional society. One example of this is that traditional health-care has not just withstood ideological attacks against superstition and spiritualism, but has also strengthened its position in recent years at the expense of modern health-care, which in turn has been prioritised by the defined goals of military destabilisation.

Today the result of the South African military development of MNR is well known. A UN agency estimated that the destruction up to 1989 amounted to at least $15 billion – an amount that would correspond to the value of 20 years' international aid or more than 100 years' export revenues according to the present order of magnitude. The same UN report calculates the number of war-related victims in Mozambique between 1980 and 1988 to be 900,000, of whom 494,000 were children.[114] The education and health-care systems in rural areas were largely destroyed. During the period 1983–89, 40 per cent of all primary schools in the whole country were destroyed or closed down.[115] Because the figures also include large towns and district centres, the situation in purely rural areas will be appalling. The worst exposed provinces were Tete and Zambezia, where 88 per cent and 81.5 per cent respectively of primary schools were destroyed or closed down.[116] As in all wars, it is the children who suffer most. The UN report 'Children in the Frontline' has studied the effects of South Africa's aggression against Angola and Mozambique. UNICEF has worked out that in Mozambique 325–75 per thousand children died before they reached their fifth

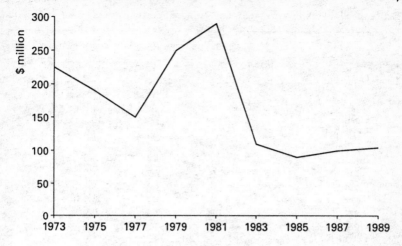

Figure 5 Total exports, selected years 1973–89

birthday. According to UNICEF the so-called one-year death rate was about 200 per thousand.[117]

Through South African destabilisation the famine in Mozambique was seriously exacerbated. Gradually over one-third of the population was forced to leave their land, move to the towns, or flee to neighbouring countries or safer areas within the country. The constant migrations and the concentration of the population in areas where security was judged to be greater entailed severe pressure on existing land and much tree-felling. In this way ecological vulnerability developed even more. For long periods about half the country's population of 15 million became dependent on external food relief for their food supply.

Figure 5 and Table 4.1 may serve as an illustration of the effects of the war on the Mozambican economy. The fall in exports was already beginning two years before independence. The figures continued to fall during the first years after independence, then rose again and reached their highest level in 1981. If this development is set relative to changes in the military situation in Mozambique, it is evident that the highest export values in 1980–82 coincide with the only period of relative peace experienced by Mozambique since independence. When South African destabilisation took off at the end of 1981 and became ever more tangible in rural areas in ever larger parts of the country from the beginning of 1982, the economy collapsed.

Table 4.1 shows how exports of different products developed during the years that constituted a turning point for the Mozambican economy. Exports of agricultural products were severely affected as the war began

Table 4.1 Exports by type, 1981–83 ($ million, current prices)

	1981	1982	1983
Total exports	280.0	229.2	131.6
Of which:			
Cashew nuts	53.4	43.6	16.1
Shrimps	52.4	38.5	31.2
Cotton	24.9	17.3	17.1
Sugar	25.1	8.8	8.6
Sisal	2.9	2.7	1.0
Copra	4.8	3.0	2.1
Tea	14.2	25.7	14.7
Timber	7.3	3.3	0.6
Coal	9.7	4.2	0.5
Citrus fruits	4.8	2.7	1.9
Oil products	52.2	37.6	21.8
Other	28.3	41.6	16.0

Source: Informação Estatística, CNP, different years.

to spread seriously over the country. Production also fell in goods for export which originated in rural areas and which required free movement of the population and access to communications in order to be obtained. This applies most clearly, perhaps, to cashew nuts, whose export figures fell by 70% between 1981 and 1983. Timber exports fell by 92% during the same period when wood-cutters could no longer work and there was no longer any transportation.[118] Sugar plantations in central areas of Mozambique were forced to reduce their production and exports fell to around a third of the previous level. Coal exports were formerly transported by rail to Beira. The railway was one of MNR's first targets, with the result that in principle exports were virtually obliterated.

Mozambican military strategy in change

According to all the evidence, the war of liberation against the Portuguese army was a guerrilla war based on close relations between the population and the guerrillas. Frelimo's supply lines from Tanzania into Mozambique were built up in close cooperation with the population and it was essential to defend these lifelines at any cost. It should be noted that in its liberated areas Frelimo organised not only social institutions, such as education and health-care, but also a commercial network with transport in both directions. This meant that if the peasants in one area were able to produce more than they themselves and the guerrillas needed for their own subsistence, this surplus could be exported to Tanzania or exchanged for consumer goods and clothing. Weapons and ammunition were probably brought along the same transport routes.

It is in this perspective that the severity with which Frelimo's *military* strategist Samora Machel attacked the *political* opposition that developed in Cabo Delgado province should be seen. When Lázaro Kavandame[119] and others started to operate private businesses in Cabo Delgado, not only was it a threat to Frelimo's socialist perspective (which was also not particularly well developed at the end of the 1960s), it threatened the whole legitimacy of the military strategy. Supply lines are central to every guerrilla war and if the people do not obtain the maximum benefit from their participation in this work, they pull out. The struggle between the two factions thus depended not only on political antagonisms, but also, and perhaps mainly, on the fact that its concrete expression threatened military action absolutely.

After independence the guerrilla army was disbanded and a standing army created. The material support and training that the new officers were offered were aimed at defence against conventional military attacks. The tanks and armoured cars placed at Mozambique's disposal by the Soviets and the Eastern bloc states have all given the impression of being passably functioning surplus materials from the Second World War. The training carried out was closely linked to the defence strategy which the supplies of materials presupposed.[120]

It was felt that the correctness of this strategic choice was confirmed by the character assumed by the aggression by Rhodesia. Air attacks and local invasions using conventional troops were normal occurrences. In several cases Mozambican troops successfully shot down a Rhodesian aeroplane. This defence strategy continued during the 1980s and it also built up a missile defence system around Maputo.

However, this military security trend proved to be misdirected. The military apparatus built up in order to ward off international conventional aggression came instead to be ranged against a sub-national security threat, and it became increasingly difficult for soldiers in the field to determine who was a friend and who was the enemy.

One of many anecdotes about Samora Machel tells how on one occasion, during an inspection of an élite company, he was asked to answer the following question: 'Suppose we are following a group of seven bandits. They enter a village where we know that 50 people live. When we arrive we find 57 people in the village. How many bandits are there in the village?' According to the story as retold by Mozambican journalists who were present on the occasion in question, Machel replied that there were seven bandits.

This illustrates a dilemma for the type of war the Mozambican army had to engage in. A military leader who does not want to massacre the population must live with the difficulty of identifying the enemy, as long as he tries to apply conventional methods of warfare.

Samora Machel later began to seek non-conventional methods. His starting point was probably his own experiences as Frelimo's military commander during the war of liberation and his analysis of what the Portuguese army had *not* succeeded in doing. The change in strategy he tried to implement had two components.

The first concerned the supply lines. The so-called territorial units which were formed after 1983–84 used the basic strategy of cutting off Renamo's supply lines.[121] The expression for this in Portuguese has a slightly broader meaning than simply supply lines. Supply lines means not only supplies of weapons and ammunition from South Africa or Malawi; in this instance it also refers to the movement patterns of Renamo groups in rural areas, between their various bases and between their own area and the population in government-controlled areas.

The second component was that government troops would 'occupy the bush', that the soldiers would become the 'lions of the bush'.[122] When one Renamo base, or a somewhat smaller hide-out, was taken, it would be occupied permanently. The military would provide housing for the population in the area and stay on with a force strong enough to defend this new outpost. In this way Machel hoped that in the long term he would be able to reduce the enemy's room for manoeuvre. Renamo's ability to move would be diminished if the area within which they were able to operate could be filled with smaller military outposts, thus guaranteeing a constant military presence. In this way he attempted to decentralise the conventional army that was built up after independence.

There were provincial commanders who managed to implement and maintain this strategy successfully for a time. They began to think more imaginatively and to make use of the heavy Soviet equipment in an unconventional way. A tank is usually heard several kilometres away if it tries to approach a base in preparation for an attack, but in one province several successful attacks were carried out against Renamo bases by moving the tanks to the correct firing position using donkeys and oxen. Firepower was thus high and the bases were easy to occupy.

However, there was a series of obstacles to the full implementation of this strategy. One obstacle was that younger middle-ranking officers had no roots in the war of liberation, but were trained after independence in strategic thinking which did not allow them to start hauling tanks using donkeys.

Another problem was that the FPLM did not manage to maintain the logistical system to feed the soldiers and provide military material to a large number of scattered military positions as required by Machel's strategy. When the soldiers in an occupied base had not received any food for two weeks, they often simply returned to the nearest district town and took French leave. The base was immediately re-taken by Renamo.

A third problem was that relations with the population at these small outposts and in the environs of occupied Renamo bases never managed to achieve the same high degree of reciprocity as during the war of liberation. This was partly because the soldiers were not voluntary guerrillas but normal conscripts, and partly because the FPLM was no longer managing to maintain its own supply lines and soldiers and officers began to run their own 'business' as the food crisis in Mozambique developed. After independence the entire military-political system had changed in a direction which did not need any 'organic' relationship with the population.

But irrespective of which circumstances at that time created problems for FPLM in relation to the type of war that Renamo represented, there were underlying factors whose significance should not be underestimated – that is, the way in which threats to national security were analysed and how people prepared themselves to confront these threats.

The military and political threat

Over many years the security situation in South Africa has mainly been assessed in terms of South Africa's military superiority and its aggression towards militarily defenceless neighbouring countries. Such a picture is correct in its military dimension. But at the same time it obscures the fact that under military asymmetry there is a more complex threat scenario, in which the frontline states have represented a far greater threat to South Africa's national security than can be discerned from their military capacity.

This relationship can be compared with relations between the USA and the Soviet Union after the Second World War. The Cold War did not arise because of the existence of a military threat from the Soviet Union against the USA and the West. The USA became a military superpower long before the Soviet Union. The threat scenario that dominated was ideological and built on a fear that the fundamental values of American society were threatened by the possible expansion of communist ideology. The point is thus that an inter-state security threat often starts as a perceived non-military threat and later acquires a military dimension. Military expressions of a security problem often first arise *after* other threat scenarios have been perceived and interpreted within a society.[123] If this analysis is transferred to the situation in Southern Africa, we can more easily understand that there have been two irreconcilable ideologically based threat scenarios behind the military security complex in the region.[124]

On the one hand is the fear amongst the Frontline States[125] that they would become totally subordinate to a South Africa that was controlled by a very strict policy of apartheid and thus be transformed into a new group of 'Bantustans' spread over the region but under South Africa's control. This threat was built into the South African government's 'offer' of admission to the 'Constellation of States' (CONSAS) under South Africa's leadership.

On the other hand the white South African population saw how country after country was moving towards black majority rule. From the South African point of view this appeared to be such a comprehensive change that it bordered on a threat of extinction. It is probable that this threat was perceived by the whites in South Africa as being far more serious than the interpretation made by the leaders of the Frontline States of the threat directed towards their countries.

But because it involved two such economically asymmetric players, the reaction to the threat led to the build-up of an extremely large military superiority by one party. We should not forget either that despite this superior military strength it is the Frontline States who have gained ground and that apartheid has disappeared. In a strictly analytical sense the South African interpretation of the threat was thus correct. The region's political development itself constituted a much greater threat to its own security (as they themselves saw it) than was revealed by the analysis of its asymmetric military strengths.

Mozambique's fundamental mistake in assessing how national security should be maintained after independence was in mainly attempting to respond to South Africa's military threat. Mozambique's economy could not possibly bear the costs that building a military apparatus able to withstand conventional military aggression from South Africa would have entailed.

Also, the Mozambican leadership was guided by a near religious belief in the war of liberation's potential for establishing black majority rule throughout the region. Frelimo's own experiences from the war of liberation against the Portuguese colonial power showed that guerrilla warfare had sufficient capacity to make the colonial power so preoccupied with combating its internal enemies that it would not be able to inflict any decisive damage on neighbouring countries that supported the war of liberation. In Frelimo's case this applied to both Tanzania and Zambia, and to a certain extent to Malawi. This principle also came to apply to Zimbabwe, where the liberation movements were able to achieve independence in a relatively short time (five years after Mozambique's independence), without serious damage to the neighbouring countries of Mozambique and Zambia. Both countries made their territories available for military activities directed against Rhodesia.

The application of the same strategy against South Africa, by giving the ANC access to Mozambican territory and strengthening conventional military forces in order to be able to withstand conventional military attacks (which had worked extremely well against Rhodesia), was unsuccessful to say the least. In no instance was Mozambique successful in withstanding a conventional attack from South Africa (apart from the shooting down in 1983 of a radio-controlled mini-plane for radar identification, an Israeli-built 'Scout'). In the main Mozambique had no counter-resources against South Africa's chosen strategy of seizing on and developing instability in the enemy camp.

Because Mozambique's government analysed its national security mainly in military terms, the opportunity to confront factors of an economic, social and cultural type, on which the South African strategy was based, was reduced. Because of the course and nature of the war, all opportunities to confront this non-military threat to national security were lost.

Domestic political capacity

The main difficulties in realising Frelimo's development strategy were indubitably due to South African economic and military destabilisation and the country's inability to defend itself from this. Over ten years it was possible to destroy completely the Mozambican economy, kill hundreds of thousands of people and put about one-third of the population to flight.

Even worse, it is clear that Frelimo's chosen policy and the development strategy contributed to the devastating effects of destabilisation. The radical development strategy and foreign policy caused weak points in several areas; this vulnerability extended not only to external intervention, but also to internal antagonisms in the absence of political and administrative capacity for the implementation of the strategy.

Prerequisites for the implementation of a strategy in practice depend, *inter alia*, on the state's ability, which can be analysed with the aid of three variables.[126] One variable is the government's room for manoeuvre, i.e. its freedom of movement in decision-making. Another is the state's administrative and technical capacity, which determines its ability to implement its development programme. The third is the government's statecraft, i.e. the degree to which it can control policy implementation by steering a course through a complex set of circumstances.

Freedom of action

A state's freedom of action is always limited by its environment. Any government that formulates a development strategy must take into consideration in planning and implementation the reactions of the rest of the world if the strategy is to have any chance of being successful.

But because world conditions are never stable, a government that has development ambitions must constantly assess and re-assess its efforts. For Mozambique and Frelimo the rest of the world changed rapidly during the years immediately after independence, in terms of the international and regional environment, Frelimo's freedom of action with regard to domestic policy and its relationship with the state apparatus it had taken over.

Frelimo's freedom of action was extensive in the period before independence, but was gradually reduced during the years that followed. As has been discussed in an earlier section, the party came to power in a period when the international political situation allowed young states in the Third World to choose socialist development strategies for their development policies. Frelimo's socialist development strategy was formulated during the period 1975–77 in a climate characterised by a certain degree of international *détente* and a positive attitude towards independent socialist-oriented development, both in the Third World and among many liberal and social democratic regimes in Europe and North America. However, when the strategy should have begun to be implemented during the period after 1978 the situation had changed. In the USA opinion had shifted and President Carter's last year in office saw a reorientation of the 'non-interventionist' foreign policy, which came to herald President Reagan's more aggressive foreign policy.

In South Africa the 'wait and see' attitude of Prime Minister Vorster's time was transformed after 1978, under P.W. Botha's leadership, into a 'total strategy' using military and economic destabilisation of neighbouring countries as its main weapon. While Frelimo was formulating its development strategy the international political scene had thus changed. However, Frelimo lacked the capacity to change the route which had been staked out in keeping with the change in the international environment.

With regard to domestic policy, Frelimo had almost total support from the population. However, it is probable that this support was mainly connected to Frelimo's near Messianic role as liberator from colonialism. A different choice of strategy would hardly have affected these domestic policy roots. The experiences of the colonial period and the war of liberation, however, limited Frelimo's ability to realise and exploit this. The socialist vision also remained completely dominant when the international environment had become openly inimical.

Freedom of action with regard to domestic policy is also bound up with the degree to which a government that is trying to attain a rapid social transformation can free itself from the short-term demands of different internal interest groups. Frelimo's dilemma in this respect can be illustrated by the relationship between the revolutionary political leadership, existing economic entrepreneurs (mainly of Asian and European origin) and black Mozambicans, who during the later years of the colonial period were allowed to pursue some economic activity. The latter are the economic equivalent of the political dissidents in Frelimo during the war of liberation.

The existing economic actors were often ambiguous in their attitude to Frelimo. On the one hand there was wide support for Frelimo's struggle for independence, and on the other hand they had individual economic ambitions which were not compatible with the socialist development strategy formulated by Frelimo. However, political support for independence came to prevail over all existing criticism of the economic policy formulated by the government. There was no real forum either for a public critical discussion or any real political alternative to Frelimo.

The intention of Frelimo's leadership was to prevent the consolidation of the colonial capitalist economy and to create new – collective – economic actors, mainly state enterprises and cooperatives. Such a policy was directed mainly against the existing economic actors. The hidden dilemma was that some of Frelimo's members themselves had ambitions to become the new entrepreneurs of independence.[127] When political decisions held back private entrepreneurs, many began to seek positions in the public sector in order to accumulate public resources by making a career in state enterprises, cooperatives, the state apparatus and the party. Their arena was transferred from private activity to the political apparatus. Becoming a director of a state enterprise came to be a coveted alternative to being a private entrepreneur.

The revolutionary party leadership enjoyed extensive political support for its role in the liberation struggle, but its economic strategy had dual enemies. Private entrepreneurs were naturally dissatisfied, but within the leadership of state enterprises as well, private ambitions dominated over the party leadership's intentions of operating a worker-friendly policy. Criticism of these *ambiciosos*[128] was common during the leadership's public appearances over the first years.

The transformation of Frelimo from a broad front to a Marxist-Leninist élite party was also an attempt to block, on a national scale, a repetition of the antagonisms of the time of the war of liberation. The 'purging' of Frelimo, which it was intended that the formation of the party would entail, would give the party the ideological unity regarded as essential for it to be capable of leading development. Amongst other things it became a strict requirement for membership that no one could own a business and employ staff. The antagonisms between the two factions dating from the time of the war of liberation were thus built into the system, because the losing non-revolutionary faction, conceived as a social force, also had a strong presence in the party even after independence. These antagonisms have also made difficult the implementation of political decisions that have not been in the interest of civil servants.

Little capability

The state administration's capability was limited. The overwhelming majority of the Portuguese population left Mozambique during the years surrounding independence, and these included nearly everyone with a higher education who worked in public administration and trade and industry. This group included many who were born in Mozambique. Many had already left the country before independence, but the wave of Mozambican patriotism during the transitional period between 25 April 1974 and independence on 25 June 1975 was interpreted by many as anti-Portuguese excess. The requirement to choose citizenship very soon after independence made many leave. Frelimo also lost a number of educated Mozambicans of African origin in connection with the internal antagonisms of the late 1960s. Many of them were expelled from the liberation front or left the organisation themselves, never to return from exile. A number of Mozambicans who studied abroad, in the USA and Portugal, also preferred for various reasons not to return to Mozambique after independence.

The capability of the state apparatus was impaired at all levels when the poorly educated labour force was forced to take on too much responsibility for activities. The inadequate level of education was reinforced by the fact that both Frelimo's leadership and people with positions of responsibility in the state administration lacked experience of the way in which a country should be ruled. The campaigns and spontaneous mobilising work methods practised during the guerrilla war had little relevance for anyone managing state activities.

Most Mozambicans entering the civil service after independence only had previous training in the administrative routines of Portuguese fascism. Through an authoritarian leadership style, strict central control and the creation of a Marxist-Leninist élite party, which would lead social development, Frelimo's revolutionary leadership tried to compensate for the lack of expertise. The combination of authoritarian work methods from the war, the colonial legacy and the principles introduced to Mozambique by East European planning advisers was devastating.

Frelimo's relationship with the state administration was characterised by the poor technical and administrative ability of the bureaucracy. Also, Frelimo had insufficient control over the state apparatus. Through nationalisation of the economy, many new economic interest groups and players had consolidated themselves within the public sector. There they had acquired a certain level of skill in business management and administrative capability at the same time as they, as public state employees, developed an extensive self-interest. It became increasingly difficult for the party to get political decisions implemented. This still applies today following Frelimo's decision to change the whole economic system, but progress is devastatingly slow. One reason, naturally, is that the state apparatus still lacks skills. This situation will be aggravated by the budget limitation imposed by donors' conditionality and the 'brain drain' to the private sector and international aid organisations in Maputo.

But it would be a mistake to underestimate the significance of conscious opposition to changes. The 'ambitious people' still need the protection of the state apparatus, control resources and the financial flow in order to fulfil their challenge to the existing private entrepreneurs. One of the party leadership's concerns today is finding a form of privatisation that gives the directors of state enterprises an opportunity to establish themselves as private entrepreneurs in competition with the previous economic actors. This is necessary if Frelimo's political unity is to be maintained.

Insufficient statecraft

If Frelimo's political freedom of action were broad and the ability of the state apparatus limited, political statecraft was almost non-existent. The party's inability to orientate itself and the lack of flexibility of its policies meant that it was unable to compensate for its deficiencies in capacity. The political process therefore came to be characterised by an over-confidence in the ideological mobilisation of the population. During the first few years many problems and bottlenecks were resolved through campaigns for 'voluntary labour'. Party, government and state never managed to shed the work methods of the war of liberation and enter into an organised administrative and political system that could function normally in day-to-day tasks. Set routines and methodical work for decision-making and implementation came to be replaced by continuous *ad hoc* solutions, which were built on personal relationships, political bonds and lines of command that the political leadership brought from the war to the state apparatus. Long-term political groundwork was replaced by 'voluntary' campaigns, in which the will to succeed would surpass the lack of capability. When political mobilisation was not enough, repressive methods were close at hand.

People's power is undermined

People's power had become a central concept for the liberation struggle in all the Portuguese colonies. Its exact meaning is more difficult to summarise briefly. In Mozambique people's power came to signify both an all-embracing policy which was operated in the poor peasants' and workers' interests and the specific institutions which were formed to facilitate popular participation in social life. Our discussion deals mainly with the difficulties in creating legitimate institutions. Creating people's power consisted not only of a simple transfer of power from the colonial structure to new organs of power. It essentially represented an attempt at a radical change of society, of people's way of thinking and relating to each other. Such a transformation is a slow process. Setting up organs of people's power thus does not mean that people's power is established, consolidated and legitimate. The first organs of people's power formed in connection with independence came to be called dynamising groups.[129] They were established during the period before independence, to become in the first instance an organisational base for Frelimo in areas of the country not reached by the war of liberation.[130] In this sense they differed from the organs of people's power set up in the liberated areas. Frelimo saw them as a defence organisation against the sabotage, thefts and disruptions that preceded the Portuguese withdrawal from enterprises and factories.[131]

The dynamising groups were direct democratic organs, whose members were elected at public meetings in residential areas, factories and rural areas. For a long time it was the dynamising groups that in practice held power in the country. They were linked to Frelimo and there were always Frelimo members within these groups, but during this turbulent period a local dynamising group was able to develop far-reaching autonomy.

Their tasks largely corresponded to the tasks of the organs of people's power in the liberated areas. They had to attend to whatever was presenting problems for the population. In factories the dynamising groups came to play a special role in that they were also forced to attempt to take responsibility for maintaining production, even if the previous owners made off. But they also had the ideological task of raising the workers' class consciousness. Later more permanent organs for organisation of the workers were established in factories – the so-called production councils. Their function acquired the clearer aim of raising production and productivity.[132] They also came to take on a comprehensive revolutionary task, namely to 'destroy the capitalist production relationships within enterprises and factories, in order to build socialist production relationships'.[133]

The institutionalisation of people's power introduced at Frelimo's third party congress in 1977 meant that the dynamising groups' political functions were distributed between other new institutions. During 1976–77, many of them disbanded when their functions were distributed among the permanent institutions being built up. Despite the public criticism directed against the dynamising groups, arguing that they had been infiltrated by the enemy,[134] they achieved a positive posthumous reputation. They had played a fundamental role in mobilising the population and they had been an important school in democracy and popular exercise of power, it was said in the Central Committee's report at Frelimo's fourth party congress in 1983. They stayed on in residential areas and performed certain administrative functions.[135]

In one sense the dynamising groups had been revolutionary organs which were able to take power locally when the colonial state ceased to function. After 1977 the party itself took over the politically mobilising role previously filled by the dynamising groups. The new people's assemblies at all levels in society were intended to become new organs for popular discussion of the policy carried out. Thus the spontaneous phase of the Mozambican 'revolution' was at an end, and people's power would be consolidated in its established institutions.

Perhaps the most important change found embedded in the institutionalisation of power was the view on leadership. It was partly shaped by the vision of the avant-garde party, which accommodated 'the best revolutionaries among the working people'. As distinct from the earlier situation, where everyone could join the Frelimo liberation front, membership was now limited to an élite. The criteria for membership of this élite constituted a great limitation to recruitment.

This élitist view was also repeated in elections to the people's assemblies. Anyone who wanted to become a member of the party or to be elected to people's assemblies could not (1) have cooperated with the colonial power, (2) be religious or (3) be polygamous. Of these criteria only one, cooperation with the colonial power, had any popular acceptance. The other two hit a large group of the population indiscriminately, and many who were keen supporters of Frelimo and independence were left without any opportunity to participate in political work. A recurrent joke is that people ask how anyone who cannot even organise his own finances well enough to pay *lobolo* (a dowry) for two wives can manage a whole village or district. More seriously, Frelimo thus lost many educated people at local level with administrative capabilities who would have been able to make far-reaching inputs into reconstruction work after independence.

Peasantry under stress

While destabilisation contributed to breaking up the development strategy's economic preconditions, the form of the strategy meant that the political alliance between Frelimo and the peasants, which was essential for the country's independence, and on which the implementation of the development strategy was built, came to be undermined. Together with the failed attempt at modernisation, this increased the material destitution of the rural population and Frelimo's diminished legitimacy facilitated the implementation of the South African destabilisation campaign.

The chosen agricultural policy determined which people were indispensable for implementing the strategy. The state farm concept required a planning and management structure, whose personnel resources were only found among the relatively well-educated Portuguese citizens who stayed on after independence and chose Mozambican citizenship, and the urbanised *assimilados*, who were found in low and intermediate positions in the colonial apparatus. The state farm concept could not accommodate the practical knowledge of cultivation and local knowledge found among the rural families who during the last years of the colonial period gained access to smaller farms and were able to initiate their own private accumulation. As it became clear that the rural strategy would not be able to satisfy the population's expectations of independence, opposition to enforced modernisation formed, and a breeding ground for slowly growing racism directed against whites, mulattos and Indians in the state apparatus and the party leadership developed.

Through the break-up of the political alliance, on which Frelimo's war of liberation and the first years of independence had rested, the peasants and the rural population became increasingly less important as a base for the policy carried out. Thus the urban population and the people in the state apparatus became more important at central and provincial levels. The rural areas were not able to supply the towns with food, and import requirements rose. At the same time access to convertible currency diminished and prioritisations were increasingly benefiting those groups who in reality constituted the government's social base.

The government thus lost its opportunity to influence production and distribution of domestic food. During the mid-1980s nearly all commercial activity outside the largest towns went over to bartering. The farmers refused to sell their surplus for cash and instead demanded to be able to exchange directly by barter. An extensive black market in food developed as the traders channelled some of the rural areas' production to areas with a food shortage and higher purchasing power, i.e. the larger towns. An attempt to stop this was made by securing food transports between different districts using compulsory permits, which further increased the alienation between town and country.

The vision of the state farms also entailed great antagonism between Frelimo and the peasantry. Frelimo considered that the land abandoned by the Portuguese belonged to the state, but the plots of land left by the Portuguese farmers in 1974–77 were not unused in reality when the state farms seized the land after 1977. During the first years after independence the small farmers had themselves implemented their own 'land reform' by taking possession of their old plots of land. As the real Portuguese penetration of the rural areas reached back less than one generation in time, the people of the rural areas still remembered very well what land belonged to whom. Whereas official political rhetoric saw a collective repossession of the plots of land which the colonial power had stolen, the farmers saw only that they had again lost the land which they themselves had already repossessed after the flight of the Portuguese. Those families who had used the land before the arrival of the Portuguese also felt that they had a right to it. Many of these farmers were evicted and the land was incorporated into the state farms. Their inputs, as land-workers and foremen, to promote production under the state farms' management in the fields which they regarded as being their own were limited, to say the least. A normal pattern was that the harvest result measured while the seed was still waving in the fields differed from the actual harvest when it was put into sacks, in round figures by the quantity that the employees' families needed for their survival. The state farms' profitability problem was consequently not a technical and economic one but a social and political one.[136] This problem mainly involved the farmers who had access to fertile plots of land that the Portuguese had confiscated. Beyond these river valleys and fertile, rainy parts of the country there were a further million small farming families. It was they who were most badly affected by the lack of hoes, implements and basic consumer goods.

It was also these farmers who were most afflicted by the new settlement pattern in rural areas. The movement into communal villages meant that some of the farming population had to walk further to reach their plots of land. The increased walking time to the fields was both a drag on the already low productivity in family agriculture and a source of a new sort of economic differentiation of farmers, as farmers lived at different distances from their fields. Increasing numbers of farmers who had fields long distances away gradually became day-labourers for other farmers with fields close by. The cooperatives also tended to use employed day-labourers to an increasing extent. Frequently the villages were located so that the area's most influential family had its traditional tract of land in close proximity to the new villages. Representatives of these families were able to become the most active local spokesmen for communal villages and they were thus able to support their economic ambitions by exercising local political and economic power in line with the official strategy. Thus Frelimo's social base changed. Its alliance with the peasants was weakened. At the same time the strategic antagonisms from the 1960s lived on in the party. When the majority faction's policy was to be implemented with the aid of the rural areas' upper class, who turned to Frelimo *after* independence, in practice it was often the 'reactionaries'' economic ambitions that came to prevail over the 'revolutionaries'' political goals.

Unequal regional development

The implementation of Frelimo's development strategy also meant that the regional imbalance within the country was strengthened. The regional imbalance which today characterises Mozambique has developed over three different periods.

The first phase in this development was initiated at the end of the nineteenth century. In the south there was the proximity to and the dependence on South Africa; the population in the south had a special relationship with South Africa through migrant labour. South Africa has always represented a source of relative wealth. Mine work was naturally hard and was managed on racist principles, but wages were always higher in South Africa than in Mozambique. Even in the nineteenth century a Mozambican migrant worker could obtain wages up to six times higher in South Africa than by working for Portuguese farmers or businessmen, or for the colonial state in southern Mozambique.[137] Industry that was created in Mozambique was mainly located in Maputo or Beira.

In the central areas of the country there were large plantations, which mainly produced plantation crops for export, such as sugar, tea and copra. These used a seasonal labour force, which was dependent for the rest of the year on the family's subsistence agriculture.

In Mozambique's northern areas foreign companies which were assigned the right of full authority over certain regions by the Portuguese Crown predominated. Their exploitation was confined mainly to forcing the farmers into growing cotton. In general, colonial penetration into northern Mozambique was limited.

Development after independence has, if anything, reinforced the unequal development shaped by the colonial period. Behind the planned economy's unequal distribution of resources and investments, three factors are apparent. The first is that the concentration of a small number of major projects swallowed the larger part of the available resources. Productive investments were thus limited to just a few areas.

The second is that, as previously mentioned, many of the large projects for which Frelimo was later criticised were themselves built on Portuguese colonial development plans. The gigantic dam installations outside Maputo, for example, are built according to old Portuguese plans. In the choice of projects Frelimo thus came to follow in the footsteps of, and strengthen the Portuguese planning that formed the basis of this unequal regional development.

The third is that Frelimo's policy was rapidly urbanised after independence. The close contact with the farming population, on which the war of liberation rested, was broken on independence. The leadership in Maputo found it more and more difficult to analyse the economic, political and cultural development of the peasantry. Policy was increasingly formulated as if politics consisted of making an immense effort of will, and Frelimo progressively lost touch with the situation in rural areas.

The pattern of economic imbalance coincides with a political imbalance. Political and economic power in Mozambique at the end of the nineteenth century had a different regional distribution. Not until about 1900 was Mozambique's capital moved to Maputo (then called Lorenço Marques).

The location of the trade centres of the time created more economic and political power, relatively speaking, for those population groups surrounding the Portuguese strongholds. This gave the central and northern parts of Mozambique a stronger position, relatively speaking, compared with the population in southern parts of the country. The southerly Gaza empire's aggression northwards during the nineteenth century reinforced the feeling of colonisation at the same time as the modern economic development potential was moved to Maputo.

Development during the period of independence was not able to alter these century-old tensions. In the centre and the north many feel that independence has consolidated a new pattern of dominance by groupings from the south.

Traditional versus people's power

Frelimo's strategy for a total transformation of society meant, *inter alia*, that the colonial state's institutions were abolished and the country's administrative divisions were changed. The Portuguese district administrators were dismissed as a first measure. However, the districts continued to be the lowest level of the state apparatus, where Frelimo considered that it was extremely important to be represented by politically reliable people. As stated in an earlier section, the war of liberation only reached very limited numbers of the population and the central leadership's interface with local supporters was small. Consequently the new administrators came to be recruited mainly from the middle ranks of the liberation army, which were distinguished in their composition by a regional imbalance. Many new administrators came to a district where they lacked political roots and could not make themselves understood in the local language.[138] Their legitimacy in the eyes of the local population was wholly based on Frelimo's general legitimacy as the country's liberators. However, this diminished in step with the administrators' inability to be flexible with regard to local matters. At the local level, under the districts, Mozambicans with roots in traditional society who filled administrative and repressive functions in the colonial system were also dismissed.

So-called 'traditional power' in Mozambique is represented mainly by the roughly 1,600 families whose chief was designated *régulo* ('regent') during the colonial period. Another lower category, which in southern Mozambique was called *cabos de terra* ('land guards'), included roughly 20,000 families.[139] Together they constitute a type of 'nobility', with deep roots in Mozambican history and culture.

People's power as an organ for an alternative exercise of power during the war of liberation directed itself towards two different power centres in colonial Mozambique: the colonial administration and the traditional power structure. During the colonial period these two power centres were closely interconnected, with the colonial structure being clearly superior. However, this subordination did not remove all autonomy from traditional power.[140] This meant that the people's power relationship with earlier forms of colonial exercise of power was different. When colonial power withdrew a vacuum arose that organs of popular power were able to fill formally without any great problems. The colonial administrative organs could easily be replaced by new organisational forms when it was a matter of registering the population, marriages, births and deaths, etc. But in relation to the structures of traditional power there were problems associated with questions concerning the legitimacy of the different systems on a deeper human level.

Frelimo's first president, Eduardo Mondlane, was conscious of these problems, perhaps as a consequence of having studied anthropology.[141] He stated that traditional leaders had roots in the cultural life of the country and that their influence during the pre-colonial period was based on popular legitimacy, not on violence. He saw that there were potential future problems with tribalism and regionalism. This view was based on the insight that the traditional institutions had historically constituted 'an adequate organisational form in order to take care of the interests of the majority', but that they provided nothing on which to base the foundations for a modern state.

The organs of people's power which were built up at a basic level in the liberated areas built on a basis of up to a couple of hundred people. This level was called *círculo*, circle. The population elected its representatives at general meetings. These representatives in turn elected representatives to the next larger area, *localidade*, locality, and so on to district and provincial organs.

Reactions to this new set-up formed a factor in the political struggle between Frelimo's two factions. There were different reasons for opposing the new organs of people's power. There were those who had their roots in the leading families of traditional society, and in people's power they saw a loss of their own power. Others felt that the question of local power should not be taken up as long as the war of liberation continued, because it could shatter unity. Yet others argued that in liberated areas there was no exploitation to combat through people's power, because exploitation was a relationship that only existed between blacks and whites. There could be no exploitative relationships between blacks.[142]

However, this vision of the development of people's power during the war of liberation, as presented in connection with and after independence, retained little of the problematising approach to which Eduardo Mondlane had given expression. Mondlane had argued that traditional power's historical legitimacy could develop into a problem of tribalism and regionalism. When in a speech ten years later[143] Samora Machel attacked tribalists and regionalists he was describing the background to their growth not as a sociological phenomenon, but as a hostile infiltration. The argument behind this was that because the war of liberation and people's power had already put an end to tribal thinking, so tribalism and regionalism had no roots in society and were therefore nothing else than infiltration. The only counter-remedy when one has lice in one's underclothes is to put all one's clothes into boiling water, said Machel.[144]

> [O]ur struggle killed the tribe. It was the first thing we killed, because enemy's strength is tribalism. So we had no hesitation in acting against tribalists, racists and regionalists. We killed the tribe to give birth to the nation.[145]

With this starting point Machel had defined away the problem of legitimacy which later came to affect the organs of people's power. Problems which arose could be dismissed as involving hostile infiltration.

The problem of legitimacy

In Mozambique we can see historically how the state's attempt to create its legitimacy has taken different forms. In traditional African 'state formations' good reciprocal relations between individuals from the same family, clan or ethnic group were the basis for the system's legitimacy. The Portuguese colonial state broke apart the fundamental features of pre-colonial reciprocity through colonial economic exploitation. As 'compensation' the citizens were allowed to retain the right to some of their own culture, traditions and religious practices. The *régulo* became the human fulcrum between tyranny and legitimacy. His capacity to carry out his balancing act became decisive for the colonial state's degree of legitimacy in the eyes of the population.

During the colonial period traditional power had two sources of legitimacy. One was the Portuguese administration, whose instructions *régulos* and *cabos de terra* had to follow. Failure to pay taxes collected from the population, or other digressions, could be punished with dismissal. It was not just a question of dismissal from a 'post' but a punishment of the whole branch of the family, who were forced to leave a privileged position in society. The second source of legitimacy was the population. This legitimacy traditionally depended on the extent to which the *régulo* could guarantee the population under his jurisdiction long-term survival and a position in relation to the world around. Historically the *régulo* has also filled a function in regulating the local use of scarce natural resources in a balanced way. The traditional leaders' role as cultural intermediaries and holders of knowledge about ceremonies and local history gave them the people's confidence, which independence has only nibbled at the edges.

Frelimo's dethronement of the whole colonial administration set aside one source of legitimacy. The fact that traditional religious worship was deemed to be superstition *in practice* made traditional ceremonies illegal, which on the surface seemed to cut the bonds of the second source of legitimacy.[146] But the legitimacy of traditional power's role as repository of knowledge about local ceremonies did not disappear in the eyes of the local population. It has survived as a strong undercurrent in all levels of the population.

Because Frelimo disregarded the force of this undercurrent it lost an opportunity to link up with the principles of legitimacy which guided the population's assessment of the measures for organising the production and distribution of social resources which they saw the new state power implement.

Traditional leadership and social differentiation

The development strategy for rural areas with its modernisation came to challenge two distinct local forces: on the one hand the dominant families who had their base in the traditional African power structure and who had been allied with the colonial administration, and on the other hand those most marginalised parts of the population, for example those having their plots of land furthest away from the newly formed communal villages. Gradually both these forces converged and together enabled Renamo to root itself in the Mozambican rural areas.

Those who had traditionally held power were challenged in that their administrative positions and political rights were taken away. They were not allowed to be candidates for the new local administrations after independence. Traditional leaders found themselves being led by people who were their subordinates in clan and family terms. The selection of new local leaders was severely limited by the criteria applied by Frelimo. As previously mentioned, no one who had cooperated with the colonial state, who was actively religious or who was polygamous could be elected to local positions of responsibility. In areas where these criteria were rigorously applied there were often fewer capable people chosen as new political leaders. They were often strongly influenced by the colonial period's administrative and repressive methods in the local exercise of power. Local harassment of the old traditional leaders often led to many of them resentfully withdrawing from public life.

Because living in villages forced increasing numbers of peasants to walk considerable distances to their fields, many gradually had their production capacity curtailed. As the supply situation worsened in rural areas, it became increasingly important for these strata of the population to remain close to their plots of land and not to be drawn into semi-unemployment in villages and small towns. In the three southernmost provinces increased unemployment among migrant workers reinforced the pauperisation of remote rural areas.

When smaller Renamo reconnaissance units began to operate in an area, this stratification of the rural population was accentuated. Those who fled with their possessions first were the ones who had most to lose and who were more able to re-establish themselves in a safer area. The poorest and the most remote families stayed on longer, because their allotments were their only chance of survival. Because their homes were scattered they came to coexist with Renamo and young boys from marginalised sections of the rural population came to constitute the mass of the perpetrators of violence in the destabilisation of the rural areas.

Local practitioners of violence[147]

The personnel taken over by the South Africans from Rhodesia in 1980 and the rest of the Rhodesian units, who still remained in their bases in various mountainous areas in the central areas of Mozambique, were trained further after the move to South Africa. South African military instructors were stationed in several bases on Mozambican territory and the commanders used in the operation were briefed on how they could exploit earlier local antagonisms in order to establish themselves in rural areas inside Mozambique. These commanders had a good knowledge of local history and possible contacts when they were stationed in various provinces from the autumn of 1981.[148]

This occurred at a stage when growing social and economic tensions in the rural areas had developed to such a degree that certain groups were prepared to countenance external destabilisation. Dissatisfied people traditionally in positions of power (*régulos* and *cabos de terra*), together with marginalised groups among the poorest rural population, were prepared to provide information and to cooperate with Renamo's commanders, who at the local level styled themselves as liberators from Frelimo's tyranny.

After an initial period of some months during which a lenient attitude towards the population was adopted, this pattern changed to attacks against all the infrastructure which represented Frelimo or the state. People who were known members of Frelimo or state employees, such as teachers or health-care personnel, were killed or mutilated. The population living in villages or in small social groups were harassed into fleeing to the bush, away from Frelimo's influence. From the second half of 1981 onwards military destabilisation was operating at full strength.

Recruitment

Renamo's role as an instrument for destabilisation meant that recruitment in rural areas built to a very limited extent on political standpoints for or against the government or Renamo. Instead recruitment can be said to have been a combination of force and the social and psychological factors connected with the growing socio-economic stratification of the rural areas, to which Frelimo's rural policy contributed.

When an MNR base was established and its armed groups began to operate in a new area, the population withdrew. But it was seldom a matter of an uncoordinated panic-stricken flight. Instead it was clear that different groups in the population reacted in different ways and chose different strategies for survival.

Some people abandoned their houses and fields immediately after the first attack, or even when they first heard that the MNR was approaching. Others stayed on and refused to relinquish their houses, fields and other assets. All in all the movements were made gradually, with people generally going no further than 5–10 km. The group that lagged behind came under the MNR base's area of influence, while the others always managed to keep themselves at a distance from direct attacks and daily demands for food supplies for the base. Within a relatively short time these different movement rhythms caused a new settlement pattern in the majority of the rural districts.

One section of the population was concentrated around district towns or larger villages, where security was satisfactory due to the presence of the government army. These *deslocados* (internal refugees) became dependent to a great extent on international food aid. The other section remained in the bush and lived around the MNR bases or within their area of influence. They thus came to be regarded with great suspicion by both the authorities and the military. Often attempts were made to move this population into the larger villages or districts by force, but this was not always successful. When it was successful they were often

Table 4.2 Pre-war socio-economic indicators among the rural population, Inhambane province[149]

	Internal refugees	Repatriated	Renamo
What they had:			
Cement brick house (%)	46	0	4
Improved house (%)	32	18	15
Grass and clay house (%)	22	82	81
Rice-growing, *machongo* (%)	84	36	35
Average harvest (number of sacks)	14	5.3	7.5
Plough (%)	78	82	43
Number of oxen (average)	8.5	3.5	3.2
Sewing machine (%)	46	45	28
Average education (years)	3.6	2.0	2.8

Source: Interviews in Inhambane province, February–March 1989.

located in their own smaller camps at a distance from the rest of the population. In the language of the authorities the word *recuperados* (repatriated) was often used to describe this group.

A closer study of both these population groups shows that the different reactions and the different ways of moving are not accidental. They actually belong to completely different strata of the rural population who consequently have to defend different types of interests. Those who made off were those who had the best economic situation before the war.

Those who stayed on previously constituted the poorer section of the rural population. To these can be added a further category, namely those who entered into close cooperation with Renamo and accepted repressive functions in relation to the population, so-called *madjibas*, as well as those who afterwards came to join armed groups. These often belonged to marginalised or stigmatised groups within the rural population's lumpenproletariat.

The socio-economic differences between these two groups are clear with regard to land ownership, living standards and education. These socio-economic differences are clearly linked to their reaction to the threat from Renamo. It may be summarised by saying that the better an individual's economic situation was, the faster he or she fled the threat from Renamo. Table 4.2 illustrates this relationship.

This shows that in the first instance it was not the prosperous rural population which attached itself to Renamo. It was rather the poorest, who purely for reasons of survival could not leave their allotments or

Table 4.3 Pre-war socio-economic indicators among former Renamo participants, Inhambane province

	Participated less than 12 months	Participated more than 12 months
What they had (%):		
Cement brick house	8	0
Improved house	17	14
Grass and clay house	75	86
Rice-growing, *machongo*	42	27
Plough	33	55
Sewing machine	33	23

Source: Interviews in Inhambane province, February–March 1989.

their huts, who came to be incorporated under the control of Renamo's bases. The paradoxical situation also arose that the prosperous rural population, who according to conventional wisdom should have been the most hostile to Frelimo's socialist development strategy, were the ones who attached themselves to Frelimo and the modern state. At the same time the poor rural population, who (also according to conventional wisdom) should have been Frelimo's closest allies in socialist construction, were marginalised.

Differences in socio-economic situation before the war also become clear on dividing the 'Renamo' category according to how long the individuals participated in armed action in rural areas. It is the poorest of the poor who stayed on the longest in Renamo as practisers of violence. Table 4.3 shows the socio-economic situation of this group in relation to the period during which they participated in armed actions.

But even more important than the material situation for the length of participation in Renamo's activities was the level of education. Table 4.4 shows that it was the least educated who stayed on the longest. As a comparison, it may be mentioned that illiteracy for men in rural areas in a corresponding age group was 42 per cent.[150] This should be compared with those who stayed on longest in Renamo, of whom 73 per cent were illiterate.

For many years diplomats and aid workers in Maputo have discussed whether Renamo has any popular support or not. Behind this question is the view that it is not possible to operate this type of warfare in rural areas without having at least a good share of popular support. This starting point presupposes that recruitment is based on political consciousness, but detailed studies of the recruitment process show that this is the wrong approach. It is based on the belief that association

Table 4.4 Education and participation in Renamo armed action

	Participated less than 12 months	Participated more than 12 months
Attended school (%)	54	27
Illiteracy (%)	46	73
Average period at school (years)	3.1	2.2

Source: Interviews in Inhambane, February–March 1989.

with all organisations, whether political or idealistic, builds on voluntary initiatives.

However, for the extremely poor peasant boys in Mozambican rural areas, enlistment 'drafting' does not occur, as they are collected more or less by force and taken to Renamo's base sites. *Real* recruitment first takes place when the individual makes a conscious decision in the choice between trying to flee back home or staying on.

The pattern in Renamo's 'drafting process' is clear and well known in rural areas in Mozambique. The overwhelming part of their recruitment is made by collecting youths from the villages in rural areas.[151] The degree of force varies between armed threats, ill-treatment and killing. But the vital point is that *this is not real recruitment*. Real recruitment does not occur before an individual has made a decision on whether to flee or to stay on and work for Renamo. Are there any identifiable circumstances which influence when this moment takes place and what the choice looks like? We can give an account of a psychological answer and a statistical one.

The psychological answer comes from an older male nurse, who was abducted and held in a Renamo base in Inhambane province for six months. He says that:

> You must understand that it needed a great deal of courage to even dare to try to get away. You have to wake up one morning and be completely convinced that that day exactly is the day you will die. That day, and not before, you can screw up enough courage so that you are no longer afraid of the violent punishment, or execution, that can result if you are caught trying to get away. If you are taken and killed, you have already reconciled yourself with your fate. If you manage to escape, then thank God that you have been able to live for another while. You must understand that different people need different times to reconcile themselves with the insight that the day of their death is set. Some get there very quickly, others can never reconcile themselves ...[152]

The statistical answer comes from interview research which, *inter alia*, investigated how long 'recruits' were active with weapons within Renamo. The average is shown to be twelve months. In bureaucratic language we would say that the personnel turnover is 100 per cent. As the tables have shown, it is the poorest of all in rural areas who predominate in Renamo's ranks.

The recruitment process can be described as a struggle between, on the one hand, the 're-socialisation' which Renamo's commanders tried to carry out using their young 'recruits' and, on the other hand, their earlier self-esteem and pattern of social identification. This struggle has great similarities with the methods for training torturers, which are known through reports from Latin America and from Greece during the junta period.[153] The goal is to transfer the individuals' identification from one social system of norms to another, in which the practice of violence of the most serious type is not a breach of valid norms.

The strength of opposition among the 'recruits' is broken down through well-known psychological methods. They are mistreated, degraded, starved and threatened with execution if they do not agree to learn to handle the weapon they are given. This harsh treatment is punctuated with moments of goodwill, friendliness and human understanding, as a reward for 'progress'. By gradually accepting new norms for human behaviour they are integrated into their new situation. Some try to escape immediately, others stay on longer and some never reach the point where respect for the lives of others becomes more important than their own survival.

Politicised ethnicity

Discussing ethnicity and ethnic antagonisms in Mozambique has been virtually taboo throughout the period of independence. The ambition of creating a single nation from Rovuma to Maputo was considered to be paramount. By declaring ethnicity and 'tribal thinking' to be non-existent in independent Mozambique, Frelimo has attempted to wish them away. When we now take up the discussion of politicised ethnicity, this is done because of a growing suspicion that the internationally dominant perspective on aid and development cooperation strengthens rather than weakens the risks of ethnic conflicts in Africa.[154]

Many ethnic conflicts in the Third World countries are associated with development after independence. Especially in multi-ethnic societies, the nation-building process has often created tensions between different areas and ethnic groups. Experiences indicate that opposition to the nation-state project grows when the state cannot deliver essential collective utilities, or guarantee the population's long-term survival, in exchange for local society voluntarily subordinating itself to the nation-state principle. This is essentially a question of how legitimacy develops for a state, or any other form of institutionalised power.

Frelimo had already learned this for itself during the war of liberation. Frelimo's first president has described very strikingly how the
population demanded two things from Frelimo and its guerrillas in
order for Frelimo to become accepted as legitimate holders of power in
the liberated areas. The population demanded that Frelimo should
protect them against Portuguese reprisals and guarantee the basic preconditions for survival. In the event that Frelimo was not able to satisfy
these demands, the population quite simply made off. This sometimes
left Frelimo in its liberated areas without a population.[155]

For a state leadership which operates a state-nation project[156] it is of
little use to proclaim the existence of a nation-state if potential citizens
of this state see themselves in the first instance as members of another
nation, of ethnic groups or local loyalty systems, which are not so close
to nation-building that they perceive themselves as participating. It is
the gradual internalisation of new patterns of social identification which
in this respect constitutes the advance of the nation-state project. In
order for this to be possible people must be given an opportunity to
satisfy their most basic needs – both needs for security and cultural
identity and material needs – under the protection of the new society.

There can be many different concrete causes for ethnicity becoming
politicised, i.e. political demands being formulated in the ethnic group's
name. The majority of causes have some economic component. Certain
regions in a country may be unfavourably treated economically, natural
resources may be exploited to the advantage of other groups or local
eco-systems may become threatened through water regulation. Ethnic
conflicts can also grow from antagonisms surrounding cultural identity,
for example the relationship between one official and several local
languages.

When after independence Frelimo came into a position of state power
in Mozambique, the analysis was made that it was a Mozambican
nation-state that they ruled. Within this state it was a matter of developing a class-based policy which built on an alliance between workers and
peasants. But this state was never a nation-state with legitimacy but a
state-nation project still engaged in nation-building. It was held together
only as long as the state's abilities to protect citizens from violence
could be maintained and as long as it could guarantee the most basic
supply requirements. This legitimacy was seriously undermined by the
destabilising war and the collapse of the economy.

For the élite in Frelimo's leadership, the formation of an integrated
nation was a precondition for the whole state-building process. Frelimo's
élite was composed of several élites, with different roots in different parts
of the country. The one-party system and the planned economy facilitated the creation of alliances between these different élites, in which the
smaller dominant groups accepted the vision of nation-building in

exchange for active participation in the process of the exercise of power.

For Frelimo the nation-building project was always about a single nation from Rovuma in the north to Maputo in the south. Through economic development and modernisation the population's material and social needs would be satisfied, ethnic and clan antagonisms would die away and traditional forms of the exercise of power would be abandoned.

At the same time, at local level and particularly in rural areas, the war has torn apart the local economy, social networks and family relationships, and the political system's legitimacy has been seriously questioned. Millions of people have left their homes. Some have moved to safer areas within Mozambique, others have sought shelter and safety in neighbouring countries. Where the political system and the modern state have no longer been able to offer either safety or sufficient emergency relief, the population has instead attempted to re-establish and consolidate traditional strategies for survival. These are based on the organisational principles of traditional society, family bonds and mutual responsibility in local society.[157]

This change in people's way of guaranteeing their long-term survival is not a totally new phenomenon, but a result of the war's catastrophic consequences. It also has roots in Frelimo's education policy, in which local languages have been suppressed, and in the definition of traditional religious worship and its ceremonies as superstitious practices that have to be combated. When the modernisation process later shows that it is capable neither of replacing the earlier value system with a new system of social norms and values nor of offering new visions for future development, it becomes even more necessary for the population to seek alternatives. In such a development the local population's dissatisfaction and disillusionment over the failure of the central power and modernisation may come to coincide with the local and regional élites' dissatisfaction with their marginalised role in relation to the leading political élite.

From somewhat different starting points the local population and the regional élites may come to have a common interest in opposing those holding central power. The extent to which such an alliance assumes political and organisational expression is linked to the élites' ability to mobilise the local society's population around the theme or demands which are regarded as being urgent in the local society.

In many multi-ethnic or multi-national societies this mobilisation takes the form of a politicisation of ethnicity. We can see three circumstances which affect such politicisation. The first involves the extent to which modernisation succeeds or fails in satisfying the material and social aspirations of local populations. The second refers to the extent to which the population have abandoned or still rely on traditional survival strategies and value systems. In times of unrest there is naturally a greater readiness and susceptibility to changes in loyalty between different élites. The third applies to the extent to which an alternative élite still retains or can re-establish its legitimacy as a leading élite with a base in ethnic mobilisation.

Politicised ethnicity in Mozambique does not necessarily have to coincide with the traditional ethnic groups in the country. It can just as easily rest on the actual material circumstances, on an unequal regional distribution of natural resources. This means that a possible deepened tension between different regions can be defined as an ethnic conflict, even though its limits do not coincide with any previously existing ethnic groups, if it is directed in concrete terms against the dominance of southern Mozambique. This ethnicity thus comes to seek new grounds for popular mobilisation. Ndau and Macua would be able to contribute the central cultural aspects of such new ethnicity, by seeking a dominant cultural position in their respective regions.

The war as an ethnic conflict

Can a discussion about ethnicity and politicised ethnicity bring us any closer to an understanding of the origins and the specific course of the war in Mozambique? Is it perhaps quite simply that the war in Mozambique has had such significant ethnic roots that it is relevant to talk of a cruel, but concealed, ethnic conflict? Has the failure of modernisation already led to an ethnic war in Mozambique? There are at least three aspects to these questions.

The first is the historical context underlying the formation of Renamo. After the Portuguese colonial army failed to put an end to Frelimo in the big offensive of 1969–70, which went under the name of 'Operation Gordian Knot', Frelimo advanced southwards in its war of liberation. Large parts of Tete province were considered to be liberated areas at the beginning of the 1970s. When the colonial power was faced with the threat that the war of liberation would approach the Beira corridor and Beira, various types of military special units were formed,[158] with the task of halting Frelimo's advance. Many black soldiers were recruited locally from the threatened areas, namely the present provinces of Manica and Sofala. It was these units that Rhodesia later had greatest need of in its attempt to combat the ZANLA guerrillas inside Mozambique. There was thus already a regional/ethnic component in operations when the Rhodesian security service developed MNR's activities in central Mozambique.

The second involves the fact that a very large number of Renamo's commanders belong to the Ndau ethnic group.[159] In conversations with people in rural areas of Mozambique, it is clear that the language spoken in Renamo bases was Ndau. This held a position that can be equated with an official language. When attacks were made, orders were often given in Ndau.

The third aspect refers to the fact that a couple of the leading dissidents in Frelimo during the period 1968–70 were Ndau, or had their roots in central Mozambique. This applies, for example, to Uria Simango, who was Frelimo's vice-president for a short period after the assassination of Eduard Mondlane. He was later expelled from Frelimo. Later on Simango was imprisoned and, as far as can be judged, he was executed. However, there is no official confirmation of this. This matter forms part of the basis for the expressions of mutual suspicion, found even within Frelimo, between people from the Beira area and others from the south.

Thus there are conditions for a possible emergence of an ethnic movement. But because Renamo's history throughout the period has been wrapped up in the interests of foreign powers, first Rhodesia's need to combat ZANLA, then as a crucial tool in the military part of South Africa's total strategy for preserving its power in the region, the ethnic element has never been developed. This ethnic identity runs as an undercurrent throughout Renamo's activities, but still has not been politicised.

However, Renamo may come to be transformed into an ethnic movement as a result, for example, of antagonisms between Renamo's leadership and the military commanders.

When it is a question of the origin and course of the war, however, there is nothing to indicate that an organised ethnic mobilisation would have played any significant role. On the local level it is rather social misery and/or intra-ethnic or intra-clan antagonisms that have produced such deep divisions in local society that some of the actors have preferred to ally themselves with Renamo.

The results of the elections and the surprisingly high number of votes in favour of Renamo give rise to another tentative question. The ethnic dimension is visible in the fact that the results differ substantially between the provinces. The socio-economic impact can be seen in the high degree of differentiation between Renamo and Frelimo supporters within provinces and districts. However, it may be the case that most of those voting for Renamo were attracted by its transformation into a political party. The increased scope for political and social affirmation that this transformation opened up in Mozambican society, rather than the party's explicit political ideology, attracted people who had been marginalised by the Frelimo version of local government. Hence the question of who allied themselves with the 'political' Renamo cannot be analysed using the same criteria as those used when studying Renamo's military strategy during the war.

5

The End of Global Bipolarity and the Price of New Alliances

The industrialised countries' answer to the demands which the Third World raised for a new international economic order took more than five years to be formulated. A reply was first presented through the Brandt Commission report of 1980, which dealt with the question of how the required massive transfer of resources could take place and be financed. The commission linked the demand for global transfers of resources from North to South to demands for arms reductions. Through the introduction of an international tax on the arms trade, it would be possible to mobilise sufficient financial funds to make the global transfer of resources possible.

One year later, however, both the demands for a new international economic world order and the Brandt Commission's proposal for massive transfers of resources were taken off the political agenda. During a non-aligned movement meeting in Cancún, Mexico, in 1981, the American administration, under President Reagan, made it clear that there could be no talk of any massive transfers of resources. The causes of underdevelopment were not to be found in a lack of capital, but were regarded rather as being due to the growth of over-bureaucratised state administrations, which through their incompetence hampered the development efforts that were actually being made.[160] According to the analysis presented, it was only through the withdrawal of the state and the liberalisation of market forces that the development process would be able to take place.

The Cancún meeting was the end of an era of development theory. Modernisation was considered in itself as still constituting a precondition for progress. But instead of an interventionist state, market forces alone would now enable poor countries to catch up with the development of the rich countries as quickly as possible.

Political reversals in Eastern Europe

As a result of the problems confronting the Soviet leadership under
Brezhnev in contributing to the establishment of stability and social
order in both the Horn of Africa and Angola, internal criticism of the
theory on socialist-orientated countries increased during the second
half of the 1970s. The difficulties in installing a regime loyal to Moscow
in Afghanistan, which finally led to the Soviet invasion in 1979, and the
spread of fundamentalist ideology in Iran, involved a serious reappraisal
of the earlier analysis within the government. Social scientists close to
Moscow began to return to a more orthodox Marxist attitude. The
idea that hardly any part of the socialist vision could be realised before
society had passed the capitalist stage again began to dominate.[161]

As a result of the Reagan administration's more aggressive foreign
and armaments policies, the Soviet state budget was exposed to further
pressure at the beginning of the 1980s. This, together with increased
internal political demands for correcting their own material problems,
meant that in practice the Soviet Union took a significantly less ambitious attitude to its commitments in the Third World.

This was clearly apparent during the 26th party congress in 1981,
when Brezhnev's speech was considerably more cautious than that of
the previous congress when it came to the description of development
in the Third World and the socialist progress of political allies. The
practical significance of this for aid cooperation with Mozambique
showed itself just one year later with the rejection of the country's
application for membership of COMECON, the Eastern bloc's organisation for economic cooperation.

This amounted to a clear signal that Mozambique now had to manage on its own. The Soviet Union considered that it could no longer
afford to prop up the socialist experiment in the Third World, when
the preconditions for progress appeared to be practically non-existent.
The somewhat reluctant attitude on the part of both parties, which had
characterised cooperation since the liberation struggle, took concrete
expression.[162]

At the 27th party congress in February 1986, under Gorbachev's
leadership, the issue of socialist-orientated countries in the Third World
was practically invisible. The Soviet Union thus ceased to constitute a
'natural ally' for Marxist-inspired and radical regimes in the Third
World. With the exception of Cuba they would now have to look after
themselves and they were advised by Moscow to adjust their economies
to the market and to seek broader economic cooperation with the
West.[163] This reappraisal of the Soviet Union's position naturally came
to have a decisive influence on the development of events in Southern
Africa.

Creating more friends and fewer enemies

Even if concrete support from Moscow had been relatively limited, the Soviet reversal at the beginning of the 1980s, in combination with several other factors which mutually reinforced each other, came to be of crucial significance for Mozambique's continued development.

First, the Soviet reversal came immediately after Mozambique's relations with the USA had seriously deteriorated. Strong forces in the US Congress were still worried about the Soviet presence in Southern Africa and the fact that Frelimo had developed into a Marxist-Leninist party. When the Mozambicans expelled several American diplomats from Maputo in 1981, accusing them of being CIA agents, demands were made in Congress that the Reagan administration should reassess its relations with Renamo, perceive it as the freedom movement it claimed to be and, as in the case of Angola, give the movement both military and economic support.

After efforts on the part of the State Department, the American administration came to a compromise with Congress. The American Foreign Administration was worried that official support for Renamo on the part of the USA would deepen the conflict in Southern Africa. Such support would increase the pressure on the Soviet Union to re-appraise its desire for international *détente* and either provide corresponding support for Frelimo itself or allow Cuban intervention in the same way as in Angola. An enlargement of the regional conflict thus also risked radicalising the opposition in South Africa, which in turn could negatively affect security and jeopardise the deliveries of raw materials to the West. As mentioned previously, the compromise was that the USA denied Mozambique part of its international development and emergency aid for a number of years. This in practice provoked a reduced multilateral input into the country on the part of UN agencies.

Second, at that time South Africa intensified its destabilisation campaign as the administrative and technical preconditions were created for implementing the 'total strategy'. Mozambique's worsening relations with the USA, with associated American passivity, allowed relatively wide international scope for South Africa to initiate something the Americans themselves several years later came to call 'one of the most brutal holocausts against ordinary human beings since World War II' in which it was alleged that Renamo had been 'waging a systematic and brutal war of terror against innocent Mozambican civilians through forced labour, starvation, physical abuse and wanton killing.'[164]

Third, the intensified economic and military destabilisation not only meant reduced foreign currency revenues from both transit trade and export goods. It also aggravated the effects of the extensive drought which afflicted the whole of Southern Africa at the beginning of the

1980s, with a resulting increased need for food imports. The country's chronic deficit in its current accounts had grown worse as a result of increased world market prices for oil at the end of the 1970s. These dramatic increases in costs for imports were further aggravated by destabilisation. The possibilities for more loans and food aid also diminished. At the same time there was an increased need for international financing in order for Mozambique to be able to respond to increasing South African aggression, maintain the level of oil imports, guarantee the population access to food and keep alive plans for modernisation.

Both import requirements and the need for international infusion of capital forced the Mozambican leadership into new external political alliances, in spite of the fact that the political price for this increased as a result of the lack of alternatives.[165] A rapprochement with the West became necessary. Thus the basis was laid for a completely new route to development in Mozambique, followed by new internal shifts in power.[166]

The political conditions for disaster relief

To embark on this new route was not an easy task. The effects of the USA's reluctant attitude to the conflict in Southern Africa were clearly expressed regarding the famine disaster in Inhambane province in 1983. Despite repeated appeals to the international donor community, it took more than a year before the first relief consignments arrived. The American decision to deny Mozambique both development support and disaster relief influenced other Western donors and multilateral aid agencies. Thus the UN agency, the World Food Programme, refused to send food aid to Inhambane province before the political problems with the USA were resolved.

The Mozambican need for support from the West in order to overcome the shortage of food was acute at the same time as the political price for this help was increasing as a result of the Soviet Union's reversal. Frustrated opportunities for deepened cooperation with socialist countries, as an alternative to the West's credit system or political support, meant that Mozambique was forced to comply with the USA's unequivocal terms. International disaster relief, as well as increased access to international credits and rescheduling of debt repayments, required the introduction of a market economy whose stability should be approved by the IMF. There were also inflexible demands for peace negotiations with South Africa and for Mozambique to cease its support for the ANC's military activities.

In order to improve relations with the USA and pave the way for the much-needed food aid, the Mozambicans took a number of initiatives. Negotiations with South Africa were opened in 1983, leading to the N'komati Accord in 1984. An economic recovery programme was initiated, with the aim of gradually liberalising the socialist economy and replacing it with a market-oriented one. This initiative included negotiations on membership of the World Bank and the IMF. As a State Department official in Washington put it:

> we made it clear to the government of Mozambique that our food aid is political. There are always conditions on aid, although they are often not explicit ... To get better relations with us, Mozambique had to demonstrate a willingness to change its economic policies. This was necessary anyway, because Africans are capitalists; Africans don't like socialism.[167]

Non-governmental distribution of relief aid

A further precondition for obtaining international relief aid was that the government would be able to guarantee that the aid reached the target groups.

In Mozambique there had been a debate about whether the disaster relief should be passed through the existing public institutions, mainly the ministry for internal trade, the state enterprise for purchasing agricultural products, Agricom, and the existing trade network in the rural areas, or through the state agency for tackling disasters, DPCCN.

The Americans imposed harsh demands. They demanded that distribution be implemented by parallel structures, separate from the state, which foreign non-governmental organisations would be allowed to build up.

But the Mozambicans stood by their demands that no parallel structures should be allowed to develop and that disaster prevention and counter-measures were a Mozambican national affair. During 1984, when famine was already a fact in Inhambane province, a compromise was reached. The American NGO CARE (Concerned Americans for the Reconstruction of Europe) would be allowed an executive responsibility for the distribution of emergency food. This would take place within the framework of the DPCCN, supported by extensive technical assistance.[168] Great emphasis would be laid on the transfer of knowledge and organisational development, according to the contract concluded between CARE and Mozambican authorities.[169]

Several other observers, not least among the multilateral donors, looked uneasily on CARE's, and thus the USA's, great influence over disaster relief distribution. For a long time there were rumours in Maputo about connections between CARE and the American intelligence service, the CIA. Through CARE's strategic role in planning emergency distribution, the organisation acquired a comprehensive picture of how the security situation was developing, district by district, and of current population movements, food production, etc. This information was naturally important for several countries' security services, which for different reasons were involved in the political game surrounding Southern Africa.

For most Mozambicans these rumours were of minor importance. At this time the country's government itself had relatively little knowledge of the internal political implications of destabilisation and saw itself as having nothing to hide. A Mozambican government official responsible for organising the distribution of disaster relief expressed it thus:

> If CARE is really informing the Americans in Washington about what is going on in the rural areas of Mozambique that would be a good thing. It will perhaps enable the American administration to acquire a more comprehensive picture of MNR's activities.[170]

The significance of American food aid, as well as the reasons for this statement, should be seen against the background of the domestic political situation in the USA.

American food aid support for Mozambique was naturally the subject of intense debate in Congress. Instead of complying with several congressmen's demands for the USA's recognition of and support for Renamo, the Reagan administration decided for political reasons to reintroduce food support for the Frelimo regime in Maputo. The administration's attitude was not just a result of the political concessions made by the Mozambicans during the negotiations. The administration had also become convinced that the Mozambican government would be able to reassume the important role of regional mediator, which it had earlier played during the Lancaster House negotiations on Zimbabwe's independence. In this way Mozambique would be able to contribute to a solution to the Southern Africa conflict acceptable to the USA.[171]

The US Congress finally approved both food aid support for Mozambique and financing of CARE. Because American policy was normally that all American food aid should be distributed to target groups by international NGOs and be clearly separated from the receiver country's own distribution network, it was astonishing that Congress also agreed that CARE would work within the Mozambican state structures and there be responsible for building up a logistic unit.[172]

But naturally it was not only this relative diplomatic victory in Washington which made the Mozambicans accept CARE's presence. The distribution of emergency goods constituted a serious problem and Mozambique needed every help in planning and implementing transports and training domestic personnel. The presence of the Americans within DPCCN would assist the regime in Maputo to increase its international credibility and to show that the disaster relief was actually reaching the target groups. CARE's presence within DPCCN would be able to help Mozambique increase its strength *vis-à-vis* the international donor community in order to maintain a minimum of national sovereignty.

The need for international financing

As a result of the drought, ecological vulnerability and military destabilisation, the country's own agricultural production was reduced to about 0.8–0.9 million tons, which corresponded to 35–40 per cent of the total requirement. This meant that over half the country's population became dependent on international food aid for its survival. This reduced supply of agricultural products thus not only reduced the country's export revenues, but also contributed to an import requirement of approximately 1.3 million tons. Even though international food aid nearly quadrupled over the period, it only covered 60–70 per cent of the requirement at most. Mozambique had to import the remainder (approximately 0.4 million tons) commercially. At the same time the country lacked the financial means for this, and had to borrow even more money on the international credit market in order for the population to have enough to eat – a fact that would further aggravate the already severely stretched balance of payments.

As previously stated, Mozambique is one of the few countries in the world to show a chronic deficit in its current accounts over the last fifty years. During the colonial era, this deficit was mainly covered by transfers from Portugal, which in turn were based on gold from South Africa. After independence these revenues fell dramatically when South Africa cancelled the gold agreement and reduced the number of Mozambican mineworkers. In this way a large part of the country's foreign currency revenues disappeared.

By closing the border with Rhodesia in 1976, Mozambique lost a significant tranche of its foreign currency revenues. The deficit in the balance of trade needed increasingly to be covered by aid and international borrowing. It was consequently not only the deficit in the balance of trade which dramatically increased during the 1980s; the sources for its financing through service exports and transfers also disappeared.

The ambitious development plans announced at the end of the 1970s disregarded these eventualities and were strongly influenced by the optimism surrounding Zimbabwe's independence. Mozambique looked forward to peace in the region and perceived no further obstacles to the growth that had been achieved since independence (17.5 per cent in 1975–81) from being maintained throughout the 1980s. Continued international borrowing would finance modernisation in the expectation

Table 5.1 Oil prices and Mozambican foreign trade, 1973–82

	1973	1975	1981	1982
Market prices ($/ton):				
Crude oil	26	91	292	273
Diesel	55	114	332	321
Import/export (million meticais):				
A. Crude oil imports	719	1, 585	5,906	8,043
B. Total imports	11,415	10,745	28,317	31,573
C. Total exports	5,540	5,050	9,926	8,655
Quotients (%):				
A/B	6.3	14.8	20.9	25.5
A/C	12.9	31.4	59.5	92.9

Source: Informação Estatística, CNP, 1975–84; *Informação Económica*, CNP, 1984.

that the transit trade would take off again and revenues from anticipated agricultural exports would increase.

Access to international credit was great, and real rates of interest were low. The excess liquidity of the American dollar had been absorbed by the OPEC countries as a result of the oil price rises for 1974/75. Large amounts of these petro-dollars were placed on the so-called Euro-dollar market in London. The international finance market's need to bring about 'recycling of the petro-dollars' created a need for willing borrowers. Interest rates were reduced and other conditions were improved.[173] In the sphere of development theory, the concept of 'indebted industrialisation' was introduced. Many countries in the Third World suddenly saw an opportunity to bring about a development process using cheap international financial means. Mozambique was one of them.[174]

But after only a couple of years economic problems loomed large. The second oil crisis, with further rising world market prices for oil in 1980/81, and the subsequent international recession, severely affected Mozambique's 'terms of trade' for the worse.

From having corresponded to 6 per cent of total imports in 1973, oil imports, share rose to 25 per cent in total in 1982. In relation to Mozambique's exports the change was even more dramatic. From having corresponded to 13 per cent of export revenues in 1973, oil imports took a total of 93 per cent of export revenues for 1982. This was mainly the result of the price of oil rising from $26 per ton in 1973 to $273 per ton in 1982.

Rising oil prices coincided with severely reduced export revenues from 1982. The reduction in export revenues was due not only to decreased world market prices but above all to reduced quantities of exports, as a consequence of the extensive drought, and the effects of military destabilisation, severely affecting traditional exports of cashew nuts, sugar, cotton and tea.

When the USA raised interest rates in 1981, it affected not only Mozambique's debt burden, but above all the terms for obtaining new credit. The available foreign currency reserves did not cover debt repayments, and within two years the country was forced to take out new loans to a value of $2 billion. The country's indebtedness thus increased substantially. Between 1980 and 1983 Mozambique's debt service ratio (interest and amortisation in relation to export revenues) quadrupled.

In 1984, although delays in payments would worsen the country's international credit-worthiness, Mozambique was forced to initiate negotiations with its international creditors on debt rescheduling. The government found itself in a situation where access to continued international credits was not just a precondition for implementing the modernisation strategy and for being able to provide peasants with consumer goods. Access to international credit was essential for the country's, and the population's, survival.

The size of the debt burden

The country's total debt burden rose in 1984 to $2.4 billion including debt arrears, i.e. interest and amortisation which had become due for payment. Over 95 per cent of the debts were bilateral. OECD countries were responsible for 46 per cent of total lending, and the OPEC countries for 21 per cent. The Eastern bloc's share rose to 27 per cent. Only a couple of per cent of the debt was commercial.[175]

The size of the debt burden was not particularly alarming compared with other indebted countries in Africa. It also consisted mainly of bilateral debts which, as distinct from borrowing from multilateral agencies, could be renegotiated. A large proportion was made up of so-called concessional loans, i.e. loans that were mixed with a gift element which gave lower rates of interest and longer repayment periods.

The concern was the size of the debt burden in relation to the country's gross domestic product or to the country's export revenues. The total debt was larger than the GDP and the debt service ratio rose to a total of 195 per cent. In other words the debt burden was unreasonably large with regard to the country's economic strength.

Especially worrying was the use made of the loans. They were partly used to pay the interest and amortisation on loans taken out earlier (so-called arrears). A very large proportion had been used in order to finance imports of consumer goods, oil and food. Any investments that had been made had great difficulties in achieving profitability. Conditions were not promising for the increases in production that would make future debt repayment possible. Debt servicing claimed an increasing share of the country's foreign currency without export revenues rising. Future import opportunities were therefore limited. The debts also had a negative effect on the state's budget deficit, with increased pressure on domestic inflation.

Economic repayment strategy

Some years into the 1980s it was absolutely clear to Mozambique's government that the country's development strategy had reached an impasse. It was argued that the economic crisis was caused by the fall in domestic production. Modernisation of agriculture had failed. The state's abilities in central planning price-setting had been overestimated, and economic and military destabilisation had affected both agricultural and industrial production.

Bilateral creditors were concerned by continued state influence over the economy and demanded that the economy be adjusted to the market. The private sector would be given an increased influence and the over-valued domestic currency would be devalued in order to stimulate exports and limit imports. This would improve the balance of current accounts and the ability to repay debts. Membership of the IMF and the World Bank, and the formulation of an economic adjustment programme in consultation with these organisations, were demanded as conditions for new credits.[176]

Mozambique's strategy was first to apply for membership of both the Bretton Woods institutions and thereafter to concentrate its efforts on reducing the bilateral debt burden.

Negotiations between the Bretton Woods institutions and Mozambique started in 1984.[177] Initially the negotiations concentrated on coming to an agreement on the causes of the economic crisis. While Mozambique emphasised the significance of South African economic and military destabilisation, the Bretton Woods institutions saw the government's financial and monetary policy as the main cause of the crisis. As for the content of the adjustment programme, the 'difficult' questions mainly consisted of coming to an agreement on the degree of state economic management and planning, the size of the budget and the extent of the social sectors, and which factors should be allowed to determine the rates of exchange. A second category of questions referred to the pace at which the measures should be implemented.

The bilateral debt to the OECD countries was renegotiated at the so-called Paris Club. As a result of the ongoing negotiations with the Bretton Woods institutions, Mozambique was able during 1984 to hold its first negotiations with its members. Mozambique was granted a respite in payments of due debts and interest payments for the period 1984–86 of $1 billion. This resulted in a considerably lower debt service paid than would otherwise have been the case. However, the long-term problem remained, as such renegotiation means only that interest payments are capitalised and deferred until a future date, which means that the debt actually grows.

N'komati and after

South African destabilisation and the drought markedly increased Mozambique's need for international support, both financial and political. As a result of the changes in Eastern Europe, the USA was able to advance its position. Commitments on food aid and international financing facilitated the American negotiations with Mozambique on the fundamental principles of the non-aggression treaty between South Africa and Mozambique, which was formulated according to an American initiative. After corresponding pressure and commitments on economic support to South Africa, the USA was able to get the parties round the negotiating table.

It was thus possible for the N'komati Agreement between South Africa and Mozambique, in which both parties pledged not to support or facilitate hostile actions against the other country from within their territory, to be concluded in 1984. Mozambique had everything to gain from such a treaty, although the country was exposed to criticism from a number of countries on the African continent.[179] After the agreement there were great expectations that the country would now be able to introduce the implementation of its development strategy in peace and quiet. In the Mozambican press the agreement was described as a victory for Mozambique's socialist peace policy.[180]

As has been made clear, this change in international alliances required considerable diplomatic endeavours from the Mozambican side.[181] Tensions within the American Congress endured, as well as the demand from several members for support for Renamo.

A conflict first developed in 1985 when the administration proposed a package of economic assistance including very limited non-lethal military supplies for the Mozambican government. By a substantial margin (247 to 177) the House of Representatives imposed conditions effectively prohibiting all but food assistance. Since then, restrictions on economic assistance have been somewhat loosened, but not those on military assistance. In 1987 Senate conservatives delayed the confirmation of Melissa Wells as ambassador to Mozambique for over 11 months in an effort to pressure the Administration to establish contacts with Renamo.[182]

As a basis for the argument against conservative Congressmen, in an attempt to win support from more undecided ones, an American consultant carried out an extensive study of Renamo's activities in rural areas, at the request of the State Department.[183]

Because of the difficulties in obtaining the US Congress's full support for the administration's expanded Southern Africa policy, the State Department increased contacts with multilateral UN agencies and the Bretton Woods institutions. For the American administration it was important, now that the communist threat was gone, to continue to work for a reform policy in Southern Africa which permitted the development of a market economy. This required financial resources over and above those the domestic political situation and Congress would allow the American aid budget to contribute. Through the Bretton Woods institutions, however, the American policy in Southern Africa could be financed through other aid donors at a rate at which they could be persuaded to support the implementation of the institutions' structural adjustment programme.[184] Mutual agreement on the introduction of majority rule in South Africa was also required before opposition groups on the left and right of the South African regime were drawn into a more extreme position which would put the future security of the region at risk.

Regional shifts of power

Even if P.W. Botha had shown an interest in political reform in South Africa, significant internal political changes had so far failed to materialise. The Americans had overestimated the prime minister's domestic political strength. Conservative forces had, during John Vorster's consolidation of the apartheid policy, grown ever stronger. Political reforms at the pace desired in Washington were perceived in Pretoria as being impossible to carry out.

Regional military and economic destabilisation was carried out consistently and over a long period. The N'komati Agreement entailed no change in this regard. South Africa would soon break the agreement in the same way and for the same reason that it had broken previous agreements, thereby incurring the disapproval not only of the international community, but of the American administration. As a result of increasing internal political troubles and the fact that the breach of the agreement attracted great attention in the international mass media, the rest of the world's demands for sanctions increased.

The US Congress, which was considerably more sympathetic to the necessity for reforms in South Africa than to the need for aid for the Frelimo regime in Maputo, became increasingly impatient. It was generally perceived that President Reagan's 'constructive engagement' had failed. This entailed a risk of deepened radicalisation of the black opposition about which Brzezinski had earlier given a warning. The state of emergency which Prime Minister P.W. Botha introduced in South Africa in 1986, as a result of increased domestic violence, was the last straw. On 25 September of the same year President Reagan decided to introduce international sanctions in order to force the political reforms of the apartheid system required for peaceful, stable development in Southern Africa.[185]

However, a great deal had happened in South Africa in the years which had been characterised by 'constructive engagement'. Trade between both countries, as well as investments, had increased. Military cooperation had been extended and now included nuclear technology guidance.[186] Throughout the period the USA had always backed South Africa within the UN's Security Council. But at the same time many black moderate leaders, previously considered able to play a moderating role, had become marginalised through the radicalisation of the black liberation struggle. 'Constructive engagement' thus militated against its own aims by strengthening the opposition on Botha's right as well as the opposition on the left.

Political development inside South Africa was influenced to a great extent by N'komati and subsequent sanctions. Through the N'komati Agreement and the deportation of ANC members from Mozambique, the ANC was forced to increase its presence inside South Africa.[187] The fact that Botha had signed the agreement also forced into the open the concealed antagonisms that had long characterised relations between business interests and the military in South Africa.[188] In this way the demands for political reforms from more liberal forces within the National Party were accelerated.[189]

As a consequence of the N'komati Agreement, and encouraged by the introduction of sanctions in 1986 by the rest of the world, the ANC intensified its political underground opposition work inside South Africa. It was this, together with the South African military's defeat in Cuito Cuanavale, Angola, in 1987, that largely caused the shifts of power in Southern Africa. There was also the South African economic decline, which obstructed costly and long-term military measures in the region. It became even more important for South African economic recovery that international sanctions were lifted. South Africa was forced to the negotiating table again and some years later, in 1990, SWAPO's takeover of power and Namibia's independence became a reality after democratic elections had been held. The Cuban troops left Angola.

The internal disintegration of the Soviet Union, and its final break-up in 1991, removed the possibility for the apartheid regime to motivate its white population into continuing their support for the 'total strategy' through the threat of the 'communist total onslaught'. It was no longer only white liberal forces in South Africa that added their voices to demands for the abolition of the apartheid system. Conservative Afrikaners also realised the necessity for political changes, especially within groups that were in need of a trained workforce and expanded domestic markets for their businesses. In the same year President P.W. Botha resigned and was replaced by F.W. de Klerk. Nelson Mandela was released from prison and opposition movements were allowed to operate freely. The changeover to majority rule in South Africa was now only a matter of time.

As a result of existing antagonisms within the Reagan administration regarding South Africa, improved relations between the USA and Mozambique did not manifest themselves immediately in increased aid cooperation. But indirectly the N'komati Agreement and the country's changed foreign and domestic policy meant a great deal. American political support changed the attitude of a number of multilateral agencies, both within the UN system and among the Bretton Woods institutions. The Americans were further successful in their attempts at mobilising international donors, via the Bretton Woods institutions, to finance the desired reform policy. In four years the aid flow to Mozambique was more than tripled.

The end of socialism in Mozambique

Through the N'komati Agreement with South Africa in 1984 and membership of the IMF and the World Bank, a comprehensive change in Mozambique's foreign and domestic policy was initiated.

Mozambique's radical foreign policy stance, which found expression within, *inter alia*, the UN system, was toned down. In several important matters the country began to play an important role as intermediary between the West and the Frontline States, not least in respect of discussions about the conditions for Namibia's independence and the withdrawal of Cuban troops from Angola. Relations with the USA were further improved.

With regard to domestic policy, a new development strategy was formulated, according to the Bretton Woods institutions' demands for structurally adjusted measures which the rest of the world deemed essential for securing the country's macro-economic balance and debt repayment ability. At the sixth party congress Frelimo abandoned its role as a Marxist-Leninist avant-garde party. The changeover from a centrally controlled planned economy to a more liberal market economy was already well under way.

6

Stabilisation and Adjustment

The heavily indebted Mozambique opted to regain the confidence of its international creditors by joining the Bretton Woods institutions in 1984 and simultaneously presenting its Economic Action Programme for 1984–86.[190] During 1987 Mozambique started the implementation of an extensive structural adjustment programme,[191] approved and partly developed by the World Bank and the IMF during late 1986.[192]

As a result of the agreement with the Bretton Woods institutions, new debt renegotiations were held with bilateral creditors within the Paris Club later that year. Debt renegotiations were also initiated with commercial creditors within the London Club. Mozambique achieved a further payment deferral. Debts totalling $700 million were re-negotiated.[193]

The conditions for more favourable debt renegotiations within the Paris Club improved in 1988, when the so-called Toronto terms were introduced for the poorest and most heavily indebted countries. Apart from a certain writing off of debts, debt rescheduling became possible. However, the renegotiations in the Paris Club did not allow any significant reduction of the debt burden itself. Interest payments were merely deferred, and this capitalisation meant that the outstanding debt increased. By 1993 the country's foreign debt had risen to $5,100 million. Of this $4,100 million comprised bilateral creditors while the majority of the remaining $900 million comprised multilateral debts, mainly to the World Bank and the IMF.[194]

The economic and social rehabilitation programme

At the consultative group's meeting in Paris, 1990, the Mozambican government presented an expanded programme which laid greater emphasis on social dimensions for the economic rehabilitation.[195]

The economic and social recovery programme (PRES) thus included four important goals:

1. to halt the decline in production;
2. to re-establish the macro-economic balance through a reduced budget deficit;
3. to strengthen the current account and the balance of payments; and
4. to combat poverty in order to ensure the rural population a minimum income and level of consumption.

In order to do this a number of financial, monetary and trade policy measures were required. State enterprises would be restructured and privatised as far as possible. Strict profitability criteria would be applied. An increased concentration on private and small-scale agriculture would occur through improved terms of trade and an increased supply of essential incentive goods. Trade would be liberalised and the fixed price system would be abolished.

State revenues would increase through a more effective collection of taxes and the countervalue created through the flow of international aid. At the same time budget expenditure would be cut by abolishing subsidies for unprofitable production units and reducing consumer subsidies.

The banking system would be rendered more efficient, the amount of credit would be reduced and interest rates would be raised. Foreign trade would be liberalised and the domestic currency devalued to stimulate exports and limit imports.

The intention of the economic and social rehabilitation programme was to deregulate the economy and gradually allow it to become market-oriented. A precondition was that it would be possible to mobilise essential foreign and domestic private investments, international credits and aid.

Implementation of the programme

Neither the Mozambican government nor the Bretton Woods institutions laid any great emphasis on the extremely difficult environment within which the programme would be implemented. In the risk analysis presented to the board of the World Bank it was however stated in general terms that the programme would be exposed to the usual political risks inherent in radical economic changes. These risks included the possibility of extensive domestic opposition to the programme, as a result of the social price which must unavoidably be paid in the short term, mainly by the urban population. The risk assessment also noted that in the transition from one economic system to another, it was possible that any privileged interest group within the party and state apparatus could obstruct the implementation of the programme. Continuing security problems could also delay an increase in production and undermine political support for continued reforms.[196]

Since 1987 the government has periodically adopted austerity and adjustment measures stronger than those required by international creditors, and this fact has undeniably facilitated international financing of the programme.

Fiscal and monetary policy

A series of different measures has been implemented in order to increase state revenues. Tax legislation has been tightened up, a turnover tax has been introduced and tax collection has been improved. Customs tariffs have been simplified and a large number of duty-free goods have been made liable to duty regardless of whether imports are financed using aid or not. Since 1987, credit availability has been determined by Mozambique's efforts to meet the IMF programme's monetary targets. Accordingly, domestic credit to the economy, measured in local currency, has stagnated over the period.

Together with the World Bank, the government has attempted to persuade aid donors to channel more aid via the state budget. This would increase payments of the countervalue, to which the aid should give rise, thus increasing the scope of the state budget despite contracted domestic issuing of credit and a reduced money supply.

Banking, savings and investments

A number of measures have been carried out which aim to create a financial system capable of mobilising savings and supplying credits. During 1992 the reform of the Banco de Moçambique was completed with the separation of the central banking functions from the commercial. Banco Comercial de Moçambique, providing the latter, has been in operation since the end of 1992. It complements the activities of the other state bank (Banco Popular de Desenvolvimento – BPD) and the privately owned bank, Banco Standard Totta de Moçambique. Two new Portuguese banks began operations during 1993.[197]

The banking system is currently facing two challenges. One is related to the required capacity of appraisal for the identification of performing debtors. Increased support to clients lacking the skill to supply the creditor with the required feasibility studies, despite viable forecasts, is of the utmost importance in order to give incentives to domestic investors. The other challenge is to establish a network with branch offices reaching out to rural areas in order to enable new traders and farmers to find outlets for savings and possibilities for credits, without their having to travel to Maputo. In order to stimulate domestic savings, interest rates were raised considerably during 1990–91, now reaching some 40–45 per cent.

In 1991, in order to stimulate increased investments, the National Assembly passed several important laws where the new owners' rights of possession were guaranteed. The first law on foreign investments had already been introduced in 1985. It had a sliding scale for tax exemption and profit export, depending on the sector in which and whereabouts in the country the investments were made. Investments in food production in the northernmost provinces yielded the highest tax exemption and a right to free profit export. Applications for permission for foreign investments rose from $26 million in 1985 to $500 million in 1993. The majority of applications refer to investments within commerce and tourism and have been made by South African and Portuguese enterprises.

Privatisation

From the mid-1980s around 130 state enterprises were responsible for about 50 per cent of the country's marketed food production. As a result of the decision in 1983 to convert the state farms into smaller units and to start extensive privatisation, the number of state agricultural enterprises fell markedly and at present totals about eighty. The land cultivated by these enterprises corresponds to 50 per cent of land formerly cultivated by the state. The privatisation process within the agricultural sector came to a standstill, however, as a result of military destabilisation of the rural areas. Few private farmers or enterprises were prepared to take the commercial risk involved in investments in rural areas as long as the war continued.

About half the country's 570 industrial enterprises were taken over by the state at the time of independence. State ownership has declined with the *ad hoc* privatisation of some 200 small- and medium-scale enterprises. Delays have been encountered in the preparations for restructuring the 13 largest enterprises, and in clarifying the legal status of some 140 intervened enterprises. Changes to the ownership structure have been complicated by a number of factors. There are great difficulties in finding criteria for an objective evaluation of assets. There are also legal uncertainties surrounding the former colonial owners' demands for recovering their properties. Also, the lack of necessary credit for acquisition, investments and working capital further reduces the number of possible purchasers. As a consequence, a number of enterprises will presumably have to be purchased by foreign interests if the privatisation is to be conducted within the foreseeable future. The objective of accelerating the restructuring of present ownership can, however, be questioned. In a monopoly situation no evidence exists to indicate that efficiency would be increased through privatisation. On the contrary, experience shows that low efficiency is often maintained through higher pricing. A more effective solution might be to reorganise the companies, replacing earlier soft budget options with strategies which induce them to become profit-oriented and to cover their own costs.

Liberalisation

A number of important measures have been adopted in order to reduce barriers for free and liberalised internal, as well as external, trade. Internal trade has largely been deregulated. In 1986 the official fixed price system included 46 different types of goods. Their combined sale value was responsible for over 70 per cent of GDP. Today only a few price-regulated goods remain, whose combined sale value is less than 10 per cent of GDP. Trade in agricultural products is almost completely deregulated. There are no longer any obstacles to purchasing food in one district or one province for sale in another area.

Prices are completely free with the exception of rice and maize, where minimum prices for producers have been introduced.

Exchange rates and allocation of foreign currency

Several measures have been adopted in order to stimulate exports and reduce imports.

Devaluations from 528 mt/$US in 1988 to 5,400 mt/$US in 1993 have gradually brought the official exchange rate closer to the secondary market.[198] During 1992 the former was replaced by a market-based rate.

With the introduction of the Free Foreign Exchange Market, FFEM, in early 1992, the various foreign exchange windows were unified under one market system. Although the administrative allocation of import support, managed by Gabinete de Coordenacão de Programas de Importacão (GCPI), has been substantially reduced, foreign exchange received through aid and classified as tied (at present estimated at some $60 million) is administratively allocated according to agreements between the donors and the Ministry of Commerce. Support in foreign currency from donors classified as untied is, together with some export earnings from goods and services (estimated at 165 million and 235 million respectively),[199] passed through the FFEM system. With the exception of a small negative list, import licences are issued on a 'first come first served' basis, provided the required countervalue is paid for. Allocation through market forces is expected to increase efficiency and transparency. In addition, counterpart funds reduce the impact of monetary policy, thus allowing a more expansive policy for priority sectors.

Macro-economic impact

Surprisingly little is known about the macro-economic impact of the rehabilitation programme. Besides methodological problems and the lack of reliable data, the length of its implementation has been too short for more substantial conclusions to be drawn as to whether or not the actual results achieved may be considered to be a result of the programme as such, or only a logical consequence of the huge increase in external resources.

Nevertheless, despite impressive efforts, the impact so far of the implementation of the structural adjustment programme appears not to be as promising as expected. On the contrary, present economic trends hint that there is a danger that short-term measures to restore macro-economic balance will destroy long-term opportunities for sustainable growth.

The statistics on economic performance provided by Mozambique and the Bretton Woods institutions are shaky and should be treated with extreme caution, as methodological and reporting restraints severely affect reliability. In addition, the recorded results are based on estimates of development in the subsistence sector and exclude the informal sector, which presently responds largely to economic activity and employment needs.

According to existing official statistics, the sharp decline in production witnessed in the period 1983–86 was arrested during the first years of the recovery programme 1987–89. A negative growth was replaced by an annual growth of about 5 per cent. As is evident from Table 6.1, however, this was reversed in 1990, when growth again became negative. This negative growth also continued during 1991 and 1992. As a result, gross output is actually estimated to be some 24 per cent below what it was in 1981, the post-independence peak, and 37 per cent below what it was in 1973, the pre-independence peak. However, growth recovered during 1993 with the end of the drought and the signing of the peace accord. This permitted the reintegration of over 75 per cent of the refugees, leading to an impressive increase in marketed quantities of agricultural surpluses, internal transport and trade, and regional transit traffic.[200] There are several explanations for the considerable fluctuations in production development

Agricultural production

There are insufficient statistics for agricultural development, partly as a consequence of the large proportion of subsistence farming. The reported growth of approximately 7 per cent over the first year of the programme is based on changes in the amount of agricultural products

Table 6.1 Production levels, 1985–93

	1985	1986	1987	1988	1989	1990	1991	1992	1993
GDP, growth (%)	-7.2	1.1	3.8	5.5	5.1	-1.3	-0.2	-2.6	19.2
Agriculture	0.8	-0.6	7.0	7.2	4.0	1.1	1.9	-7.5	21.3
Industry	-18.6	-4.3	8.9	7.5	6.8	-9.6	-5.6	-9.2	-6.7
Construction	-4.4	44.8	-16.0	0.1	3.0	1.5	3.0	-1.8	7.0
Transport & communication	-11.8	1.7	-9.8	6.2	10.2	0.5	-2.3	13.6	16.7
Trade & other services	-6.8	-0.7	3.5	4.5	4.0	2.5	2.0	2.0	22.3
GDP, growth/capita (%)	-11.2	-1.7	1.9	2.8	2.7	-1.3	-1.8	-4.7	16.2

Source: Anuário Estatístico, CNP, 1991; *Plano Económico e Social*, CNP, 1993–94.

sold on the official market and not on changes in actual agricultural production.

The increase in marketed agricultural products was mainly due to better access to consumer goods and improved producer prices, which channelled an ever greater quantity of food to the official market and not via the formerly very extensive parallel market. It is extremely uncertain whether the increase in marketed production was actually due to an increase in agricultural production. There is much to indicate that the peasant farmers sold their reserves in order to save their assets during the war. During 1989–90 this positive growth within agriculture was halted. It was negative for 1992 as a result of the worsening drought, but increased in 1993 as a result of heavy rainfall at the right time and the peace accord. However, the agricultural sector showing the greatest decline was also the private sector, which was not as vulnerable to drought as the peasant sector. This fact points to more structural problems in increasing agricultural production, namely difficulties for the farmers and traders in getting access to required credits for inputs and marketing agricultural surpluses, as well as to the negative impact of external food aid which forced the commercial farmers to reduce areas under cultivation.

Industrial production

On the introduction of the recovery programme both private and state industry had great problems. Technology was obsolete due to a lack of investment since the end of the colonial era. The shortage of foreign currency did not allow the importation of raw materials and spare parts. Production costs had increased as a result of the security situation and constant breakdowns in electricity and water supplies. The result was an extensive debt to the Banco de Moçambique.

Domestic industrial production increased by 9 per cent during the first year of the recovery programme. This large increase should be seen against the background of the low starting point and the very low utilisation of capacity in the industry sector. Through access to foreign currency, imports of raw materials and spare parts could increase and production be raised. During 1990, however, industrial production fell again and negative growth, between 5 and 10 per cent annually, continued during 1991, 1992 and 1993, reducing industrial production to some 44 per cent of the 1981 level.[201]

There is a range of explanations for the fall noted after the initial increase in production. In the face of severe constraints in getting access to credits for paying countervalue, imports of required inputs (estimated to be in the realm of 80 per cent of the total requirements for the industrial sector), as well as spares and equipment for the required rehabilitation of the war-stricken infrastructures and the upgrading of technology, were substantially reduced. The reduction of imports, together with decreased internal demand as a result of reduced real wages, has reduced capacity utilisation in the industrial sector to about 10–20 per cent.[202] Accordingly, confronted with low efficiency and high production costs, national industry could not withstand the increased international competition as a result of the ongoing liberalisation, above all from South African enterprises. Industry's total processing value amounted to barely 20 per cent of GDP. Employment fell by over 17 per cent during 1991 alone. In 1990 there were 472 manufacturing industries which employed approximately 86,000 workers. One year later the number of manufacturing enterprises had fallen to 369 and the number of workers to just over 70,000. Over 100 manufacturing enterprises had gone bankrupt or had transferred to purely service production.[203]

Domestic industry had thus been faced with the structural problems created by the colonial production type and choice of technology. It had been possible to avoid these problems previously under the protection of the planned economy, but they were now appearing in the light of ongoing liberalisation and increasing international competition.

Transport

During the period 1982–89, as a consequence of South African de-stabilisation, over 300 engines, 660 railways, 35 bridges and 244 km of railway track were destroyed, which drastically reduced transport

Table 6.2 Transit trade, 1975–91

	1975	1977	1979	1981	1983	1985	1987	1989	1991
International rail freight (1,000 tons)	11,200	5,900	6,800	5,350	3,100	2,200	1,900	3,700	2,700
International handled goods in ports* (1,000 tons)	13,850	9,460	9,700	7,700	5,300	4,000	4,200	5,100	4,900
Revenues in foreign currency for international rail transport and handling of goods ($ million, current prices)	110	60	80	113	40	21	17	n.a.	n.a.

*Including oil.
Source: Own calculations from Stephens (1991) and *Informação Estatística.*

capacity.[204] As a result, freight revenues from transit traffic fell by a total of 90 per cent.[205]

Despite the fact that over $4 billion has been invested in order to rehabilitate and modernise the country's transport infrastructure and thus reduce the landlocked neighbouring countries' need to use considerably more distant South African ports, the region's exporters and importers continue to use the South African transport network. However, it was not only for security reasons that neighbouring countries chose to transport their goods via South African ports. Just as important is the restructuring of the international transport system which has been carried out since the middle of the 1960s, where the full impact for the region of Southern Africa was felt a couple of decades later.

As a consequence of the international manufacturing sector's need for more efficient transport, so-called 'integrated door-to-door transport' was introduced. The regularity and punctuality of transportation became just as important as the sea freight lost itself in the total cost picture, requiring a continuous flow of information and a well-developed international agency network. At present Mozambique lacks commercial transport enterprises which can exploit the investments made effectively and offer the region's transport purchasers high-quality integrated door-to-door transport solutions.

The South African transport organisations and ports offer a substantially better service in this respect. Despite the higher direct costs for inland freight, total transport costs can be reduced. The result has been that the investments made in Mozambique's transport corridors are under-exploited and revenues from the transit trade have not developed as expected.

During 1992, however, utilisation improved significantly as a result of the drought that afflicted the whole region of Southern Africa. Substantial quantities of imported maize were transported to Zimbabwe via the ports in Maputo and Beira. Even if the investments in the transport corridors were not made with such a reversed cargo flow in mind, this increased transit trade entailed substantial, even if temporary, revenues for Mozambique.

National accounts

As is made clear in Table 6.3, state revenues increased from 13 per cent of GDP in 1985 to 26 per cent of GDP in 1992. In particular, the increased significance of the aid-generated countervalue should be noted.

The state's expenditure on consumer and enterprise subsidies fell sharply. Public wages were not allowed to develop in line with inflation. Defence expenditure was cut from an amount corresponding to 35 per

Table 6.3 State budget, 1985–93 (billion meticais, current prices)

	1985	1986	1987	1988	1989	1990	1991	1992	1993
GDP	146	167	423	657	966	1,388	1,871	2,556	5,462
Total revenue	19	22	70	130	225	300	447	660	1,092
of which tax revenue	13	16	60	110	200	265	379	574	995
Total revenues as % of GDP	13	10	16	20	24	22	24	26	20
Total expenditure	31	52	160	290	460	690	958	1,490	2,308
of which:									
current expenditures	24	42	90	150	245	345	466	764	1,171
investment expenditures	7	9	70	140	215	345	491	726	1,137
Total expenditure as % of GDP	21	31	38	44	50	50	51	58	42
Investment as % of GDP	5	5	16	21	23	25	25	28	20
Overall deficit before grants	-12	-30	-90	-160	-235	-390	-510	-829	-1,215
as % of GDP	8	18	21	24	24	28	27	32	22
Grants (i.e. countervalue)	3	4	40	90	160	230	397	645	932
as % of GDP	2	2	9	14	16	16	21	25	17
Deficit after grants	-9	-26	-50	-70	-75	-165	-113	-184	-283
as % of GDP	6	16	12	10	9	12	6	7	5

Source: Own calculations from *Informação Estatística*, CNP, 1989–93; *Plano Económica e Social*, 1993–94.

cent of current state expenditure in 1985 to 18 per cent in 1993 (an amount which corresponds to approximately 10 per cent of GDP).[206]

Despite these measures, as is clear from Table 6.3, state expenditure increased markedly during the first year of the recovery programme, and rose from 21 per cent of GDP in 1985 to 58 per cent in 1992. Altogether the increased state expenditure resulted in a large budget deficit, which increased from 8 per cent of GDP in 1985 to nearly 32 per cent of GDP in 1992. The deficit was largely financed through aid. The actual deficit, including the aid-generated countervalue, fluctuated between 6 and 12 per cent during the period.

Inflation, savings and investment

During the first year of the implementation of the programme, 1987, the rate of inflation increased from some 30 per cent to 170 per cent as a result of devaluations carried out.[207] Since then the rate of inflation has gradually fallen from 170 per cent to an average of about 40 per cent. However, during the last few years, delays in aid disbursements have created a temporary dollar shortage, inducing unplanned devaluations. The delays have further reduced counterpart funds and increased the need for domestically created credits at high interest rates. Consequently, inflation increased to over 50 per cent, compared with the planned target of about 30 per cent, thus severely undermining government efforts to create a positive real interest rate, and thereby stimulating private savings.[208]

Gross domestic savings remained negative during the period, i.e. at present public revenues do not cover public current expenditure. This is possibly because the continued aid inflow covers the main part of current as well as total deficits.

The scope for increasing government savings is limited, particularly in the light of costs for servicing external debts and existing needs in priority sectors. At the same time, given Mozambique's extremely low levels of per capita consumption and incomes, the negative non-governmental domestic savings (equivalent to over 20 per cent of GDP in 1992) can hardly be reversed in the medium term.[209] The restrictive monetary policy, in combination with devaluations and price increases, constitutes a severe constraint on private savings.

Thus the savings–investment ratios continue to reveal profound macro-economic imbalances. As both the public and private sectors continue to be sizeable net losers, international aid provides the bulk of resources for domestic investment.

In spite of the impressive number of approved applications for foreign investments, totalling some $500 million during the 1990s, the previous security situation and the present prevailing political uncertainty make foreign investors reluctant and hesitant. However, in the light of the prospects for political stability, foreign investments in tourism and agro-processing in particular have now slowly started, reaching some $25 million in 1992 (equivalent to 5 per cent of total investment).[210]

The investment ratio reached 47 per cent of GDP in 1992.[211] This seemingly high ratio is explained by the extremely small GDP and by the fact that foreign-financed investments tend to be overvalued in local currency, due to the devaluations carried out. However, with the present budget constraints, the investment ratio nevertheless limits the country's capacity for absorption from a monitoring point of view and, above all, it prevents expansion in overall public expenditure, keeping recurrent public expenditure as a percentage of GDP relatively unchanged. This situation, presently considered grossly inadequate to satisfy minimum quality standards, particularly in the social sectors, will be insupportable in the near future given the required recurrent expenditure for the demobilisation of soldiers and the resettlement of the population.[212] Although a re-allocation of funds from investment to this sector would probably enhance efficiency, this has proved difficult as the composition of external aid continues to favour investment projects instead of untied budget support, in spite of the country's limited capacity for absorption.

Short-term stabilisation (i.e. reduced budget deficits and inflation through restrictive monetary policy and tightened credit ceilings) has tended to contradict the long-term purpose of adjustment to increase production. During 1991, the IMF started to base its ceilings not only on domestically sourced credit, but also on externally sourced credit (i.e. aid). However, due to substantial increases in import support, the need for domestic credits for payment of countervalue increased simultaneously (by some 50 per cent approximately). The credit ceiling has since led to a severe shortage of more long-term credit for productive investment (including supply-orientated import support). Distortions of credits towards trade in fast-turnover consumer goods can be noted. Estimates claim that over 10 per cent of the total import value during 1992 remained idle in ports and customs bonded warehouses due to importers' liquidity problems.[213]

Current account and balance of payments

As is clear from Table 6.4, in later years it was possible to halt the sharp fall in exports. Export goods' share of GDP increased from 2 per cent in 1985 to 9 per cent in 1993. However, the impact of the adjustment programme in terms of increased export production was limited. Effectuated devaluations have not achieved the desired results. The price elasticity for Mozambique's traditional export products is low, i.e. the world market demand is fairly constant and does not immediately

Table 6.4 Exports, selected years, 1981–93 ($ million)

	1981	1983	1985	1987	1989	1990	1991	1992	1993
Total exports of which:	280	132	77	97	105	126	162	139	132
A. Traditional export goods (cashews, shrimps, cotton, sugar, tea, copra, etc.)	252	116	70	86	88	81	111	110	96
B. Other, mainly non-traditional export goods (lobsters, clothing, medicinal plants, semi-precious stones, etc.)	28	16	7	11	17	45	51	29	36
B/A quotient (%)	11	14	10	13	19	56	46	21	38
Exports as % of GDP	12	5	2	6	8	8	12	10	9
Imports	801	636	424	642	807	877	898	887	955
Imports as % of GDP	35	28	12	42	62	57	69	77	65
Exports/imports (%)	35	21	18	15	13	14	18	16	14

Source: Own calculations from Informação Estatística, CNP, different years; Plano Económico e Social, 1993–94.

respond to decreased prices. Instead, devaluations continue to increase profits for individual enterprises (often international) as well as the inflation rate for the national economy due to increased costs of imports. Special measures were taken to increase non-traditional exports, mainly textiles, but cancelled purchase orders from the former Soviet Union and the lack of alternative outlets reduced the impact far beyond expectations.[214] Insufficient investments in upgrading equipment for the production of traditional export crops, combined with a reduction in world market prices (especially for cotton and copra) are reasons behind declining export revenues which, in contrast to initial expectations, stagnated over the period, contributing to only 15 per cent of imports.[215] The majority of exports went to Spain, the USA, Japan and Portugal. Imports came mainly from Western Europe, the USA and Japan. While 10 per cent of exports went to South Africa, over 20 per cent of imports came from there.

Despite many regional coordination meetings at supra-national political level and extensive investments in the infrastructure, the region's economic dependence on both the Western countries and on South Africa increased over the period. The region's internal trade was very low, corresponding to roughly 4 per cent of the member countries' total foreign trade. On the other hand, the member countries' trade with South Africa increased, especially over the last few years.[216]

The SADCC countries' dependence on South Africa should principally be understood against the background of their reciprocally low complementarity. The countries' trade mostly consists of agricultural products and raw materials, for which there is a limited demand in the region. Their imports consist of oil, input goods for agriculture, capital and consumer goods. Goods which can only be processed to a very limited extent by the member countries.

Increased regional trade has not been stimulated either by the government's initiatives. Few investments have been made in order to change the colonial production structures, which were mainly directed towards exports according to the colonial powers' needs. On the contrary, the member countries' macro-economic imbalances, with large balance of payments deficits and the concomitant debts, have increased the importance of export revenues from the traditional production structures. The economic recovery programme's emphasis on increasing exports from the modern sector has thus contributed to reducing the resources available for increased intra-regional trade and production.

Because export revenues have not increased as expected, while costs for imports continue to rise, there is still a high level of deficit in the balance of trade. Poor domestic production of raw materials for domestic industry and the high demand for input goods for agriculture mean that a large import requirement must be satisfied in order for the

Table 6.5 Balance of payments, 1985–93 ($ million)

	1985	1986	1987	1988	1989	1990	1991	1992	1993
I. Trade balance	-347	-464	-545	-633	-703	-751	-736	-748	-823
Exports	77	-79	97	103	105	126	162	139	132
Imports	-424	-543	-642	-736	-808	-877	-898	-887	-955
II. Services	-93	-159	-148	-103	-145	-136	-154	-157	-122
Service receipts	107	119	137	157	167	173	203	222	240
Transport	39	45	35	42	53	63	60	69	78
Migrant workers	41	50	58	72	71	70	56	58	60
Other	27	24	44	43	43	40	87	95	102
Expenditures	-200	-278	-285	-260	-312	-309	-357	-379	-361
Interest	-117	-155	-148	-117	-170	-165	-180	-195	-165
Other	-83	-123	-137	-143	-142	-144	-177	-184	-196
III. Current account, excluding grants and transfers	-440	-622	-693	-735	-848	-887	-890	-905	-944
as % of GDP	13	15	47	59	65	59	68	75	65
IV. Transfers	139	215	310	460	476	547	608	609	628
Grants	139	213	304	377	388	448	501	499	503
Other	–	2	6	83	88	99	107	110	125
V. Current account, including grants	-301	-407	-383	-275	-372	-340	-282	-295	-316
as % of GDP	9	10	26	22	29	26	22	28	22
VI. Capital account	-40	-52	-83	-131	-58	-83	-187	-123	-146
Foreign borrowing	239	284	301	248	257	261	167	227	186
Amortisation	-279	-336	-384	-379	-315	-344	-354	-350	-332
VII. Other	-13	-29	40	34	9	3	-34	-15	27
VIII. Balance	-354	-488	-426	-372	-421	-420	-503	-433	-435
IX. Rescheduling, debt relief and deferment of payments	354	488	426	372	421	420	503	433	435

Source: Own calculations from *Informação Estatística*, CNP, different years, and *Plano Económico e Social*, 1993.

recovery programme to be implemented. Even though the economic squeeze has reduced domestic demand, it has not been possible to reduce imports to a sufficient extent. The import/export ratio presently amounts to some 600 per cent (i.e. the volume of imports exceeds the volume of exports by seven times), and the balance of trade deficit corresponded to a total of 65 per cent of GDP for 1993.[217]

Most of the current account deficit, amounting to some $900 million per year, could be financed through external aid (over 50 per cent). The current deficit after grants is calculated to remain constant at around $300 million per year throughout the second half of the 1990s, corresponding to approximately 25 per cent of GDP, emphasising the need for debt relief.[218]

Despite an increased total inflow of grants and soft loans, a balance in the country's foreign transactions can only be achieved after considerable debt rescheduling. In spite of the fact that a number of donors have either written off their debts or converted them into grant aid, the measures taken to reduce the outstanding debt and the actual debt servicing ratio have been inadequate. In 1993 the actual debt servicing ratio amounted to 25 per cent, which means that a total of $80 million (approximately 10 per cent of total grant aid) was used to pay interest on the outstanding debt. Simultaneously effectuated devaluations and increased domestic interest rates have considerably raised the local costs of debt service repayments. The state has been forced into considerable domestic borrowing in order to be able to purchase, via its own banking system, the foreign currency required for the international interest payments. At present some 20 per cent in the state budget has to be allocated for debt service payment, obviously reducing the scope for combating poverty and satisfying social needs.

Poverty reduction

Mozambique, with a GDP per capita estimated at below $100 and about 60–70 per cent of the rural and 50 per cent of the urban population living in absolute poverty, is one of the poorest countries in the world.[219] The realisation that the process of stabilisation and structural adjustment would lead to further hardships for the already vulnerable majority of the population should lead to poverty alleviation interventions in the social sectors being given full priority status.

However, government efforts to combine a restrictive monetary policy with efforts to alleviate poverty have been unsuccessful. Motivated by the concern shown by a number of donors, the government has tried to leave social expenditure unaffected when cuts in expenditure have been carried out in the budget preparation process. Nevertheless, given that the structural adjustment objective of increasing and sustaining economic growth is considered to be essential for any poverty alleviation, in practice the former has been prioritised at the expense of the latter. Most of the poverty alleviation carried out has therefore been through various emergency programmes financed by foreign aid. At the same time, the free distribution of food aid has resulted in distortions in allocations and negative impacts for local food production, tending to reduce purchasing power and increase poverty.

Living standards of the rural population

The prolonged drought and the war economy have had a severe impact on rural areas. A number of very productive agricultural areas have been completely abandoned by the population or cut off from the trade network. Destabilisation has meant that some districts have been almost totally isolated from the world around. Popular migrations have given rise to increased pressure on militarily secure areas, with a resulting increase in ecological vulnerability. A whole generation of children of peasant farmers has been forced to grow up in refugee camps with different soil conditions, a shortage of agricultural implements and a lack of knowledge about the conditions necessary for subsistence agriculture. In addition, rationalisation and workforce reductions within state industries and agricultural units are reducing access to seasonal employment and thus the rural population's purchasing power and level of consumption are being reduced.

Despite a liberalisation of trade and increased producer prices, the peasant farmers' terms of trade have not been improved either. The measurements that form the basis of Table 6.4 are uncertain, but several studies show that the terms of exchange became worse during the first years of the structural adjustment programme.[220]

Table 6.6 Peasant farmers' terms of trade, 1976–89 (index 1986=100)

1976	1980	1983	1985	1986	1987	1988	1989
88	69	74	97	100	111	62	45

Source: Eduards et al., 1990, Appendix 9.

Social services

Indicators on social development, presented by the World Bank, are low in comparison with the African continent in general. Life expectancy is 49 years, compared with 51 years for Africa south of the Sahara. Similarly, infant mortality is 137 per thousand compared with 107 per thousand. UNICEF has presented figures which indicate a so-called one-year mortality rate for infants of 200 per thousand.[221]

Due to budget constraints, development expenditures for the social sectors have generally declined during the 1990s, presently amounting to around 3 per cent of GDP, although the allocation has been fairly constant in real terms.[222] However, this is unsatisfactory bearing in mind the destruction of the social infrastructure in rural areas as a consequence of destabilisation.

Since 1980 most of the primary school network (68 per cent) has been destroyed or closed by the war, giving under 50 per cent of the school-age population access to education. As a result of the massive destruction of over 1,000 units in the health infrastructure in rural areas, the density of the health network decreased from some 10,000 persons per health unit in 1985 to around 13,000 seven years later.[223]

This reduces the peasants' desire to move back to their original settlement areas, even if the security situation permitted it. There is a risk that the migration from the rural areas to the towns will continue.[224] The lack of development inputs into rural areas may negatively affect the conditions for implementing the economic and social rehabilitation programme and reinforce the difficulties in bringing about increased security and peaceful development in rural areas.

Living conditions of the urban population

Mozambique's decision-makers and international financiers were aware that the implementation of the recovery programme would worsen living conditions for the population in the towns, at least in the short term.

> In this setting, the ERP is having certain painful social consequences in the short run. The combined effect of wage restraint, increases in the prices of consumer goods, and lay-offs in civil service and public enterprises is reducing urban purchasing power and may be increasing urban poverty.[225]

This has actually been the case. Reduced consumer subsidies, together with a greatly increased migration into towns, has increased the supply burden and the strain on families' household budgets. Many families are forced to take care of relatives who moved to the towns to avoid the war, and charges for electricity and water supplies have risen sharply. Since 1985 real wages have declined by about 25 per cent, aggravating the problem still further.[226] Nurses and teachers feel obliged to demand extra payments for services illegally, be it from patients for providing necessary remedies or from parents for passing the children through examinations. This process of informal privatisation of public activities affects the poorest most drastically, as they are not capable of paying. Several investigations have shown that, taken as a whole, the food intake for the urban population has fallen.[227]

The political and social unrest which ought to be a natural consequence of the worsening living conditions in urban areas has not yet developed into any great threat to the country's leaders. Apart from a number of strikes and some extensive demonstrations, affected population groups appear unexpectedly passive. One explanation for this forbearance shown by Mozambicans in general is assumed to be an awareness of the lack of an alternative, due to the prevailing security and political situation and the drought which again struck the whole region in 1992. The effects of the economic cutbacks carried out by the government are still interpreted in popular parlance as a result of external factors, over which the decision-makers have no control. However, the question remains of how long that forbearance will last. There is reason to fear that social unrest in urban environments will increase in the near future.

7

The Impact of
International Aid

During the 1980s the direction of international bilateral aid to the African continent changed. As a result of the international debt crisis and the necessity for macro-economic structural adjustment, a much larger share of bilateral aid was converted from sector support and project support into general import and balance of payments support. At the same time increasing material destitution for large population groups increased the need for short-term disaster relief.

The industrial countries' fear that the effects of migration and environmental degradation would spill over from the African continent and increase social tensions in the West meant that at the end of the 1980s the goal became one of finding conditions under which Africa's problems could be contained within Africa. Hence aid gradually changed from being development-orientated to becoming disaster-directed, with an emphasis on creating and maintaining social security. The question of long-term sustainable economic development was therefore deferred to the future.

The direction and orientation of aid has been further homogenised and made subordinate to multilateral UN agencies to an increasing extent. While the international financial institutions, the IMF and the World Bank, increasingly monitor the use of import and balance of payments support, a growing amount of emergency support has been channelled via various UN agencies and voluntary organisations which have built up their own distribution channels locally. This has strengthened the aid donors' influence over the economies and development policies of the recipient countries.

This development is also a distinctive feature in Mozambique. From emphasising the importance of aid cooperation on equal terms and in accordance with the recipient country's priorities in the first years after independence, Mozambique has now become completely dependent on the donors' goals and ambitions. This is largely explained by the simple fact that the country's most vital imports exceed exports almost tenfold and are almost totally financed by international aid. Thus Mozambique has become the world's most aid-dependent country.

Growth and composition of aid

The Bretton Woods institutions' ambitions to mobilise international donors to finance the implementation of the country's economic structural adjustment have made great progress. During the period 1986–90, the flow of aid into the country trebled. Grant aid amounted to over $950 million in 1990, according to figures published by the UN agency, UNDP. This corresponds to around $62 per capita, which can be compared with the average of $27 for countries south of the Sahara. Grant aid corresponded to 75 per cent of GDP, being eight times larger than the country's exports of goods and nearly four times higher than the state's other revenues.[228]

Table 7.1 Growth of aid, 1985–90 ($ million)

	1985	1986	1987	1988	1989	1990
Grants:						
A. UNDP's calculations	200	328	655	880	840	970
B. Mozambique's calculations	140	215	305	380	390	450
B/A quotient (%)	70	65	47	43	47	47
Soft loans:						
UNDP's calculations	345	362	250	130	110	145
Total aid:						
UNDP's calculations	545	690	905	1,010	950	1,115
Share grants (%)	37	47	72	87	88	87
Share soft loans (%)	63	53	28	13	12	13
DAC's calculations	300	422	651	893	788	946

Source: UNDP, 1989–90; *Informação Estatística*, CNP, 1990; DAC *Annual Reports*, 1986–91.

The largest donors

One of the dominant features of the flow of aid is the large number of donors. At present there are 33 multilateral donors (of which 27 are UN agencies), 44 bilateral organisations and 104 NGOs in the country. The majority of the aid (77 per cent), however, comes from the ten largest donors (EU, Italy, Sweden, France, Great Britain, the USA and Norway, in the order stated). Among the UN agencies, the World Bank was responsible for over 50 per cent of multilateral funds disbursed, followed by WFP, UNDP, IMF and UNICEF.[229]

Motives behind aid

From independence until the presentation of the economic rehabilitation programme in 1987, aid to Mozambique was mainly motivated by foreign policy reasons.

The Soviet Union saw Mozambique as one of its allies in the Third World; extensive technical aid would make the socialist transition process possible. The West attempted to limit the Soviet Union's influence through aid. For the Nordic countries the apartheid policy in South Africa had a decisive influence on the extent of the aid. The extensive drought in the region during the first half of the 1980s was a further motivating factor for international aid during that period.

The presentation of the economic and social rehabilitation programme created a new motive for aid. More market-adjusted economic development in Southern Africa was considered as being able to contribute to more stable political development in the region. At the same time the country's repayment of debts was seen as being necessary in order not to create disquiet on the international credit market.

Forms and direction of aid

Aid to Mozambique can be divided into four main groups: import and balance of payments support, sector support with project aid, technical assistance, and food aid including disaster relief.

At the beginning of the 1990s import and balance of payments support was responsible for approximately 25 per cent of the flow of aid. This form of support is intended to finance the country's deficit in the current account and to support the implementation of the economic rehabilitation programme. The majority of import and balance of payments support is not tied and is allocated to end-users through market forces. Project support amounted to around 25 per cent of aid. This financed almost 75 per cent of the government's investment programme and covered over 500 different projects. Sector support in the form of foreign personnel and equipment amounted to another 25 per cent. There were over 3,000 expatriates in the country at a cost of $250 million. Food aid, together with disaster relief, was responsible for around 25 per cent.

An analysis of the direction of project and sector support shows the current priorities. Most of this support at the beginning of the 1990s went to the productive sector (68 per cent). Agriculture is responsible for the largest share (24 per cent), followed by transport (21 per cent). The education sector received 13 per cent, while just 5 per cent went to health-care.

Aid to Mozambique can be divided into three different phases:

1. *Project aid for development 1975–82* From independence until the beginning of the 1980s, socialist countries and the Nordic countries were responsible for the largest flow of aid. During this period aid was concentrated on import support, capital-intensive development projects and the expansion of the physical and social infrastructure.

Aid from the socialist countries mainly consisted of long-term loans which were often repaid in the form of export goods. The Nordic countries' import support (mainly paper and school materials), project activity and technical assistance comprised purely grant aid.

2. *Disaster relief for survival 1982–87* During this period the direction and scope of aid was altered. Several large investment projects continued to swallow up large chunks of aid, especially where extensive construction work had already been started. After criticism at the fourth party congress in 1983, the large-scale and technically advanced aid projects were toned down. Greater emphasis would be laid on small-scale projects in rural areas and on the rehabilitation of existing industry. Through a law on foreign investments passed in 1985, an attempt was made to convert some of the flow of aid into commercial cooperation.

At the same time the drought at the beginning of the 1980s meant that large amounts of the development aid were converted into disaster relief and food aid. Aid cooperation with the socialist countries remained close.[230]

The signing of the N'komati Agreement with South Africa in 1984 and the application for membership of the World Bank and the IMF in the same year opened the way for aid from the USA.

3. *Adjustment support for economic and social rehabilitation 1987–92* In 1987 the economic and social rehabilitation programme was presented, and in the same year the first international disaster conference was held in Geneva on the initiative of the UN. These two events, together with the changes in Eastern Europe a few years later, would come to have a decisive influence on the direction of future aid cooperation.

The economic and social rehabilitation programme meant that import and balance of payments support increased sharply in extent, with the aim of improving the macro-economic balance. At the same time project aid was further toned down. Several planned large-scale projects were mothballed or taken over by international commercial capital. The most notable was the agricultural project in Cabo Delgado province, covering 400,000 hectares, which was partly taken over by the Lonrho company group. The disaster conference in Geneva resulted in larger amounts of traditional project and development aid being converted into disaster relief.

During 1990/91 in practice all aid from the Eastern bloc ceased. It is difficult to establish its total value, but information from different sources indicates that the total involved was approximately $150 million per year in long-term credits or grant aid. Subsidised oil supplies from the Soviet Union ceased. Migrant workers from East Germany returned home. Investment projects were finished and Mozambique had to start to pay international market wages in foreign currency to the aid workers from the Eastern bloc who remained in the country.

Countervalue of aid

The importance of the countervalue generated from aid, as a financial source for government spending, has increased as a consequence of increased aid flow.

Aid in the form of grants should constitute a grant to the recipient country, not to a company, a project or an individual. Accordingly, in most cases the recipient project, enterprise or individual has to pay a corresponding amount in domestic currency to the Ministry of Finance before the aid can be used (the so-called countervalue). Aid therefore has a direct positive effect on the state's revenues. If the aid donor does not tie the countervalue created by their aid, the state can use it as normal state revenues in the state budget to cover its expenditures. This reduces the need for domestic state borrowing and the risk of inflation entailed by borrowing in order to finance the deficit in the state budget.

There are, however, several problems with regard to payment and use of the countervalue. Only 70 per cent of total aid is registered, because large amounts of disaster aid, project and technical assistance are channelled outside the state budget. At the same time studies from the World Bank show that only 75 per cent of the registered counter-value is actually paid into the Ministry of Finance.[231] Thus in total only 50 per cent of aid generates countervalue.

One further problem is that the use of large amounts of the counter-value is tied by the donors. This restricts the government's opportunities to dispose freely of revenues in its state budget even if the countervalue is paid to the Ministry of Finance. Some countries demand that the countervalue should be used to finance in domestic currency the current costs of their own project activity. Others present a negative list of domestic activities for which 'their' countervalue cannot be used.

If donors channelled all their aid through the state budget the payment of countervalue would increase. If donors also ceased to impose

Table 7.2 International aid generating countervalue (billion meticais)

	1985	1986	1987	1988	1989	1990	1991	1992
A. Received grants according to Mozambican calculations	6	8.5	90	200	290	420	720	1,210
B. Paid countervalue	3	4	40	90	160	230	380	650
B/A quotient (%)	50	47	42	46	55	55	53	53

Source: Informação Estatística, CNP, 1989–92.

conditions for the use of the countervalue, this would mean a great deal for the macro-economic balance. State revenues would increase, and hence their ability to pay off state debts. The credit ceiling would be raised, interest rates would be lower and the state would more easily be able to finance the extensive infrastructural investments that would be necessary, without the risk of increasing inflation. The implementation of the economic and social rehabilitation programme could be eased considerably, as the scope for carrying out social rehabilitation work and poverty alleviation activities increased.

Aid planning and coordination

During the second half of the 1980s the role of planning as an instrument to control economic development was greatly reduced. The Ministry for Planning was closed down and the national planning commission functioned more as an information-gathering and statistics-processing authority. The lack of long-term development plans setting out the framework for aid and governmental priorities made the coordination of international aid difficult.

With regard to disaster relief, in 1980 the 'Departamento para a Prevenção e Combate às Calamidades Naturais' (DPCCN)[232] was formed, after a series of droughts, floods and cyclones. There was a great need to be able to better predict, prevent and combat the effects of natural disasters. DPCCN was subordinate to the planning commission.

The lasting effects of natural disasters increased the need for external food aid. Through the rapid growth of the number of donors, overall coordinated planning became necessary. In 1986, therefore, DPCCN was transferred to the newly created Ministry for Cooperation.

Also, in 1987 an executive committee was formed at national level (CENE, Comissão Executiva Nacional de Emergência) with the central task of collecting information on the disaster situation, mobilising international support and coordinating the donors' inputs. The commission was subordinate to the Ministry for Cooperation and was headed by its deputy minister.

At central level there were regular coordination meetings in Maputo between CENE, DPCCN, UN agencies, bilateral donors and representatives of the NGOs. Increasing mistrust of the Mozambican administrative capacity led donors to hold their own meetings over the last few years in order to discuss necessary measures, without inviting government representatives. This has naturally further worsened the climate of cooperation between donors and recipients.

During the first period, 1975–82, the more long-term development aid was channelled through a national directorate for international cooperation which was subordinate to the planning commission. Aid activities were, however, never totally integrated into the work of the planning commission. The majority of aid inputs were made according to the various aid donors' identification and prioritisation in direct cooperation with the different sectoral ministries.

During the second period, 1982–87, the national directorate for international cooperation was reorganised and in 1986 it became a separate ministry, the Ministry of Cooperation. The ministry did not manage to bring about better coordination of aid either. Different aid inputs still continued to be implemented according to the initiative of the aid donors themselves, in some cases after consultation with different sectoral ministries.

During the third period, 1987–91, several measures were implemented in order to improve coordination. In May 1989 the government attempted to strengthen the Ministry for Cooperation's role and to increase its responsibility in relation to the Ministry of Finance which, through the rehabilitation programme, came in practice to take over most contacts with the donors.

This attempt did not have the intended effect. The Ministry for Cooperation's influence over aid cooperation or its coordination has not been strengthened – rather the reverse. In the dialogue with international aid donors Mozambique is represented by the sector ministries involved. The system using coordinating ministerial committees has ceased. Instead, on the Ministry of Finance's initiative, an attempt is being made to get the dominant aid donors within each sector to take on a leading role in order to achieve the coordination necessary among the donors and improve communications with the government.

In order to function, international adjustment support requires effective coordination of the bilateral donors' inputs. With regard to coordination and dialogue with different donors, the Mozambican government has chosen first and foremost to allow this to happen through the donor meetings which were introduced between representatives of the Mozambican government, the World Bank and the international donors (the consultative group meeting in Paris). The Mozambican government is represented by the prime minister and/or finance minister. The minister for cooperation seldom takes part.

This has entailed a relative monopolisation of the aid dialogue by the World Bank and the Mozambican government. Corresponding monopolisation has also occurred on the Mozambican side through the Finance Ministry representing the government to an increasing extent. This monopolisation has had negative effects.

The Mozambican decision-makers who are 'linked-in' to the external financing flow have obtained an increasingly strong position in the internal political debate. Their dependence on the external base for the continued exercise of power has simultaneously reduced their interest in critically examining the implementation and result of the rehabilitation programme.

Bilateral donors and sector ministries are also becoming increasingly marginalised from the decision-making process and the development dialogue. This marginalisation does not contribute to stopping the 'brain-drain' which is so troubling various government departments at present – rather the opposite. The administrative capacity of government departments is diminishing more and more, like their ability to formulate overall sector development plans, and they are becoming more divorced from the dialogue and political decision-making.

At the donor meetings the results achieved and the experience gained from the implementation of the economic and social rehabilitation programme are discussed, together with the identification of necessary measures and available aid resources for the coming year. In this way communications between donors and recipients has also been improved. However, the lack of coordination between international creditors and aid donors still constitutes a problem.[234] Mozambique's decision-makers often receive different signals from creditors and aid donors, depending on the importance these attribute to different measures. It is natural that the creditors' and aid donors' views on how to resolve the problems differ, because they represent different interests. For the creditors, their basic interest consists of being paid back the capital lent out, or at least obtaining debt servicing payments with as little delay as possible. This perspective weighs heavily on the formulation of the rehabilitation programme's conditions within the IMF management and in the Paris Club. For international aid donors the long-term development perspective often weighs more heavily, which is reflected in the consultative group meetings between aid donors, the World Bank and representatives of the Mozambican government. There are also problems in that debt matters and the content of the rehabilitation programme are handled by several different departments and authorities in the donor countries.

Knowledge of Mozambique's economic and political realities naturally varies among these different authorities. Unfortunately it happens
that a decision taken at an IMF board meeting is not always rooted in
the knowledge possessed by the various aid donors and the World Bank.
This increases the Mozambican requirement for preparation and
competent representation in a range of different forums. The government needs to create an increased understanding of the economic and
political environment that prevails in the country and thus greater
efficiency for the measures drawn up. The preparation of such work
often exceeds Mozambique's administrative capacity.

Mozambique's capacity for absorption

Mozambique's absorption capacity is affected by the aid donors' criteria
and goals for the use of the aid. Each and every one of over 180 active
aid organisations has different requirements for the formulation of
agreements, purchasing and reporting routines, as well as government
obligations and the use of countervalue. Aid planning and reporting is
also rendered difficult through the donors having different fiscal years.

These conditions impose heavy demands on Mozambique's absorption capacity, which for historical reasons is very low. The Mozambican
workforce is both untrained and inexperienced in comparison with other
countries in Africa south of the Sahara. There are less than 2,500
university-educated people and only 150 are examined annually. Within
the state administration a third of employees have a basic school education, and fewer than 15 per cent have any form of higher training. This
substantially affects the conditions for economic restructuring.

This means that Mozambique in its present position often lacks the
capacity to identify development projects, assess the proposals for inputs
presented by donors or execute its own evaluations.

Also, the country's decision-makers can neither afford nor have the
knowledge to say no thank you to aid, even if the long-term effects of
that aid could be measured and predicted. The lack of capacity within
the central administration often has adverse consequences at local level,
as the aid is seldom adjusted to locally prevailing conditions. The
provincial governments are often faced with a *fait accompli* when the aid
project is to be implemented. They have rarely had an opportunity to
participate in preparing the project.

In order to carry out project implementation, the country has therefore been extremely dependent on expatriates ever since independence.
During the latter half of the 1980s the extent of foreign personnel was
estimated to be about 3,000–4,000 persons. This number is expected to
fall during the first half of the 1990s as a result of reduced cooperation
with the Eastern bloc. Some 2,000 domestic officials with minimal

academic preparation can hardly match the influence of over 3,000 expatriates.

Both the government and the World Bank point to the importance of strengthening the Mozambican administration's capacity for it to be possible to implement necessary reforms and manage the increasing flow of aid. The problem has been observed by international aid donors, and at various 'consultative meetings' in Paris different measures have been presented to 'put the government back in the driving seat'.[235]

Negative effects of relief aid

As a result of the drought which struck Southern Africa during the 1980s, an increasing share of the flow of aid to Mozambique comprises disaster relief. As has been made clear, comprehensive political conditions often have to be satisfied before this food aid support is issued. The price Mozambicans had to pay for US food aid and its distribution to the starving population through CARE proved to be higher than anticipated.

At the end of the 1980s DPCCN was badly shaken by extensive rumours of corruption and abuse of disaster relief resources. A special investigation committee was set up, and the Mozambican authorities acknowledged the existence of corruption in the sense of theft and abuse of disaster relief food. The loss was calculated to amount to approximately 20 per cent and a number of DPCCN officials at middle level were dismissed. However, donors who obtained full access to the investigation material and who participated in summarising it for the international aid community estimated the loss at a total of 50 per cent. In the joint report that was published, a large number of the explanations for the existing abuse of disaster relief related to the control system which had been developed within DPCCN and also to deficiencies in the quality of foreign technical assistance obtained through CARE.

> LSU is equipped with computers and adequate working equipment. It has a reasonable number of staff, including the CARE advisors. However, its level of functioning does not appear to be in proportion to the resources available.

An evaluation of Swedish logistical support for disaster relief inputs, however, shows that DPCCN functioned considerably better at provincial and district level than the host of rumours among both Mozambican decision-makers and aid donors in Maputo gave reason to believe.[237]

At the same time the evaluation revealed serious deficiencies in the administrative system and control functions developed by CARE at central level. These deficiencies seriously affected the efficiency of the use of resources and the magnitude of existing losses and theft. Several investigations, like the spot-checks undertaken by the evaluation team, showed a shortfall which could amount to 30–40 per cent. The calculations were hampered by the fact that, despite all the computers, there was no systematised information at central level on what happened to the food after the sacks left the provincial stores. The donors' mistrust of the Mozambican administration's capacity to manage future distribution of disaster goods was therefore not totally groundless.

The deficiencies in information systems and methods which the team discovered were largely explained by the fact that the technical assistance which CARE provided to DPCCN over the years had been inadequate. The self-imposed main task for CARE became resolving short-term distribution problems without regard to efficiency/costs or to the need for a more long-term transfer of knowledge and organisational development. This attitude proved counterproductive. Incorrect transport solutions have been chosen, resulting in price increases and delays. More money than necessary went on covering the costs for transport. These are funds which should have been used to purchase more food or to strengthen the existing transport capacity and make it more efficient. There is also the fact that in several cases the choice of modes of transport resulted in losses and a smaller part of the disaster relief food reaching its target groups than would otherwise have been the case.

The most serious aspect for Mozambique is that for eight years the country has not succeeded in building up any efficient organisation which can take on the implementation of future disaster inputs using its own resources. In several cases competent Mozambican personnel have moved to better paid government departments, to the private sector or to foreign NGOs, and in the main the staff staying on have not taken part in any transfer of knowledge.

Over the years a series of evaluations and studies referring to CARE's work has pointed out these matters and proposed changes.[238] No Mozambican authority has had the power to intervene to carry through or monitor the implementation of the stated recommendations. This series of evaluations has never come to be used as an instrument for improvement. It may be worth noting in particular that the financiers, USAID, did not react to the deficiencies in quality revealed.

But a representative of the American financiers, commenting on the Swedish evaluation team's presentation of its conclusions, indicated, on the contrary, a passive acceptance of CARE's inadequate capacity:

We are fully aware of the shortcomings mentioned. However, it has never been the USA's political and aid-related intention to go in and strengthen Mozambican public administration by helping to establish a national state organisation to counteract emergencies. Quite the opposite; the faster such attempts erode, the easier it will be for private interest and non-governmental organisations to assume responsibility for the distribution of emergency aid and to reach targeted groups. You can quote me on this point.[239]

There is no evidence that CARE consciously created deficiencies in the control systems for distribution of disaster relief food in order to stimulate the growth of losses, thefts and increased mistrust on the part of the international donors.

Through CARE's participation, however, the country was taken back to its starting position for the distribution of disaster relief goods which prevailed at the beginning of the 1980s. The donors again repeated their earlier demands that distribution should occur through parallel structures, separated from the state and DPCCN, which could instead be monitored by multilateral UN agencies or foreign NGOs. These demands reduce Mozambique's sovereignty and its right to independent decision-making with reference to the direction of disaster relief, and the implementation entails a range of negative effects at local level.

Decreased local food production

Even more serious are the long-term forms of dependency that disaster relief creates. International food aid often drives out locally produced food. One reason for this is that the aid donors have been unwilling to purchase surplus production in Mozambique, despite the fact that there are areas in Mozambique which have not been afflicted by the drought and which, despite the war, have been able to maintain some surplus production of food. International food aid most often has a direct connection with the donor country's own agricultural policy and any surplus production. Food aid is not usually made available to the recipient country in the form of cash to purchase food locally or on the world market and transport it to the starving population according to needs and priorities identified by the country's government. Instead the donors often make food available on their own terms, with little opportunity for the recipient countries to have any influence.[240] Through supplying the surplus from their own domestic agriculture, the donors have been able to finance some of their own agricultural subsidies with the help of their aid budget.[241] Free purchase on the world market for cash granted would give considerably more food to Mozambique than the delivery channels preferred by the donors.

Non-governmental organisations and parallel structures

The negative impact of aid is aggravated by the local authorities' inability to monitor and control the local activities of foreign NGOs. Several of these work with different political overtones and several in direct opposition to the government's policy.[242] As a result of the different

THE IMPACT OF INTERNATIONAL AID

problems which these antagonisms entail and which afflict the local population, the legitimacy of state power is increasingly undermined.

An expressed goal of Mozambique's government has been that the fight against disasters should be led by Mozambican institutions. One ideal is that society's normal institutions should handle disaster situations within respective sectors, with the necessary coordination. Another ideal has been that the fight against disasters should be organised so there can be a smooth transition to development work when the situation ceases or eases. In this perspective the state would also 'learn' to handle disasters, at both local and central level. The build-up of the donors' parallel structures poses a constant threat to these goals.

At district level the local administration's ambitions often encounter different goals within foreign NGOs, which are given responsibility for the distribution of disaster relief food by the donors. The donors demand that food aid should be distributed through 'their' organisations. In this way a large part of the available logistical resources ends up in the hands of these organisations instead of the Mozambican institutions. Local Mozambican authorities and officials thus become increasingly dependent (for transport, for example) on resources belonging to foreign organisations or local commercial interests in order to carry out their normal work. In some districts foreign organisations have assumed responsibility for food supplies and airlift these into the area without being controlled by or informing the provincial authorities. In several cases deliveries have been omitted, and because the authorities at provincial level have not been informed, this has resulted in cases of acute starvation.

The more foreign organisations take over the local management of disaster relief, the more society's normal administrative system is divorced from reality. Expertise and experience is 'archived' within foreign NGOs and not within society's normal administration.

Free distribution versus sale

The donor community's demands that disaster relief should reach its target groups are natural. There are few areas where public opinion is so sensitive as when food disappears on the way to suffering people who are starving. As earlier accounts attempted to show, demands from donors to monitor and implement distribution themselves involve several economic and political dilemmas.

The existence of several different channels for the distribution and management of food, and the fact that these channels are controlled by different principles, creates several difficulties. One fundamental problem is that the food shortage affects both internal refugees and peasant farmers and the urban population and civil servants. This means that certain population groups are completely without any purchasing power and are in need of free distribution of food. Other groups have purchasing power, more or less, and should thus to some extent be able to purchase their food.

But the international donor community is interested in the first instance in satisfying the needs of destitute people who are starving. The need for food for free distribution is thus satisfied more easily than the need for food for sale. In Mozambique's case (1990–91) around 90 per cent of the need for free distribution among disasters was satisfied, while only about 45 per cent of the requirement for the commercial network was satisfied using food aid. This imbalance between the two distribution systems creates a couple of problems.

On one hand, the price difference between locally produced and imported food becomes too great, as normally demand for local produce is much greater than supplies. This difference in prices is heavily reinforced by the fact that imported maize is subsidised. This in turn reinforces the above-mentioned disadvantages for locally produced maize. In the long run this price difference also tends to change the population's pattern of consumption through imported yellow maize being much cheaper than locally produced white maize.

In addition, the existing demand for maize for sale creates a strong incentive for leakage from the disaster relief distribution to the commercial network, i.e. theft and losses are stimulated. The total demand for food in the commercial network is then satisfied on the 'black market', where the leakage from disaster relief goods ends up.[243]

The identification of need rarely takes into consideration what can be done using local resources. Inputs are planned according to short-term need without regard to the effects on long-term economic and political development, and often without coordination with other donors.

Aid dependency

As has been made clear, Mozambique's aid dependency is very great. The international flow of aid corresponds to over 75 per cent of GDP and finances over 80 per cent of the country's imports. Aid dependency of this magnitude reduces the country's sovereignty and ability to take independent political decisions.

At the same time as the state has been forced to reduce its political and economic role, domestic entrepreneurs appear too weak to bring about the development of a market economy. The economic vacuum, which arose as a result of the difficulties in changing from a centrally planned economy to a more market oriented economy, has given international aid donors an unusually strong influence over the country's economic and social development.

The donors' special interests and special expertise, together with the lack of donor coordination, have, however, sporadically reduced support for the implementation of the adjustment programme. As has been made clear, aid is not always channelled into the most highly prioritised sectors. The donors' development ambitions and choice of technology mean, against the background of the shortage of a skilled workforce, that several projects are being implemented without an opportunity for Mozambique to manage the activity further after the expiry of the project period. Sometimes there is no scope in the budget to cover the operating costs, a fact that of course increases the risk of so-called white elephants.

The large flow of aid has, against the background of the scarcity of consumer goods and prevailing political uncertainty, increased the scope for crime and corruption. Disaster relief food is stolen and increasing numbers of officials within the administration are demanding a commission for speeding up bureaucratic processes. The situation is being experienced by parts of the population as so troublesome that the economic recovery programme (PRE) has been translated in common parlance to the programme for individual recuperation (PRI).

Simultaneously, aid donors are experiencing great 'aid fatigue' as a result of the prolonged crisis. While waiting for the new government to take power following the recently carried out election, several donors view the current government as a transitional government. In recent years they have therefore preferred to plan and implement the various aid inputs under their own auspices with as little involvement of the Mozambican administration as possible. Hence, bilateral donors were invited to meetings by UN agencies to discuss the disaster situation and the measures required without the Mozambican aid or disaster relief authorities being extended a corresponding invitation. Donors hold their own meetings and discussions regarding questions which involve democracy without any Mozambican representative participating in the discussion. In this way the donors quite simply ignore altogether the fact that regardless of which government comes to power there will be a very great future need for a strong administrative state apparatus.

At the same time Mozambican decision-makers appear to lack the power to take their own initiative to involve the donors in planning and thus reduce the alienation. They are experiencing heavy pressure as a result of the rapidly increasing number of donors whose demands for regular meetings and own reporting routines are taking up ever more time and to an increasing extent exceeding the capacity of the administration. Also, more Mozambican decision-makers are feeling superfluous at these meetings. They do not have time to study the donors' questions more than very briefly. They assume that the donors will decide everything and that there is little room for Mozambican points of view. There is also the fact that the officials themselves, as a result of the economic crisis and the political uncertainty, are forced to look after themselves and downgrade the donors' never-ending demands for reporting.

These facts raise the question of whether or not the dimension of external assistance ought to decrease. An international flow of aid corresponding to 75 per cent of GDP is obviously not sustainable in the long run. However, in the case of Mozambique, the aid/GDP ratio is more a result of an extremely low GDP, measured in current US dollars (which is probably very much underestimated) than a result of a too extensive aid programme. The country has been at war since independence and the human and material destruction is devastating. But endorsing the need for continued and extended external assistance makes it important to reassess the present orientation of external aid. The objective of present external assistance should be to increase national ownership and to reduce external dependency in the long term.

8

State and Market
in Distortion

One of the economic and social rehabilitation programme's overall goals is to bring about a transition from a centrally planned economy to a market-orientated economy. For several reasons this transition process has proved harder to accomplish than originally anticipated. Some reasons are based on the fact that the rehabilitation programme has not been consistent and designed in accordance with Mozambique's realities. Others are based on the fact that the programme could not be implemented as originally thought.

A well-functioning market requires a competent state, capable of creating developmental norms and rules which, if followed by the market actors, contribute to the legitimacy of both the state and the market in their relations to the society as such. Hence the role of the state will be to do less where the market functions, and to do more where market imperfections prevail. The present phase of transition from state to market in Mozambique is characterised by disturbing distortions which have thus far prevented such a development from taking place. In fact earlier government failures have been aggravated and complemented at the same time by a number of market failures.

One reason for this situation, besides the over-ambitious pace with which the programme is being implemented, is the different attitudes to the role of the state represented by Mozambique's government and its international creditors. For a long time Mozambique sought a third route between a centrally administered economy and a pure market economy. According to this line of thinking the state would henceforth also play an important role. But instead of being directly interventional in production planning and allocation of resources, the state would be responsible for constructing the framework of rules and institutions required for a market economy to be able to function.

According to the government's perception several areas lacked the right conditions for market forces to be developed. The state therefore had to support the growth of a market. This applied in particular to the rural economy, where low productivity and distorted production structures from the colonial era greatly limited the population's productivity and purchasing power. In order for the demand to be developed strong economic support was needed. Corresponding support was required for constructing functioning trade and credit systems. These were tasks which the market could not tackle itself.[244]

According to international creditors, represented by the IMF, the state's role should be limited as far as possible. This was considered to be not only of economic importance in order to reduce the state's expenditures and thereby be able to balance the state budget. Above all this perception was determined ideologically. In order for long-term economic development to be brought about, it was considered necessary to give market forces as much scope as possible with the minimum of state involvement.

Through the restrictions on the budget deficit imposed by the IMF on the government as conditions for continued international financing, the state's area of activity came to be limited. The budget limitations restricted the state's ability to retain its educated personnel, which resulted in a serious administrative gap in capacity. The wage cake was only allowed to grow by around 10 per cent per year in 1987–89, which was significantly lower than the increases in the cost of living resulting from the devaluations. In comparison with other countries in Africa, Mozambican civil servants are extremely underpaid.

The reduced budget scope did not lead to the administration's personnel being reduced to the extent planned. It is mainly the qualified personnel who are leaving the public sector and looking for higher-paid employment in the private sector. Because of this the administration's qualitative capacity is diminishing. The remaining personnel largely lack the ability to execute all the administrative and legal measures the rehabilitation programme requires in order to achieve its full effect.

Especially worrying is the 'brain-drain' to which the international aid donors, including the World Bank, have given rise through their more flexible wage structures. There are many examples of well-educated Mozambican personnel being hand-picked and offered important and well-paid posts within the aid agencies' administration and project activity. In some cases both aid donors and the World Bank demanded that personnel within the Mozambican administration working on the World Bank's programme or project should receive extraordinary emoluments.[245] Such benefits deviate from the decision on wage structures taken by the government in consultation with the World Bank at a general macro-economic level.

The market and its failures

Independent Mozambique suffered from a lack of a skilled workforce. Colonial shortcomings within education were reinforced by the fact that the Portuguese colonial administration largely prohibited Mozambicans from carrying out business activities. Few Mozambican entrepreneurs were allowed to operate within productive businesses or within commerce. On independence there were few Mozambican owners of capital or farmers who could take over the properties the Portuguese left behind them. Those existing, particularly in the southern areas of the country, were exposed to extensive political control and limitation of activity. No domestic capitalist class would be allowed to develop, and so none arose.

The section of the population that today aspires to belong to the new class of entrepreneurs, which the economic rehabilitation programme is striving for, consists largely of well-educated administrators within the state sector. This involves a dilemma. The same officials within the state administration who have the task of promoting an administrative framework of rules for state monitoring and management of the market economy themselves aspire to develop into entrepreneurs and become new actors in the market economy.

The impact of the restrictive monetary policy

At the same time the civil servants' transformation into productive entrepreneurs is limited by precisely those measures being implemented by the economic rehabilitation programme. The fixed credit ceiling limits access to credits for private investments and increases the cost of working capital. This has meant that private entrepreneurs have difficulty in creating profitability quickly enough for the productive resources which aid, *inter alia*, places at the country's disposal. Private investments therefore move into commerce, speculation and unproductive businesses instead of imports of raw materials, spare parts and equipment for rehabilitating domestic industry.[246]

The rehabilitation programme's aim is to correct the budget deficit and limit inflation through a restrictive monetary policy and a tight credit ceiling has thus come into serious conflict with the programme's more long-term aim of increasing domestic production. This contradiction not only threatens economic growth in the long term. Through the business climate which it created due to private entrepreneurs preferring more short-term speculation in currencies, commerce and unproductive businesses in order to achieve the desired returns, the programme is also threatened in the short term.

This distortion is stimulated by the current short-term, profit-oriented commercial banks, which prefer credits to activities with fast turnover, yielding higher interests and decreased risks. In this way the banking system also tries to compensate for credits tied up in non-performing loans issued in earlier years. This posture also reflects the banking system's inability to assess projects' and enterprises' credit-worthiness. Accordingly, statistics at Banco de Moçambique show that net credit for internal commerce has increased rapidly (from 15 per cent in 1988 to 27 per cent in 1992), while credits to industry and agriculture have stagnated or declined, thus reinforcing the prospect for long-term stagflation.[247]

Free-market allocation of foreign currency

As the market forces unfortunately do not behave in accordance with the donors' expectations as regards the allocation of foreign currency, they began to question the programme's continued financing. Severe doubts about the macro-economic effects created by the allocation of currency through the Free Foreign Exchange Market (FFEM) have contributed to the decision among some donors to keep their import or balance of payment support tied in some way or other.

A number of donors still show concern that a substantial part of the importation of durable consumer goods, earlier imported through the parallel market, could reduce the scope for required importation of the equipment and raw materials needed for intended supply responses, as well as for the necessary importation of inputs to the social sectors. The first assessments carried out of the composition of imports through the system supported this concern, finding that only a relatively small proportion of FFEM funds has gone to industry (around 8 per cent), transport (3 per cent) and communications (6 per cent), and virtually nothing (less than 1 per cent) to agriculture.[248] The study also pointed to the fact that a number of foreign exchange applications for social sectors and productive investment purposes had to be cancelled due to unplanned cuts or reallocations in government expenditures and reduced credit facilities, thus creating constraints in obtaining required countervalues.

Simultaneously, the World Bank is trying hard to persuade donors to reinforce the process of untied import or balance of payments support channelled through the FFEM. Data compiled by the Bank of Mozambique on the use of IDA funds under the Economic Rehabilitation Credit aim to show that the funds allocated through the market were in fact absorbed into productive activities, contrary to earlier findings. Some 70 per cent of the funds were estimated to have been used for the importation of equipment, spare parts and raw materials.[249]

The study is not without problems. The classifications used do not provide any guidance to more detailed analyses of either composition or end users. Furthermore, it is based on only a fraction of the currency allocated through the system (some 15 per cent). There is reason for serious doubts about whether the demonstrated pattern of allocation is due to market performance and applicable to the majority of foreign aid. Suspicions have been raised regarding whether or not the recorded structure of imports only reflects the creation of an informally administered allocation system, based on regular contacts between the banking system and concerned donors in order to obtain a consensus on utilisation before an allocation is made. Until relevant information on the market's allocation of balance of payments support is available, the present delays in supply responses from the real economy, i.e. the productive sectors, emphasise the need for close monitoring and regular assessment of allocations.

Empirical evidence exists showing that a restrictive monetary policy, which increases interest rates and reduces credits, has dramatically increased costs for the immediate payment of countervalue beyond the realms of economic viability from the enterprises' point of view. Accordingly, economic actors involved in trade and fast-turnover activities substantially reduce the enterprises' opportunities for such activities. The fact that a number of productive enterprises are presently transforming their activities into trade emphasises the need for concern.

Aid and exchange rates

The implementation of the economic rehabilitation programme is dependent on a continued large flow of aid in the form of balance of payments and import support. The country, while waiting for the growth of domestic production to become adequate, has to import raw materials, spare parts and various implements for industry and agriculture. Not least important are imports of consumer goods to satisfy the rural population's needs and to provide an incentive for increased production of cash crops.

From a macro-economic point of view, increased aid in the form of balance of payments and import support means that the conditions for payments of countervalue increase.[250] Increased access to foreign currency also reduces the price of the currency, the exchange rate falls and imports become cheaper. Through holding down prices of consumer goods, the peasants' terms of trade can thereby be improved, with the precondition that the prices they receive as payment for their cash crops do not fall by a corresponding degree. An increased flow of aid can thus in theory counteract some of the negative effects which devaluation entails without a negative effect on the macro-economic balance.

However, in practice various factors make it extremely hazardous to draw any scientific conclusions regarding the long-term macro-economic impact of the devaluations. Doubts can be raised, however, as to whether the speed, size and timing of the devaluations have permitted international competitiveness to increase, thereby reinforcing the comparative advantages of the country and making the exchange rate more fully reflect the effective domestic costs of production.

On the one hand, the market valuation of the local currency is strongly influenced by the increase in the amount of international aid available. International aid tends to maintain the overvaluation of local currency (the so-called Dutch disease), thereby reducing the domestic capacity to face competition from imports and aggravating the de-industrialisation process even further.[251]

On the other hand, these tendencies are simultaneously counteracted by the effects of the capital flight presently going on in the region, which reduces the availability of foreign exchange. During the last few years, movement of capital from South Africa has been facilitated through the export of South African commodities on favourable credits to Mozambique. These commodities are paid for in Mozambican local currency, converted into dollars through the parallel market and illegally exported to the banking system in Portugal or England. The sizes of these transactions are not known, but well-informed observers estimate the amounts to be some 100 millions of dollars annually.

The empirical basis for determining the influence of aid on exchange rates is thus very fragile. Economists' warnings point, however, to the important dilemma which the present direction of the rehabilitation programme entails, with its emphasis on increased exports for increased debt repayments, as a result of a market-based exchange rate being implemented in combination with far-reaching liberalisation and a large flow of aid.

Limited domestic demand

One of the fundamental problems for the Mozambican economy and the supply-side policy carried out is that supply has not managed to create its own demand, which is a precondition for a supply-side policy producing dynamic effects. Domestic industry is finding it increasingly difficult to find a domestic outlet for its own production. The reason behind this is that so few measures have been adopted to expand the domestic production structure, and the existing industry lacks sufficient strength to compete with the imported goods. Increased imports are the result of both the ongoing liberalisation and the large flow of aid. Because the supply of goods is being mainly generated through imports, no basis for internal demand – i.e. increased employment and purchasing power, which would normally be the consequence of a concentration on increasing domestic supply – is being created either.

Current Mozambican economic development indicates that a clear-cut supply-side policy in a country with such a poor domestic production structure and weak demand as Mozambique, as a result of the almost non-existent market integration of 80 per cent of the population, also requires extremely large amounts of credit in order for sufficient demand to be created. In order to function and expand, a developed market economy requires sufficient purchasing power and can only be developed with difficulty in a situation where the majority of people are so destitute that they have no purchasing power at all. In order to create the preconditions for a market economy, the supply-side policy must therefore be combined with an active demand policy. Such a policy, however, requires extensive debt forgiveness and an increased concentration on rural development, which will be discussed in the concluding section of this chapter.

The dilemma of free trade

The liberalised imports necessary for implementing the programme are killing off domestic industry, which is too weak competitively, thus reducing employment and the population's purchasing power. This makes it impossible to maintain the domestic demand on which the supply-side policy is building. This indicates further conflicts between both theory and practice in the long- and short-term perspective in the rehabilitation programme.

The programme, which was formulated by the Bretton Woods institutions, is striving to stimulate increased exports through the liberalisation of trade and devaluation of the currency. In the long run a liberalisation of trade is necessary to bring about efficiency in production and international competitive enterprises. As a result of falling world market prices for traditional export goods special measures have been adopted to increase exports of so-called non-traditional export goods. The problem is that at present the Western world's trade restrictions and protectionist measures are making access to international outlet markets difficult, even with regard to these types of goods.

There are also the negative effects of the international food subsidies on domestic food production. As long as the structural adjustment programmes of different countries are implemented in an international environment, where the equivalent liberalisation of trade is not occurring, then the programmes will be virtually counterproductive.[252]

In the short term domestic industry, with its poor initial position and obsolete technology, needs to be allowed to be built up and developed under tariff protection with the aid of protectionist measures. In order to prevent a state of ill-health it is important that all endeavours are made for the country's foreign currency to be available to the productive sectors so that the domestic production base can be strengthened and develop an improved internationally competitive force. As has been indicated, a concentration on rural development and increased domestic food production ought to produce most of the necessary conditions for this.[253] It is extremely unlikely that the market forces operating today in Mozambique would operate in this direction. No doubt the European experience after the Second World War, with 15 years of grace before the opening up of international competition, provides important elements for an understanding of this reasoning.

The interaction of state and market

The lack of a commercial infrastructure and the reduced presence of traders created by the war constitutes the most important factor behind the breakdown of the rural economy. In many areas there is no longer anyone to provide the peasantry with implements, seed or consumer goods, or to buy up their surplus production. In this way not only the marketed surplus production but also the ability of the peasants to maintain production at a subsistence-level is being reduced.

In some areas existing traders have ceased their economic activities or have only maintained a minimum activity through taking out extra profits as compensation for the risks they are exposing themselves to. Many traders have been severely affected by the effects of destabilisation through having their goods, means of transport, businesses and storage premises destroyed without any possibility of financial compensation.

As a result the number of traders fell to about 2,000 during the latter half of the 1980s. The majority are operating in urban areas. Several measures have been adopted in connection with the economic rehabilitation programme in order to reopen markets and stimulate traders to resume their rural activities. The uncertainty regarding the future security situation, harsh credit terms and ignorance of current legislative conditions for establishing themselves has meant that many traders are still hesitant.

Markets in Mozambican rural areas are thus imperfect to a high degree. In many areas there is only one active trader, which creates a monopsony situation (many vendors and one purchaser) in the marketing of peasants' production. The only areas with reasonable competition are around the district and provincial towns. Several studies indicate that a form of 'godfather' system has begun to develop – a wholesaler with a monopoly situation (one vendor and several purchasers) supplies consumer goods at district level only to 'his' retail agents. The wholesaler supplies transportation, credits and consumer goods on condition that the retail agents accept the wholesaler's rules. This naturally limits the opportunities for more traders to enter the market.

The current economic and social rehabilitation programme risks reinforcing this situation. Despite the steps towards liberalisation, the restrictive monetary policy implies too high costs for procuring transportation and the required working capital (= credits) for it to be possible for the number of traders to increase. The lack of inter-province transportation, both on land and by sea, increases the credit requirement because of the long transport times. In the northern Cabo Delgado province the purchasing campaign for agricultural products over the last few years has been forced to a halt because the wholesalers have neither cash nor storage premises. At the same time disaster relief food has been transported into the districts in order to cover occasional shortages.

Discussions on reduced state intervention and greater scope for the market have taken as their starting point the view that state and market stand opposed to each other. This is a misconception. In fact Mozambique today needs both more state intervention and an increased scope for market forces in order for the development of rural areas to get going. The liberalisation of trade can only achieve the intended effect of increased food production if it is supported by a state which can establish the framework of rules and institutions in the form of laws and regulations, banking and credit systems, etc., needed in order for the market to be able to operate.

The lack of rules

The difficulties for a domestic class of entrepreneurs in developing and creating a domestic long-term accumulation base depend not only on the monetary and fiscal policy measures included in the rehabilitation programme. Their economic performance is also affected by the prevailing gap in capacity within the administration, not least through the shortage of information which this gap creates. The development of market forces and the rules of the game require that the market has access to information. This is not the case in Mozambique. Information on current prices does not reach the rural areas. There is great uncertainty at provincial level about the legal conditions, requirements for registration, tax rules, etc., involved in applying for small enterprises. This does not create an economically friendly climate. Willingness to invest in improved land or in premises and buildings will be small as long as uncertainty prevails about rights of occupation or exploitation.

'Wild West'-type capitalism

Macro-economic measures, backed by a strong political will, are far easier to implement and less time-consuming than the employment of reforms required for institution-building. As a consequence, a kind of 'Wild West'-type capitalism has emerged in Mozambique over recent years, which permits increased illegality, corruption and opportunities for the strong to line their pockets at the expense of the weak.

Extent of corruption

Increasing corruption is hampering the implementation of the economic and social rehabilitation programme because it tends to redistribute important resources according to unplanned individual interests. There can be no doubt that corruption in Mozambique increased very rapidly during the latter half of the 1980s. Before that it was generally acknowledged that corruption was rare in the country. There is no concrete information on the extent of the corruption and its growth, as very few studies have been carried out on the subject.

Crucial for an assessment of the extent of the corruption and its growth in Mozambique is the way in which the concept of corruption is to be defined. In Mozambique the word has a wide significance, possibly through the influence of the word's Latin origin, *corruptio*, which has an implication of degeneracy. This is reflected in, *inter alia*, a phrase used frequently in Mozambican Portuguese – *corrupção sexual* – sexual corruption, which signifies everything from extra-marital digressions to the sexual exploitation of minors, for example teachers who exploit their position with regard to female pupils. Also arrogant attitudes and abuse of resources through negligence or theft are often placed under the term corruption. It would be easier to identify measures to combat corruption if theft and morally condemnable behaviour could be distinguished from corruption in the sense of officials abusing their power for personal gains.

The majority of international observers consider that corruption in Mozambique has still not reached the level of other African countries. What is worrying is its rapid growth and the fact that the Mozambican government has been restrained with regard to measures to correct the situation.

There are several different explanations for the lack of concrete proof of corruption in 'high places', referred to by the host of rumours in Mozambique, and the lack of publicly published measures to combat corruption. Some refer to deficiencies in the country's legislation, audit capacity and legal system. The inadequate number of judges and minimal public audit activity make it difficult to detect improprieties.

There is also the political situation until recently resulting from the peace agreement between the government and Renamo. A possible exposure of higher party and government members' participation in corruption could seriously have reduced the possibilities of holding Frelimo together until the recent elections were carried out.

Causes of corruption

There is a range of different explanations which can be used with regard to the origin of the corruption 'phenomenon'.[254]

The first builds on a historic perspective and involves a view of corruption as an almost unavoidable phenomenon at a certain stage of every society's development. This perspective is valid in the sense that Mozambique, like so many other countries, is still dominated by what could be called an economy of affection[255] built on kinship principles. Families and clans impose demands on those who hold office, positions or just a post within private or public activity, in order to draw as many resources as possible from this position – for distribution within a wide family circle. This is common in Mozambican society.

The other point of view directs its attention towards the responsibility of the individual and therefore emphasises the moral implications of corruption. The unscrupulousness of civil servants is consequently a central element in the anatomy of corruption. An individualised view in an analysis of corruption in Mozambique would rapidly fill a catalogue of examples. Individual officials who request payment from the public to carry out their normal tasks are perhaps the most common examples of corruption in Mozambique. There is a conspicuous lack of institutional control and it is remarkable that attempted bribery is not punishable at all.

A third viewpoint is that corruption is an obvious consequence of an incorrect economic policy. An economic policy with state regulations, incorrect exchange rates, etc., is always considered to give rise to shortage economies where corruption becomes a method for controlling distribution of scarce resources.

This economic point of view is supported by numerous examples. This applies not least to the handling of international aid, for example within the agencies which administer import support or food aid. The slowness of the structural change process indicates that there are many people who wish to retain the present structure for economic administration, as well as keeping up the high level of the flow of aid.[256]

It is not difficult to identify some of the driving forces behind the growing corruption in Mozambique. Above all, there are three important social and political circumstances behind the fact that corruption has increased since the middle of the 1980s.

First, it has become more difficult for officials in public administration to take care of their own and their families' survival on ever smaller wages. This has been accentuated since the introduction of the economic rehabilitation programme. Extra incomes have become essential for survival. This situation has entailed an extraordinary development of the informal sector. Originally the informal sector, then called the black market, apart from currency transactions mainly involved the sale of food. After the introduction of the rehabilitation programme the informal sector expanded to become a part of the pattern of corruption in society, mainly through theft of state property and 'privatisation of service production' within the framework of the public institutions.[257]

Second, the political uncertainty prevailing today in Mozambique has put many 'orthodox' state functionaries in an awkward position. Having spent 15, 20 or 30 years of their life on a revolution which failed, they are now looking fearfully at the future. A pertinent question for them is what possible new ministers from Renamo will do with the ministries' civil servants. Many of them feel a great need to put themselves first for the time being.

Third, the new economic policy and liberalisation are extending ever more economic activities to private entrepreneurs. Large numbers of civil servants at different levels are looking at the possibilities for starting their own businesses in order to participate in this transformation process. Because their personal capital is non-existent or very small, they have no resources to invest in privatised state activities. The temptation to exploit their positions in order to procure resources has for many been overwhelming, especially in a situation where the liberalisation of the economy is being driven at a faster rate than is required for legal supervisory institutions to be able to develop. The result is a completely uncontrollable 'Wild West' capitalism, where everyone is trying to exploit the legal framework of rules as much as possible.

This last circumstance is probably also the most common background to the corruption found at higher levels within the Frelimo party and state leadership. For politicians and higher officials with roots in the central and northern areas of the country, this driving force is combined with the demands of kinship principles for moving resources to their home provinces. Future family, clan or ethnic projects can thus be financed through the present extensive flow of aid.

During 1991 the country's Attorney-General took up the problem of corruption in his annual report to parliament. He demanded strong measures to correct the problem. A number of new investigations into corruption were initiated, but there have not been any concrete results yet. It has been reported that the Attorney-General has been exposed to death threats after his public action.

The real danger of increased corruption and illegalities is rooted in the conditionalities imposed by the international requirements for structural adjustment and debt repayments. Because of economic restrictions, individual civil servants may include that their only option is to engage in non-conventional economic activities and to try to attract the attention of the rapidly expanding illegal international network – the production of narcotics, the illicit drug trade, arms trafficking, the unregulated storage of toxic waste or money laundering. The vacuum created by the organic crisis of the Mozambican state, in combination with the blocked market expansion of the national class of entrepreneurs as a consequence of the structural adjustment programme, tends to facilitate such a development.

The programme's rhetoric and practice

The lack of economic actors who, through private investments in the real economy, can bring about a dynamic market economy, may explain the meagre results achieved so far. There is also the inability of both government departments and aid donors to implement the programme as intended.

The main problems with the actual timing and sequencing are multifold. The extreme speed with which the programme has been carried out has not permitted the required capacity-building within public administration to take place. The administrative capacity of the state has, on the contrary, been eroded as a consequence of cuts in expenditures, thus forcing the few existing educationally prepared officials to search for alternative and better-paid employment, at a time when the implementation of the programme needs, in order to be successful, an increase in state capacity through time-consuming institution-building. Accordingly, a number of monetary and liberalisation policies are being conducted before the required fiscal reforms have matured, thus enabling the achievement of the desired results. The current general sales tax is only one example of measures that have a negative effect on Mozambique's international competitiveness and makes local production more expensive than imports. This situation will only be rectified when the administrative capacity exists to replace the actual tax with the implementation of a value-added tax. Hence increased support for capacity-building is strongly advocated. However, such support must be supplemented by a gradual transfer of financial resources from the technical assistance that finances expatriates to the recently created salary incentive fund for domestic civil servants.

The struggle for a macro-economic balance in the short term has further implied an overtly emphasised concentration on monetary policies at the expense of measurements required to rehabilitate the real economy, i.e. the measures taken to achieve the short-term objective destroy the possibilities for achieving the long-term objective.

The economic structures established during the colonial era, with little domestic production and a chronic current account deficit, require extensive structural and long-term economic changes in order for the rural areas' production conditions to be utilised and developed.

The programme's challenge is thus to successfully *adjust* the country's economy in the *short term* through increased exports of goods and reduced public expenditures (so that a macro-economic balance can be achieved) in order to create preconditions for a *structural transformation* of the rural areas in the long term and thus achieve the improved productivity and purchasing power required for an expanding market and lasting economic development.

This challenge, like the description of the market's imperfections recorded above, coincides in essential respects with the analysis made by the World Bank's resident representation in Maputo. According to the World Bank's perceptions, however, only the market itself will correct this, and the structural transformation of the rural areas will come about as the market creates the right conditions for increased private investments. The state is considered to be too weak to correct the current imperfections.

This perception can be questioned. It is of course correct that the state is weak and that the market's economic actors within several areas are better equipped in the short term to bring about a certain dynamic in economic development. But at the same time the economic actors lack any motive for such action in some important areas, not least with reference to the structural transformation of the rural areas. Demand in rural areas is weak or non-existent, which means that it must first be created. This requires increased public investments, equally regionally divided.[258]

In theory the economic rehabilitation programme includes a range of urgent measures in order to bring about the necessary structural change and allow long-term economic and social sustainable rural development. Apart from the aid resources being channelled in the form of balance of payments and import support in order to correct the macro-economic balance in the short term, the country is also receiving, as previously mentioned, considerable sector support for the implementation of the measures.

In practice, however, very little is being done. Instead, government departments, together with international aid donors, are continuing to use the development aid for large-scale modernisation projects, often with the aim of increasing exports in the short term and frequently without coordination with other activities in the rehabilitation programme.

Table 8.1 Public investment by sector (per cent)

	1978–81	1982–86	1987–90	1991–93	1992–94
Agriculture	19.6	23.8	13.0	12.5	12.4
Industry/Energy	12.8	22.6	12.1	6.3	7.0
Transport	1.8	9.8	14.9	37.9	26.1
Education/Health	3.4	3.8	8.5	11.2	18.1
Construction/Public works	n.a.	n.a.	n.a.	11.3	11.0

Source: 1978–86 *Informação Estatística*, CNP, 1987–90; Sharpley (1991); 1991–93, 1992–94, PTIP.

This is absolutely clear if one studies the different investment plans for the period 1991–95. As made clear in Table 8.1, sector imbalances that the programme was intended to change remain. Although the strategy documents lay great emphasis on the development of rural areas, few public investments are allocated there, and private businessmen are hesitant. The rehabilitation of 'feeder roads' to rural areas in the plan for 1991–93 can be taken as one example. Between 30 and 40 per cent of investments during the period have gone to the transport sector (cf. agriculture 13 per cent). Only 0.6 per cent is intended for road transport, of which the largest amount is for the Beira and Maputo transport corridors respectively.

An analysis of the investments for the rehabilitation of the social infrastructure of rural areas shows the same depressing result. Investments within the education sector amount to a total of 6 per cent, of which only 0.9 per cent is going to primary schools and literacy, mainly in the Maputo area and Beira. Health-care is receiving 5 per cent, of which 0.5 per cent is going to health-care institutions in rural areas.

Today the rapid development of the market economy appears to be further reinforcing the imbalances from the colonial period and the planned economy. Economically better developed regions and the country's centre of power have greater opportunities to take a larger share of the total cake, with the support of the rules of the market economy. It is thus the already most developed areas of the country, together with the two largest urban areas around Maputo and Beira, that have taken up the lion's share of the external resources which have streamed into Mozambique since 1987. Public investments are still concentrated in the southern areas of the country.[259] Only a couple of per cent of the whole goes to the northern provinces. There is a great risk in this imbalance of social and political turbulence, which may come to over-turn all attempts at economic rehabilitation. These regional imbalances have been noticeable and have been criticised to an increasing extent by provincial political leaders and other social and economic actors at provincial level. Explicit criticism has naturally come mainly from the élites who have not felt integrated into Frelimo's nation-state project. The tensions resulting from this have not yet developed into actual ethnic conflicts. However, they may quickly develop if no measures are adopted in order to strongly counteract regional imbalances.

The difference between rhetoric and practice clearly points to a dilemma with regard to implementing the rehabilitation programme. The triennial public investment plan is no plan in the real sense of the word. It is rather a compilation of the different activities which different donors have undertaken to complete together with different government departments. The Planning Commisson and the Ministry of Finance have little influence over this. A very large part of the aid to Mozambique is not even included in the state budget, but consists of direct separate agreements with different government departments.

However, the aid's sectoral distribution shows the same sort of planning gap as characterises the country's investment plan for the period 1991–93. Although the rehabilitation programme prioritises, in theory, rural development, with the relevant build-up of the physical and social infrastructure, in practice few aid resources are allocated for this purpose. The share of aid to agriculture actually increased by nearly 50 per cent during the years 1989–90. However, a third of the total support to the agricultural sector was channelled to a single project, namely the construction of the Corumana dam in Maputo province.

The main share of aid to the transport sector went to the rehabilitation of the transport corridors within the SADCC programme. Very little of the aid that went to the sector was intended for the rehabilitation of the road network in rural areas. The international aid organisations must thus assume a great deal of the responsibility for the economic action programme not being implemented in accordance with the plans presented.

In consultation with the government of Mozambique, the World Bank has recently presented some guidelines for a reorientation of international aid.[260] In general terms, the guidelines now emphasising the importance of rural development, a shift towards sectoral programmes and strengthened local participation through decentralisation, can be fully endorsed, although the importance of a regionally balanced allocation must be further underlined.

Similar intentions for development can in fact be found in most PFP documents produced during the 1990s.[261] The problem is, however, that experience so far clearly shows that such intentions differ considerably from what is happening in practice. Continued large-scale investments in projects which are identified and implemented from above aim to increase export production and are primarily located in the southern

Table 8.2 IDA credits: allocations and disbursements, 1985–91

	Planned allocation		Actually disbursed	
	($ million)	(% of total)	($ million)	(% of total)
Macro-economic structural adjustment	224	36	220	78
Energy	42	7	13	5
Urban rehabilitation	60	10	28	10
Health	27	5	3	1
Education	70	11	13	4
Beira corridor	40	6.5	5	2
Industry	82	13	0	–
Administration	21	3.5	0	–
Agriculture	50	8	0	–
Total	616	100	282	100

Source: IBRD Report, No. P-5775–Moz., 27 August 1992.

part of the country. An assessment of the application of the IDA credits provided by the World Bank during 1985 to 1991 does not show any exceptions from this trend.[262]

Since Mozambique joined the World Bank in 1984, 15 projects involving IDA credits corresponding to approximately $600 million have been planned. The majority of the bank's planned investments are concentrated in important economic and social infrastructure. As is made clear by Table 8.2, which shows detailed planning for the use of these funds, a total of 35 per cent went towards macro-economic structural adjustment, while 7 per cent was allocated to industry, 10 per cent to urban rehabilitation, 6.5 per cent to the Beira corridor, 13 per cent to industry, 4 per cent to administration aid, 8 per cent to agriculture, 11 per cent to education and 5 per cent to health. According to the plans, only 24 per cent of the funds would go to the sectors which the World Bank says are priorities.

If one looks further at what has been done, the situation becomes even more disheartening. Of $616 million planned, only $282 million have been disbursed. Of this 78 per cent went to support the economic recovery programme. The social sectors received 5 per cent, while nothing was used with regard to agriculture.

This leads to a serious questioning of the possibilities for implementing the rehabilitation programme and achieving the desired production result. An increase in food production requires that the peasant farmers are able to return to their original homes and go back to a normal life when the security situation and rainfall conditions so permit. In order to stimulate the peasant farmers to move back it is necessary not only that they can guarantee their own food supply, but that the physical infrastructure is rehabilitated and preconditions for the trade network are created. The social infrastructure must also be rebuilt in the long run so that the new generation will not be motivated to leave the rural areas and move into the towns.

Economic adjustment and political democracy

The experiences until now put into question not only the implementation of the programme, but also its feasibility. In the same way as the colonial era, like Frelimo's modernisation strategy in general, did not succeed in changing the distorted structures and the extremely low productivity of the rural areas, the current rehabilitation programme does not distinguish sufficiently the extensive structural changes required in order to bring about long-term and sustainable rural development. The criticism which can therefore be directed against the programme goes beyond the usual unease that the weaker population groups will be economically and financially worse off, and questions whether its orientation can possibly bring about the production increase required to close the financial gap and restore the macro-economic balance in the long term.

Problems with the implementation of the economic and social rehabilitation programme are, however, not solely of a national economic or social nature. First and foremost they are political. While the programme is creating social differentiation and new conflicts of interest, it is not providing any scope for the growth of different political parties, which through different economic programmes would be able to attempt to take care of the needs of different socio-economic interest groups. At the same time as the international community has been strongly pursuing the question of the introduction of Western democracy, parliamentarism and a multi-party system, international creditors' demands for an economic balance with attendant credit restrictions are restricting the elaboration of an alternative economic action programme.

As the recent election has shown, there is an obvious tendency for the different parties to establish their political base in ethnic allegiances. Because several ethnic minority groups will thus be marginalised further and their élites removed increasingly from participation in the exercise of power, the risk of social and ethnic tensions is increasing at a time when the rehabilitation programme requires a consolidation of the nation state in order for implementation to be possible.

Different ethnic élites risk not only being marginalised from political power. The ability to mobilise the capital necessary for the growth of domestic entrepreneurs is, as discussed, very limited. A few groups are therefore seeking to exploit traditional commercial relationships with foreign regional interests in order to obtain resources for necessary investments in cooperation with them. At the same time as these élites (mainly Indians and white former Portuguese) thereby accept subordinating themselves economically to foreign capital interests, other ethnic élites, lacking these traditional commercial contact networks, are being further marginalised.

This leads us to the conclusion that democracy in the Western sense as an absolute precondition for economic development can be questioned. Most historical experience shows the contrary: that economic development, combined with reasonable social equality, is essential if a sustainable democracy is to emerge and be consolidated. In many cases, accelerated economic growth has been registered in countries where the lack of democracy has been the dominating political feature of the society. Thus there are no obvious causal links between democracy and economic growth. Furthermore, there are no clear signs that an imposed implementation of multi-party systems in the Third World will lead to the development of either a sustainable democracy or a viable nation-state.

On the contrary, it could be argued that the mainstream structural adjustment programmes currently being implemented in immature market economies are undermining those economies' long-term sustainability. These programmes are biasing the social distribution of the economic growth to the extent that the states – both one-party and multi-party – are losing their legitimacy. They are therefore making unfeasible the consolidation of both the multi-party system and the vision of the nation-state.

In the next chapter we will look further into the concept of democracy in a Mozambican context. While questioning whether the concept of democracy is applicable, we will emphasise the importance of a more inclusive participation by different ethnic groups in the political decision-making process.

9

Democracy and Civil Society

Democratic transformation

In parallel with the implementation of the rehabilitation programme, a range of political measures has been adopted with the aim of adjusting the country's political constitution to economic deregulation and liberalisation.

The first proposal for changes to the Mozambican constitution was presented in 1988, and consisted of minor changes within the framework for the existing political system.[263] This did not lead to any more extensive debate. A comprehensive proposal for changes was presented in January 1990. This proposal was constantly discussed over the whole year in the mass media and at meetings in workplaces and institutions around the country.

The most visible question in the constitutional debate concerned who could be a Mozambican citizen. The text of the proposal had no racist language, but the content was such that it could not be guaranteed that several ministers of Portuguese origin would be able to retain their Mozambican citizenship. The most extreme position in this debate was taken by one of Frelimo's classic guerrilla commanders. He wanted the question of citizenship to take as its starting point the population which lived in Mozambique when Vasco da Gama arrived in 1498. Only those who had Mozambican forefathers for three generations back would be able to become Mozambican citizens. The new text for the constitution, however, has a broader definition of citizenship. It was approved by a vote of 110 to 1, but a total of 71 members of the People's Assembly abstained. This level of abstentions was at that time unique in Mozambique's political practice.[264]

The new constitution means that Mozambique changed its name from the People's Republic of Mozambique to the Republic of Mozambique, and simultaneously a multi-party system was introduced. The design of the one-party system in the earlier constitution built on the fact that Frelimo's president was also automatically the president of the republic. Now the president would also be chosen in a general election. A presidential candidate must be at least 35 years old and of Mozambican parentage. This means that no 'naturalised' Mozambican can be elected president. A presidential candidate must be nominated by 5,000 enfranchised citizens. Of these every one of the ten provinces must contribute 200. The president is elected for five years at a time and can be re-selected twice.

The multi-party system and parliament do not have the same strong position in the constitution as in a traditional parliamentary democracy. Power flows from the president, who appoints both the head of the government and ministers. If parliament twice does not accept a proposal from the government, the president may dissolve parliament and call a new election.

The constitution also changes the centralised structure of the state apparatus. Formerly all local authorities were subordinate to their provincial and central institutions. Now a decentralised structure is being created in which there are two different election processes. One is directed towards electing a president and members to parliament. The other system will elect local institutions which will be sovereign in their territory within the limits of their stated responsibilities.

The constitution abolishes the death penalty in Mozambique for the second time. Frelimo abolished the death penalty on independence in 1975. Its reintroduction after several years was motivated by the expansion of the war and growing economic crime.[265]

The constitution also contains rules on the freedom of the press and citizens' rights to information. The right to strike is also written into the constitution, while the employers' lockout weapon is prohibited.

This new constitution establishes that the Republic of Mozambique has a market economy. After a debate and a supplementary proposal in the People's Assembly, the final text was that within the framework of a market economy the state would have a regulatory function and promote social prosperity.

Multi-party system

The new constitution means that it is possible to form political parties in Mozambique and that these parties may participate in an election. However, the constitution in itself gives no concrete advice on the way in which the election system should function. The concrete design of the multi-party system is regulated by a special party law and a specific electoral law.

The party law[266] stipulates certain restrictions in the new multi-party system. Politically the most important of these is that parties must have a nationwide composition. In order for a party to be officially registered, the law requires that it has at least 100 members from each province. A party may not operate a separatist policy or have its membership base in regional, ethnic, tribal, racial or religious groups. The law establishes that policies must aim to consolidate the Mozambican nation. The supreme court has the right to dissolve a political party operating in conflict with the rules of party law.

The law also requires that party leaders should be Mozambicans resident in Mozambique. At least two party leaders of new parties, Máximo Dias and Domingo Arouca, had Portuguese citizenship at the time of party registration.

The parties will be allocated a state activity grant, the size of which will be determined by the number of seats in parliament the party wins in an election. They may also receive other contributions, but each party should make public its accounts every year. Fourteen parties or coalitions of parties participated in the first elections in October 1994.

The electoral law which controls the organisation and form of the recent elections was passed in December 1993. The electoral process was discussed in negotiations between the government and Renamo and the parties agreed on certain principles for the election.[267] After continued discussions between the government, Renamo and the other political parties, a proposed bill was achieved which was acceptable to all.[268]

One of the significant differences over the outline of the electoral process in the Peace Agreement is the level of the minimum percentages of votes required for a party to have a seat in the Assembly. Renamo had proposed 20 per cent of the votes at national level as the limit, while the government argued for 5 per cent as the minimum requirement to obtain seats. This became the choice for the Electoral Law, which stipulates 5 per cent.

The number of mandates in the legislative assembly (Assembleia da República) is 250. There are 11 constituencies (ten provinces and the city of Maputo), among which the candidates will be distributed according to the number of registered voters in each constituency.

In the distribution of mandates only party or electoral coalitions obtaining more than 5 per cent of the votes at national level will be entitled to seats. In each constituency, mandates will be distributed through a method for proportional representation called de Hondt's method. This method favours the big parties at the expense of smaller ones.

This is confirmed by the outcome of the elections held in October 1994: Frelimo received the highest number of votes (44 per cent), followed by Renamo (38 per cent) and a three-party coalition called the União Democrática, which received 5 per cent. The distribution of the 250 parliamentary seats followed the general bias in d'Hondt's method:

129 to Frelimo, 112 to Renamo and 9 to the União Democrática. Thus, with 44 per cent of the votes, Frelimo got 52 per cent of the seats; Renamo, with 38 per cent of the votes, got 45 per cent of the seats; and the União Democrática got only 3 per cent of the seats, in spite of receiving 5 per cent of the votes. In the presidential election Joaquim Chissano was re-elected with 53 per cent of the votes, followed by Afonso Dhlakama, with 34 per cent.

This outcome, and the exemplary way in which the elections were held, are essential ingredients for the success story so badly needed by the UN system. However, more needs to be done to contain societal violence in order to create and consolidate the conditions necessary for future development.

Africa and parliamentary democracy

Parliamentary democracy is the political form of governance which developed in parallel with the emergence of nation-states and industrialisation in Europe. The multi-party system has come to function in order to balance economically defined interest groups in society and to counterbalance the tensions entailed by that economic development. Attempts have been made to correct regional imbalances as they arose.

Many African leaders have argued the advantages of a one-party system in African society. One important argument for the one-party system has been that a multi-party system in Africa would come to be based on ethnic allegiances and thus counteract the consolidation of the nation-state. Within the framework for one-party rule it would be easier to balance different interest groups against each other in the name of national unity. This means that one function of the one-party system is considered to be to contribute to the creation and maintenance of a functioning nation-state. The one-party system is thus set against a multi-party system in the sense that it is seen as being more effective for the development of the nation-state, through blocking regional and ethnic splits. This argument has had its main features accepted in the international community and in the aid donors' world. There has been a common interest in bringing about functioning nation-states in Third World countries as well.

Criticism of one-party systems during the 1980s has *not* referred to the fact that one-party systems have not succeeded in their goals of contributing to the development of stable nation-states, but have been formulated in terms of democracy and dictatorship as global ideological conflicts between the great powers intensified during the 1980s. In this, the transition from a one-party system to a multi-party system was connected with the transition from a planned economy to a market economy. This meant that mainstream criticism of the African one-party system took as its starting point the same ideological criticism that the West directed against the dictatorships in the Soviet Union and the Eastern bloc. We must remember that the Eastern European one-party system was ideologically motivated in that it represented the 'dictatorship of the proletariat', i.e. the power of the working class over other classes in society. African leaders intended to reduce internal non-class tensions using one-party systems in order to be able to create nations and nation-states. The majority of one-party states in Africa which attempted to maintain planned economies are now on the road to market economies and multi-party systems. But this has not reduced their difficulties in nation-building.

Vision of the nation-state

Those newly in power saw one of their main tasks as being the creation of 'a nation' within the borders of the state which they had just inherited. In other words, a 'national consciousness' was seen as being something which could be created from above. This is sometimes called a nation-building project. In practice it was very seldom that the new states succeeded in formulating and implementing a policy which was capable of creating this 'nation'.[269] That a government started nation-building did not necessarily mean that it ended in progress. Development can both come to a halt and regress. As we have seen in Europe, very long periods of attempts at integration can prove to be inadequate.

The prevailing development ideology – modernisation – has presupposed that Africa will go the same way as Western Europe, but later. The nation-state as a form of management has almost achieved the status of a 'natural law'. If the European nation-state is a relatively new phenomenon whose existence is not assured once and for all, the position of the African nation-state is much more precarious. In most cases it has not yet been formed. This has consequences for attempts to analyse the political and administrative breakdown which we now see going on in a number of African states.[270]

Modernisation and state-building have not been a monopoly of socialist-orientated regimes. Neither have the crises for political systems in different parts of Africa been limited to countries where Marxist-Leninist governments have been on the brink of ruin. The crises constantly recurring in Africa tend to become acute in situations where the *state* loses its legitimacy. This has occurred completely regardless of whether that state's activities are based on a socialist or liberal government policy. In the majority of African states, where the population's identification with the nation-state project is still very poor, each policy which has failed also represents a crisis for the nation-state's possibilities for development. A nation-state project which is breaking down can hardly provide a sufficiently strong framework for the development of a functioning democratic multi-party system.

Restored legitimacy

The Mozambican transitional period, in which the one-party state's institutions, gallery of personalities and political practice function within the framework of a pluralistic constitution, has been characterised by three circumstances. The first is that the state apparatus is increasingly weakened. Basic activities within medical services, education, the administration of justice and administration have gradually ceased to function. The second circumstance is that the economic actors are not strong enough to fill quickly the void left by diminishing state economic activity. The extreme poverty in the country is not creating any demand to motivate extensive productive investments. The third circumstance is the remaining political uncertainty after the elections.

The challenge for Mozambique is, with the support of international aid, to form an institutional framework within which democracy can grow and be consolidated. Hitherto the discussion on support for the democracy process in Mozambique has focused on support for the mass media, new political parties and financing of the first election. Less attention has so far been directed towards questions concerning the legitimacy of a democratic system.

The discussions on democracy look different in towns from those in rural areas. The intellectual and urbanised middle classes are the groups who have mainly come to embrace the nation-state perspective. This urbanised political discussion also involves ideologies and party political programmes. Political failure is analysed in terms of the failure of political parties. If a party is unsuccessful it can be replaced by another. This form of analysis presupposes that the institutional framework is not eroded, that the state's legitimacy is maintained.

In rural areas the political discussion largely involves the legitimacy of the state. The alternative to an unsuccessful political party is not in the first instance another political party. In fact, one party is often considered more than sufficient. Instead of seeking party political alternatives, over the years people have sought an alternative to the state. When state medical services no longer function traditional medicine remains, with its mixture of herbal decoctions and magic. When the police and the legal system can no longer punish crime, people take justice into their own hands. Countless petty thieves have lost their lives in this way over the last few years. When schools collapse the demand for initiation rites for the young increases. Parents wish to give children some form of organised socialisation.

The preconditions for a rapid democratic transformation in Mozambique consequently lie in the modern state finding a democratic form of governance, so that it can regain the legitimacy it has lost in the eyes of the population. This requires inputs at two different levels. First, the state apparatus must be given the capacity to live up to the expectations of the population for improvements after peace. Democracy and a free election must lead to visible improvements in order for the elected government to be perceived as being legitimate. This is not only a matter of security and the satisfaction of basic material needs. The importance of the social sectors for restored legitimacy and future peace is great. Second, there is also a need to implement a far-reaching decentralisation of the political decision-making process.

The role of education and of the state

For such a process of democratisation to take place, the role of education is of course paramount. Despite the fifth party congress' (1989) decision to permit NGOs to set up and administer schools and the recent (1990) authorisation for the functioning of private schools, education in Mozambique is still offered almost exclusively by the public sector. Although in the near future it can be expected that the Protestant and Catholic Churches and the Muslim associations will make a more active contribution to non-public education, the role of the state as a provider of education will continue to be predominant.

However, there is no doubt that the implementation of PRES has simultaneously reduced the state's room for manoeuvre. The decision taken by the third Frelimo congress to expand basic social services – notably literacy and primary health-care – to be generally available to everyone had to be abandoned with the implementation of the structural adjustment programme. Although Frelimo never promised free access to either health-care or education, the prices for these services were at that time symbolic. With the structural adjustment programme, education became privatised in the sense that each family had to cover a far higher proportion of the actual costs, so that access to these services was for the majority limited. The state has scope in its budget neither for maintaining the present state of affairs nor – in fact far less so – for reconstructing what has been destroyed in the war.

In 1983, expenditures in education accounted for about 10 per cent of the state budget as against 15 per cent in other low-income countries in sub-Saharan Africa. Since then expenditures have experienced a sharp decline. In constant 1980 prices, per capita government recurrent expenditure per pupil in primary education dropped from about $18 to about $11 ten years later; and this in a situation where the requirements have doubled as a consequence of the destruction created by the war of destabilisation. These figures should be compared with an annual expenditure of $32 per pupil in primary education in sub-Saharan Africa in general.

However, users of the system did not bear the full burden of the decline in education expenditures in the 1980s, as cuts also seriously affected teachers' salaries (provoking a 50 per cent drop in 1986–87). In order to increase the quality of education, a boost in teacher salaries is urgently needed.

Hence, due to human and severe financial restraints, the Frelimo objective of access to formal education for all children and adults will not be attainable. Furthermore, the objective of achieving an enrolment rate of more than 80 per cent during the coming five years seems far beyond the scope of prevailing realities.

As a consequence, growing contradictions in the decision-making process concerning the critical issues in the overall education policy in general, and in the textbook policy in particular, can be expected. Who should have access to education, and to what kind of education, are important questions on the political agenda.

The question of content

One of the main features of the formulation of the education policy of Mozambique has been, and still is, the strong interaction between the concept of development and the concept of modernisation. In this sense, education directly determines the eventual success of modernisation.

However, neither development nor modernisation can be seen as only a technological and economic growth process. Modernisation also entails a change in society's social and political institutions, as well as in people's beliefs, both religious and moral, and their way of looking at the world and explaining the inner cohesion of the human mind.

This distinction determines the way one looks upon the failure of modernisation: what was a failure and why. At the same time, it is a precondition for our understanding that modernisation, in terms of technological and economic growth, has to adapt to the pace and content of development and change in the other spheres noted above. If this is not the case, the chasm between vision and reality grows.

The role of the school in this context is twofold. One role concerns socialisation, in the sense that schooling prepares children for the kind of life they will live for the foreseeable future. This includes learning to internalise the basic values which constitute the normative system ruling society and relations between human beings. Another role concerns the transfer of knowledge, i.e. education in specific disciplines which will give children certain intellectual capabilities they need in order to facilitate their long-term survival. These two roles are normally inter-twined, in the sense that they influence one another. The socialisation process will not be successful if the children are not provided with knowledge that is able to give them a productive role in the economic life of society. At the same time, the transfer of knowledge will not work properly if the knowledge provided is not relevant to the specific forms of production and distribution of societal resources that are dominant in that specific society.

The very strong imperative of modernisation in Frelimo's development strategy meant that the forms of organisation in the society the new government inherited in 1975 were considered obsolete. Therefore society had to be deeply transformed in order to be modernised. This view of modernisation had one material and one social and cultural dimension: both human beings and society would be transformed on the path to modernity.

Therefore, Frelimo's education policy did not intend to socialise the children into the norms and way of life of the existing society. The objective was the opposite, i.e. to present the children with a vision of another kind of society that they should strive towards. However, the vision was described as though that vision was an existing reality, while in actuality it was a dream. In official documents, as well as in schoolbooks, a desired future was often described in the grammatical form of the present.

The failure of modernisation, in this sense, means that on the one hand material growth never matched the image of the vision as it 'existed' in the books and, on the other hand, the children were left without being socialised, in the sense that they were not prepared for the society in which they came to live. In this sense, the difference between vision and reality became extremely clear in the policy for education. This, in turn, means that other features and institutions of modernisation may come to be looked upon as being of no concern to rural people. Thus local participation in the activities of modern civil society, as well as the democratisation process, may be hampered. This has meant that it is no longer an automatic imperative for parents in rural areas to send their children to school. Experiences over the last 20 years have shown that formal education is no guarantee of employment in the modern sector. At the same time, it has become clear to the parents that the 'socialisation' provided by schools implies that the children will not return to manual agricultural work even if they fail to obtain a job or continue their studies after completing their primary education. Sending children to school can therefore mean that they are lost for ever as contributors to the family's economy. One of the main changes in educational policy aimed at remedying this situation is to adapt the content of schoolbooks to the pupils' experience of reality.

Policy-making in transition

The prevailing difficulties faced by the Mozambican government in its efforts to formulate a coherent long-term education strategy should, accordingly, not only be seen as a consequence of the competition over scarce resources, or as a result of the fact that the institutional framework within the education sector is politically fragile. The difficulties in developing a comprehensive and coherent strategy should also be understood in the light of the ongoing transition from war to peace and the political instability and insecurity that the country is currently facing. In order to cope with the present contradictions and future challenges, be they the problem of language or the problem of relevant content, the development of a coherent education policy requires long-term expectations for a stable development process and a vision of the society one wishes to create. The failure of the modernisation strategy and the search for an alternative strategy, which is more territorially orientated and which integrates the vision of modernisation with the prevailing cultural/traditional values, make this formulation a very complex process indeed.

Two simultaneous processes – increased 'privatisation' of education (reduced economic capacity of the state), on the one hand, and increased difficulties at the central level in formulating and implementing a coherent education policy on the other hand – tend to create a situation in which a number of donors and decision-makers withdraw from supporting the central level and existing structures and instead try to dynamise the role of the civil society and NGOs from above.

No doubt the civil society is taking on an increased and complementary role in education as the state capacity diminishes, but the civil society can never constitute any viable alternative to the state as the provider of education.

Decentralisation and democracy

One of the explanations for the ability of Mozambican local society to survive the failure of modernisation, destabilisation, war and drought is its traditional forms of organisation and distribution of scarce resources.[271] With the starting point that the democratisation of Africa must come from within African society itself and build on its own traditions, Mozambique's government seems to be seeking African social and cultural models as a basis for successful democratisation – after a convergence between the present forms of 'African consciousness' and modern political and economic decision-making.

One question is in what way it will be possible to incorporate broader groups from the population into a really democratic governance, and how it will be possible to consolidate democracy in order to become an all-embracing legitimate system in an African context.

The risk of rapid democratisation, where surface phenomena may come to be perceived as its real nature, is that democracy is made synonymous with a multi-party system. In order for a multi-party system to function according to democratic intentions, a well-developed defence of human rights, and a society which allows everyone to make use of their economic, social and cultural rights, is also required. If a new political governance is to achieve legitimacy, a prolonged process of popular education, and a consolidation of a functioning legal system, in which people can cherish a deep-rooted trust, is required.

The democratisation process requires extensive resources and a strong state with the capacity to implement this transformation. An immediate risk lies in the economic rehabilitation programme failing to improve the citizen's material conditions, and widespread poverty and social instability becoming an effective obstacle to genuine popular participation in a democratic system.

Decentralisation and political inclusiveness

Decentralisation is mostly understood as a remedy for inefficient and top-heavy administration. As such it dichotomises the weaker concept of deconcentration, which can be defined as a handing-out of responsibility for the implementation of central decisions. Decentralisation should, then, be a more thorough solution as it is meant to bring both resources and political power to lower levels of the political system.

Decentralisation is also, and maybe even more so, a political issue linked to the societal power struggles within different élites. It aims to make local élites politically visible in their local surroundings. This is an important feature of Mozambican decentralisation. It will give constitutional room for manoeuvre to alternative élites who may otherwise look for opportunities for political and economic affirmation in the tribal or ethnic mobilisation of their constituency, in order to be able to challenge the élite presently dominating state power.[272]

Hence the ultimate goal for decentralisation is, on the one hand, to involve more alternative élites in local power participation and, on the other hand, to make priorities and decisions on the utilisation of resources closer to the reality of Mozambican life. In the present centre–periphery tensions or in the urban–rural conflict, the periphery and rural people tend to be constant losers.

The pace of the decentralisation reform has been slow. One fundamental internal contradiction has been the extent to which political power should be handed out to local authorities. One argument has favoured a very limited decentralisation of political power, but an increase in the responsibility for implementation at provincial and district levels (deconcentration). Its main argument has been that only a strong state is able successfully to promote a societal decentralisation. Therefore, the central state apparatus has to be a priority for the foreseeable future. Another argument has claimed that a strong state can only be built from below, based on strong and self-confident communities as pillars of legitimacy for the state. Political power therefore has to be decentralised in order to provide local communities with instruments to develop their capacity to deal with their own affairs. This argument is also inclined to embrace a certain cultural traditionalism.

It seems as if development of the peace process during 1994, as well as in the internal government deliberations for the elections, has provided some decisive arguments for the 'traditionalists'. The main argument stems from the comprehension of the role the traditional authorities may play as intermediaries between the political parties and the rural population. Any party with ambitions of achieving a reasonable result in the elections had to take into consideration how to approach traditional authority, or other leaders considered legitimate in the eyes of the population. It is clear that this turned out to be a main strategy of various political parties, including Frelimo and Renamo. The increasing pace of the decentralisation programme should be viewed in this light.

Civil versus traditional society

An area which has strong points of contact with questions of democracy is the role that civil society can play. It is thus important to define the concept of a civil society in a Mozambican context. One view of a civil society is that it is a bridge between the state and citizens which brings about legitimacy.[273] In this respect the organisational principles of traditional society functioned as a carrier of legitimacy for the colonial state in Mozambique. However, this does not mean that these principles can simply be said to have constituted the basis for a civil society in the sense that it has come to acquire in the West. A civil society is very much a Western concept, like Marxism-Leninism, democracy and nation-state, and thus cannot be used without reservations for an analysis of African societal formations.[274]

In the Mozambican (and African) context the view of civil society may become clearer if it is set against a 'traditional' African society's different principles for distribution of societal resources. Karl Polanyi has written about society's distribution models in terms of principles.[275] He describes four different principles for the way in which a society's total resources are distributed. He talks about reciprocity, redistribution, householding and barter principles.

Reciprocity is, to put it simply, a system where different families or groups take mutual responsibility for each other's long-term survival. It can be illustrated by everyone giving each other ten kilos of maize a year at certain ceremonies, which means that one shows 'societal responsibility'. Inherent in this is that even if you have a crop failure some years, you and your family receive ten kilos of maize from a number of families. This implies security for long-term survival. In Africa this is bound up with the way in which, for example, the pattern for marriage is organised, i.e. forms of marriage are an important institutional framework for the principle of reciprocity.

Redistribution means that there is a chief within the group who receives parts of every family's surplus and stores it so that it can serve as the group's reserve food in hard times. This can mean that he stores it in the physical sense, but also that he has complete information about a respective family's stock situation and enough authority and legitimacy to ensure that no one disposes of food without informing the clan leader and following his instructions.

Householding is the principle that builds on production for one's own use within the production group or production unit. It means that the group that produces is also the one that consumes the produce. The group does not need to be very small, but the principle means that it is limited.

This thus deals with different principles of behaviour, which are in turn linked to different institutional forms of management in order to maintain the observance of the rules in order for the societal form to endure and survive in the long term.

Most societal formations consist of combinations of these different principles in different mixes. What they have in common is that they all build on what we could call *non-economic* rules for distribution. This means that they are controlled by factors other than those applying to the fourth principle – the *barter principle*, which builds on the growth of a market economy. The capacity to maintain oneself in a market determines the distribution of resources in a society. It is people's value in the market exchange that determines what share of the society's total resources becomes each and everyone's.

The concept of a traditional society is related to the first three principles, which build on non-economic control mechanisms and institutions. It is this that we mean when we talk about traditional society in Africa.[276] This differs from the civil society created by people as a defence against the negative effects of the market economy and the transition to principles of barter.

This means that the civil society's organisational forms and institutions, as we know them in Europe, are historically and functionally linked to the growth of market forces and to a political system which is in turn linked to class and economic stratification, and the consolidation of the nation-state.

The transition does not offer a quick break between one system and another. It is in this sense that a traditional society and a civil society can be said to fulfil similar functions, although in relation to two different modes of production and their respective institutional frameworks.

In the absence of clearer definitions we can use civil society for the norms and organisational forms which coexist with a state-market relationship, i.e. a market economy which manages to maintain a suitable level of survival and long-term confidence and where the market's institutions dominate societal life.

We can call traditional society the corresponding norms and organisational forms which controlled production and the distribution of resources in pre-industrial and pre-colonial societies. In this context modernisation may describe the process in which the gradual growth of a market economy leads to people voluntarily choosing new survival strategies and organisational forms, which prove to be more effective and relevant for the new material circumstances.

What is happening in the present crisis in Mozambique is that people today cannot depend on modern society's institutions (either state or market functions) for their long-term survival. Therefore guarantees for survival which have their roots in pre-modern times are acquiring greater importance. According to our analysis, these principles fulfilled the same function for the people as what we call civil society does in Europe and North America. But it shows other forms than those we usually associate with the growth of a civil society, namely NGOs in the Western sense.

Growth of non-governmental organisations

Because the number of voluntary organisations is increasing in Mozambique, this does not necessarily mean that civil society is being strengthened. There is a tendency in practice for Mozambican NGOs to be mainly partners in cooperation and project implementors for foreign voluntary organisations or bilateral aid donors.

Civil society in the Mozambican version is something other than the sum of NGOs that can demonstrate sufficiently advanced administrative reporting routines in order to be able to become a possible choice for external support from different aid donors. The development of a genuine Mozambican civil society must consequently be sought in other environments than those where NGOs with foreign support are active, namely in contexts where people themselves try to resolve their fundamental problems.

A decisive point is the way in which new organisational forms and their leaders develop. A distinction one sometimes tries to make is between formal and real leaders of communities, movements or organisations. It is obvious that those of Frelimo's district administrators who did not speak 'their' district's local language had some problems in becoming perceived as the districts' real leaders, even if they were very articulate as formal leaders. The same difficulties may come to afflict the aid donors who appoint the most articulate formal leaders to different NGOs without asking themselves whether the organisations' activities at local level are integrated into the sphere of the local society's real leaders or are endeavouring to satisfy a locally identified need. A local society's real leaders can have roots in the traditional society, but equally they can have another background, from which they have created their own legitimacy. This may involve religious leaders, doctors, health-care personnel or any worthy citizen.

There were also formal leaders and real leaders during the colonial period. Not all *régulos* were real leaders in local societies. When Frelimo abolished the whole function of *régulos* on coming to power, the state was left with no contact with the principles of traditional organisations and legitimacy. In one of several attempts to create its own bridge of legitimacy between the state and the population, Frelimo started a women's organisation and a youth organisation (Organização de Mulheres Moçambicanas, OMM, and Organização de Juventude Moçambicana, OJM), through which Frelimo hoped to be able to strengthen the legitimacy of the new state. They thus tried to introduce the organisational forms of a civil society from above, and this was naturally doomed to failure in the short term.

Legitimacy versus legality

Over the last few years relations between the state and Mozambican local society have become increasingly unbalanced and the state's legitimacy has diminished by a corresponding degree. The renaissance of the institutions of traditional African society, indicated by Mozambique's new constitution, is an expression of Frelimo's attempt to find a point of contact between the political institutions of modernisation, with its need for legitimacy, and traditional society's real expectations of the state. This has led to a situation where the norms which today control daily life for very large numbers of the population have deep roots in African society. A paradoxical situation has thus arisen where the legal systems have weak legitimacy, while there are legitimate systems for the distribution of resources and the administration of justice in local society which are not legal. It is crucial for the state's future legitimacy that this paradox is resolved.

These circumstances provide some examples to show that discussion about a civil society is ineffective, because no civil society in the form which the European and North American discussion recognises yet exists in the country, or at the least it is very embryonic. In the Eastern European debate the non-existence of NGOs has been a sign of the lack of democracy, as the dictatorial state had suppressed civil society. The existence of a broad spectrum of NGOs, which constitute a civil society, has consequently come to be the nucleus of the definition of democracy.

When a similar discussion was introduced in the countries of the Third World, which are in a transitional stage from a planned economy to a market economy, it was thus also assumed there that the state had suppressed civil society and banned these organisational forms. In Mozambique the preconditions for the emergence of a civil society were missing and the population's self-organisation has taken other forms, which were considered to be more adequate for resolving local problems than those usually associated with the Western concept of a civil society.

Many of the NGOs developed in Mozambique have, however, very little or nothing to do with the majority of the population, except that they *address themselves to the population* in the implementation of a number of externally financed development projects. These new organisations are structures from above, from the capital's urban élite, who are seeking roots in broad strata of the population. In this respect they do not differ from Frelimo's earlier attempt to create 'democratic mass organisations' for women and youth.

A development of democracy in Mozambique can never jump over the self-organisation with which the citizens *de facto* live and which fulfil those functions which we usually associate with civil society in a modern Western version. Today these functions are largely found in traditional society's surviving organisational forms, and provide one of the few forms of the population's self-organisation from which a growing civil society can obtain its sustenance. In keeping with the changing fundamental principles for the distribution of societal resources, another type of civil society is developing. Perhaps this will become more like the Western type.

The Western democratic institutions, parliament and political parties which are already being formed in Mozambique will obviously not necessarily come to be perceived as a legitimate replacement for Frelimo's system and thus gain legitimacy for the political system. In an environment where fragmentation of societal life and a revival of traditional values are the dominant tendencies, Western institutions risk meeting the same fate as that which befell Frelimo's 'mass organisations', if they are not able to link up with the principles of legitimacy that apply in Mozambican rural areas.

10

Transition in Turmoil

Future development in Mozambique is at least as insecure as that in Africa as a whole. Several different factors affect future nation-building and future state-building. This chapter presents three different scenarios for the country's long-term political development.

The first scenario discusses the tendencies for Mozambique to be largely subordinated to foreign regional political and economic interests. The second scenario discusses the risks that exist for the country's division or disintegration. In the third scenario, the different attempts being made to consolidate nation state-building are discussed.

One crucial question is whether it will be possible to develop the present political transitional society directly towards a stable future, or whether society will first experience yet greater social turbulence. In spite of the elections there is still a risk that development will lead the country into ever deeper chaos in the short and intermediate term. Whether development towards a more stable future must pass through such a state on its way towards stability depends on how the conditions necessary for stabilisation develop.

Development in the short term

Several interacting factors at international, regional and national level will determine whether the country's unstable political situation can be stabilised in the short term. These include:

— development of the international political economy;
— regional cooperation;
— development in South Africa;
— demobilisation and the progress of the peace process in Mozambique;
— the implementation of the country's economic and social recovery programme; and
— the government's regional distribution policy at national level.

The development of the international political economy

At the time of Mozambique's independence in 1975, Third World governments made demands for a new international economic order. Radical African leaders recommended a collective self-reliance in their, at least rhetorical, attempt to break out of the capitalist world order. At the beginning of the 1990s these same heads of state are making efforts to ensure that their countries remain within the world order, with strengthened economic links with the West.

One important factor behind this change is the break-up of the Soviet Union and the Eastern bloc. The illusion of a possible co-operative partnership in the East, which theoretically at least would help some countries in the Third World to find a way outside the existing world order, has been shattered. The debt burden has increased the African continent's dependence on the West's economies, at the same time as it has undermined the conditions necessary for the nation-building projects.

At the same time the African continent has, in the eyes of the West, lost most of its earlier importance. In terms of military strategy Africa now plays a marginal role. International commercial interests see no profitable future in Africa. Investments in the continued essential production of raw materials have already been implemented or are financed by aid. New investments in industrial production require a skilled and disciplined workforce, and a developed infrastructure where communications and electricity and water supplies can be guaranteed without breakdowns. The African continent has no internationally competitive advantages in this respect – rather the opposite. New investment projects in Europe, OSS and South-east Asia provide better prospects for a good return.

These conditions are clear from the international statistics. The share of foreign direct investment in the Third World going to the African continent has fallen from 25 per cent in 1970 to 15 per cent in 1989. It is still falling. At the same time the African continent's share of world trade fell from 3 per cent in 1970 to less than 1 per cent in 1990, despite a persistent attempt by the countries during the second half of the 1980s to export their way out of the economic crisis.[277]

The international environment that characterised the development of the Asiatic newly industrialising countries (NICs) in the middle of the 1970s no longer exists now when several African countries, in accordance with the recommendation of the IFIs, will follow the same export-led strategy. Worsened terms of trade for traditional raw materials, rising debts, changed patterns of investment and ever increasing obstacles to trade have had a negative effect on the African continent. One result is that few African countries show any signs at all of sustainable economic development. For the majority of countries on the continent, development has continued downwards with increased inequalities, ecological destruction, de-industrialisation and increased poverty. During the 1980s economic growth drastically declined and since the middle of the decade the continent has experienced a net outflow of financial resources.[278]

Despite this, and despite the fact that international commercial actors are now tending to leave Africa to its fate, the continent still appears on the agenda of the West's political decision-makers. However, it is no longer a matter of development and nation-building, but of survival and security. Growing chaos in Africa, with tens of millions of people starving, and the consequent migration, together with a galloping increase in AIDS and the constant threat of ecological disasters, will also threaten the security of the West if it is allowed to spill over into other continents. There is also the risk of disruptions in the West's supplies of minerals. The question of how best to keep Africa's problems in Africa has been raised.

As far as can be judged, the flow of aid to Africa will therefore not cease. But its direction will probably change from development support to disaster relief channelled through NGOs. This aid will become more short-term and increasingly less developmental. In this way it will be more difficult to mobilise external financial resources essential to correct the distorted production structures established in rural areas during the colonial era. In the light of the marginalisation of the continent, aid to Africa may develop in a way that in the short term contributes to increasing instability. If aid is 'disaster-directed' it does not contribute to the desired extent to increasing the rural population's productivity and purchasing power in order to create preconditions for long-term and sustainable rural development. There is a considerable risk that the instability will continue indefinitely.

However, in the long run, the shared interest of the Western countries and Africa in creating social stability on the continent will most probably open up a more development-oriented aid. Sustainable conflict resolution and economic development require both poverty alleviation and state capacity-building.

Regional cooperation

Even if there was a political will for regional cooperation in Southern Africa at the beginning of the 1980s, the region's geopolitical and economic realities did not allow the SADCC cooperation to be developed into a real alternative to the West or to the former apartheid regime in South Africa. The attempts at increased cooperation made hitherto in Southern Africa were also characterised by an endeavour coming *from without* to bring about, with the support of political decisions *from above*, a more *outward-directed* economy. The member countries' nation-building had hardly started and they lacked an economic base in order for the political decisions to be effective in practice. Moreover, there were many examples of individual member states attempting to hold the door open to South Africa through bilateral commercial agreements, at the same time as regional agreements on different measures were left lying in desk drawers. The region's dependence on South Africa has increased. Its regionally dominant role is indisputable.

SADC[279] member countries will be forced in the future into a balance process between two different trends in regional cooperation. On the one hand SADC has recently admitted the majority-ruled South Africa to the organisation. This should increase the region's internal complementarity and preconditions for increased intra-regional trade, at the same time as providing access to the South African enterprises' international network of contacts and negotiating experience. On the other hand, there may be cause to reduce dependency on South Africa even after the introduction of black majority rule, in order that regional development does not become too unequal and South African influence too great.

The need, and preconditions, for increased regional cooperation are also influenced by international political developments. The new multipolarity that developed after the break-up of the Soviet Union may come to create a new pattern of alliances. Increasing rivalry between the industrialised countries, strengthened regionalisation and increased risks of a trade war may open new routes to alliances with countries in the south. Future international marginalisation of the African continent could create an economic need for strengthened regional cooperation in Southern Africa. For the commercial actors in the region access to the neighbouring countries' markets and workforce will become the only alternative to a reduced space on the world market. This indicates that regional cooperation may be forced to increase significantly during the 1990s. SADC may prove to be a suitable organisational form for this regional cooperation. An increased marginalisation of Africa would thus be able to bring about from below the result that the political decision-makers have not succeeded in creating from above. In the short term, however, this prospect of future regional cooperation does not offer any stabilising development.

Developments in South Africa

One significant question for future regional cooperation concerns the kind of role which a democratic South Africa may come to play. At the same time as a continued supply of minerals, mainly of so-called strategic metals, is of great importance, world dependence on minerals from South Africa is diminishing as a consequence of ongoing technical development. The political and economic changes in Eastern Europe and the former Soviet Union may also increase the world market's supply of minerals, of which South Africa was previously the dominant producer. Reduced mineral production and growing unemployment would diminish South Africa's possibilities for becoming an economic engine for Southern Africa.

A peaceful and harmonious consolidation of the majority-ruled South Africa may otherwise lead the country to obtain a dominant role in future regional cooperation. South Africa could become the region's economic power centre. South African membership would thus change the low level of complementarity which presently characterises SADC's members and thus radically change the conditions of regional trade.

A precondition for this would be, however, a rapid growth in purchasing power for the population in the region. However, there are no signs that such development would go any faster or become more extensive than the expected growth in demand for consumer goods and social services in a future democratic South Africa. It will probably be more urgent in South Africa to satisfy the black South African population's pent-up needs for material improvements and increased living standards than to try to find new wide markets in countries like Mozambique.

The political democratisation of South Africa is also by no means secure. Observers who believe that there will be continued difficult social unrest, economic sabotage and destabilisation see little possibility for South Africa to dominate regional cooperation. Because its economic base is regarded as being far too weak to cope with any regional challenges, Mozambique will become, within a foreseeable period, a market, even if a marginal one, for certain South African consumer goods.

It is also true that black majority rule will come to entail measures with high capital needs, and that both South African and foreign capital may come to be concentrated in South Africa at the expense of investments in the region as such. This applies to the country's economy in general terms. A branch and sector analysis, however, provides scope for a somewhat different interpretation. It is quite probable that economic cooperation with Mozambique, for example, will increase, especially within agriculture in connection with the large dam constructions in the southern areas of the country and within the transport sector in connection with the modern transport corridors. The energy sector is also of interest through the gas deposits in Pande and electrical power from Cabora Bassa. International aid donors have here already financed large parts of the investments needed for the infrastructure in order for profitable production to be brought about. Investment requirements in these sectors are therefore relatively marginal. They mainly refer to improving administrative and organisational skills in order to be better able to exploit the irrigation plants and the transport infrastructure being built up.

However, it is not particularly probable that this commercial co-operation will be born out of any multilateral negotiations within the limits of expanded SADC cooperation. This cooperation will rather be developed from negotiations between South African economic players and Mozambican authorities involved on bilateral terms. Also, in this context there are no clear signs of any development that will lead to short-term increased stability in Mozambique. It is naïve to believe that the abolition of apartheid will make the region the first one without internal conflicts. A new and different pattern of conflicts will emerge and require special management

Demobilisation and the progress of the peace process in Mozambique

All future planning in Mozambique depends on whether the peace agreement, signed on 4 October 1992, will quickly lead to a stable peace or whether its implementation will drag on. With a few exceptions the ceasefire has held.

The question of demobilisation is of crucial importance and should not be viewed as an isolated activity. Demobilisation is a process whereby soldiers are gradually reintegrated into civil society. A number of soldiers who are what is termed 'middle-range officers' have been in the army for a large part of their professional lives. Most of them have not only cut off their own links to civilian life, but have also brought their own families into the military camps and further increased the role of the army in their lives.

It is of the utmost importance that these officers are not conventionally demobilised. If opportunities for long-term educational or professional development are not offered, there is a risk that after some time the officers will take up arms again and turn into warlords indulging in small-scale and low-intensity armed conflicts on a 'freelance' basis. At the same time, measures to facilitate non-conventional demobilisation and adequate reintegration into civil society of this category of soldiers should not be too selective, as this could create a new special social grouping and new tensions with the civilian population.

The security situation in Mozambique is also dependent on developments in South Africa. The prospects for an improved security situation in rural areas are dependent on the degree to which the present, or future, government in South Africa is able to control political and individual interests, which still have room for manoeuvre within police and military units. Many of these interests have a Portuguese past and ambitions for regaining properties lost in Mozambique. This component in the war in Mozambique will not disappear automatically. Security problems will probably be found in rural areas in Mozambique over the next few years. Thus, in spite of the peace agreement and recent elections, development will not lead unequivocally towards stability.

Implementation of the country's economic and social rehabilitation programme

A further precondition for peaceful development in rural areas is that the economic and social rehabilitation programme leads to improved living conditions for the peasant population. Without peace and opportunities for the rural population to return to active agriculture there will not be sufficient economic growth. The most important contribution to Mozambique's macro-economic balance would be quickly to achieve self-sufficiency in food, thereby reducing import requirements. At the same time a larger share of the workforce in rural areas could be directed towards increasing production of export products within agriculture. However, there is no visible consequent concentration on a strategy that aims rapidly to achieve self-sufficiency in food.

Mozambique's government must formulate an economic strategy, which will obtain the aid donors' committed support, in order to finance the extensive rehabilitation of the physical, social and commercial infrastructure in the countryside required in order for the population to be able to return to a normal life after the peace agreement. Such an undertaking is considered necessary before any structural adjustment programme can be fully implemented and a macro-economic balance achieved. International political and economic developments indicate, however, that countries such as Mozambique will most probably find it hard even to maintain the aid they have obtained up to the present. In this area there are no trends clearly pointing towards stability.

The government's regional distribution policy at national level

There are at least two important circumstances behind the fact that several presumptive parties in Mozambique have appeared to be defenders of regional or ethnic interests. One is that the war has isolated different areas of the country from each other. As mentioned earlier, a constant criticism of political leaders and state functionaries at all levels is that they do not travel around the country. In the districts it is thought that the provincial government does not leave its office in the provincial capital, and the provincial government itself thinks that ministers sit in Maputo and do not know what is happening in the country. The second important circumstance is the outcome of the regional policy carried out by Frelimo during its nearly twenty years in government. The concentration of resources in a few larger projects has meant that many parts of the country have been treated unfairly. The large projects still require great resources in maintenance and reinvestments in order that earlier inputs should not be wasted.

At the same time as the present pattern of investment is regionally unbalanced, it also shows an imbalance in the distribution between urban and rural areas. The investments made in more remote provinces have tended not to benefit the rural areas, but instead have favoured urban centres in provinces and districts. The political opposition thus has opportunities to mobilise popular support based on dissatisfaction with the central distribution of resources to provinces and regions. The assessment is that ongoing development will tend to lead towards instability. This trend is probably the most serious threat to future stability in the rural areas of Mozambique.

Towards continued instability

Development at international, regional and national level will therefore not lead unequivocally towards short- and medium-term stability in Mozambique. Continued instability in the country would increase the probability of chaos and anarchy. Such development is a threatening vision which, if it comes about, will lead to extensive disintegration of modern societal functions, and permanent violent regimes in rural areas through local warlords and bands from both the former Renamo and the government army. In such a development it would be impossible for the international community to provide anything other than disaster relief to the victims of violence and famine. Mozambique would probably cease to function as a political unit.

Not even a consolidation of the peace accord and a successful demobilisation of the soldiers of the middle-range officers is a guarantee against instability in rural areas. Today there is a true lumpenproletariat in the rural areas and on the edges of the towns. Several million people are on the way into, or are already in, a situation where they are forced to steal to survive.

The extensive lumpenproletariatisation of large groups of the rural population has strengthened the economic and social stratification which was already found before the war. There is an imminent danger that this new socio-economic stratification will become permanent in rural areas and that the poorer groups will be treated unfairly in the redistribution of cultivable land following return migrations.

It is from this type of local conflict that a new rural violence may develop. Together with bands of former soldiers and 'leftover' Renamo groups, this population may form an environment in which a socially conditioned violence may be developed. The solutions to these problems involve neither the police nor the military, but must build on a serious attempt at social and economic development in the most remote parts of the country as well.

This solution at local level may have its counterpart in the regions and provinces. A continued unbalanced regional policy, combined with strongly centralised decision-making, may lead to both provincial governments and administrators at district level gradually ceasing to 'take orders' from Maputo. The central government will become increasingly isolated from the development of events in rural areas, and no nationally organised power has the capacity to take over the leadership. If such conflicts are militarised and set against the central government's demand for national unity, a state coup by authoritarian members of the government could lead to a very authoritarian regime being established. The motivation would be the classic one: the military must take control in order to preserve national unity and maintain law and order.

A military coup, however, is not likely. The Mozambican army today lacks the capacity to become any real alternative, on a national scale. Its material situation is precarious, and the loyalty of local troop units to coup leaders from Maputo would be very uncertain. If, on the other hand, a larger group from the new government found support from the military or police leadership in a 'palace coup' against the rest of the government, it would be possible for a civil government of a strongly repressive nature to be established.

Foreign support for a coup in this direction cannot be excluded. Developments in South Africa may come to change the Portuguese component's, and other interested parties', options for the continued destabilisation of Mozambique. Their endeavours to regain their assets and societal positions in a 're-colonised' Mozambique may also form the basis for the possible future destabilisation of a democratic South Africa.

Probable and desirable scenarios in the longer term

Subordination of the state-nation

The rehabilitation programme's 'social and economic carrier' has consisted of an alliance between large numbers of the Frelimo leadership, a broad stratum of leading state functionaries and international aid donors. They have all had a common interest in maintaining the inflow of resources that is generated by a Mozambican adherence to the principles of the structural adjustment programme.

The political uncertainty and dejection caused by the war and the restrictions of the present economic policy have forced other alternative points of view to the fore. Functionaries and decision-makers with private ambitions at a high level within the administration are troubled, like the country's private owners of capital, by the danger of continuing political and economic turbulence. This would render more difficult their ambitions for developing private entrepreneurial skills. Many are trying instead to develop cooperation with South African and Portuguese businessmen.

In this scenario there is an ethnic dimension, which emphasises 'Mozambicanness', in the sense that the political and economic development should favour black Mozambicans in the first instance. In order to be able to challenge economically the Asian trade capital that today dominates Mozambique, and in order to be able to face a possible massive Portuguese return, this political tendency wishes to promote a Mozambican class of entrepreneurs to a dominant position in the political life of the country.

Many of the resources that can attract foreign enterprises are today state-owned or under state control. This applies not least to the large state farms' agricultural land and the country's mineral assets. Closer economic cooperation with foreign interests would improve the preconditions for a domestic class of entrepreneurs, who would be recruited among higher civil servants, from the management of state enterprises and among politicians. The aim is to exploit this political control of the sale of state enterprises and the formation of new joint ventures for private objectives and ambitions.

A rapid and extensive sale of internationally demanded domestic resources, in exchange for personal positions in the new enterprises for politicians and state functionaries, would quickly erode all visions of a democratic and modern nation-state. Such a development could come to be called 'Bantustanisation' and resemble former relations between South Africa and its so-called homelands. Faced with such a development many aid donors would gradually reduce their development aid and limit themselves to financing the voluntary organisations' disaster relief work. The Mozambican state apparatus would become increasingly weakened and its possibilities for gaining legitimacy for democracy and a multi-party system would be minimal.

Those Mozambican groups which have an interest in acting in accordance with this scenario also needed a quick end to the war. Many of the areas that can be exploited were militarily insecure. They were therefore prepared to make very far-reaching concessions in the peace negotiations, for example to accept territorial divisions which would undermine future nation-building.

There are several reasons for such Mozambican interest groups continuing, at least rhetorically, to support the new government and to rally round the recovery programme. Continued support from international aid donors is regarded as being an absolute precondition for the rehabilitation of the infrastructure and industries required for creating an interest in an international sale of these resources.

Another reason is that the inflow of aid can be drained through corruption to finance the individual projects which many dream about. A marginalisation of Africa would limit the commercial flow of capital that can be made available for a market economic transformation in Southern Africa.

This works against a state coup of the 'palace type' discussed earlier. Few of these interested parties would then be able to come into possession of international political support and an international flow of aid of the present magnitude. The country's current aid dependency thus has a very important stabilising effect on the present political leadership through reducing the domestic policy room for manoeuvre for the opposition both within and outside the government.

Macro-regionalism

This chapter has thus far proceeded from the fact that the main trend for the whole of Southern Africa for the next few years indicates continued instability. It is assumed that instability at regional level will thus also imply that development in Mozambique will continue to be unstable.

But another kind of subordination in relation to the region may also be the consequence of a more stable development. A regional subordination which takes the form of a far-reaching integration, which involves all the countries in the region, would produce a different regional scenario.

The preconditions for the region to be able to meet such stable development depend on whether the peaceful democratic process in South Africa can be consolidated and that the South African export-dependent economy succeeds in maintaining its position on the world market, making the required resources for expansion in the region available.

One step towards regional stability would be a rapid integration of all national economies within SADC countries, including a democratic South Africa. This presupposes that all nation-state projects in the region are subordinate to a regional development perspective. Unlike regional cooperation hitherto (an endeavour from without to strengthen an outward-directed economy through political decisions from above), such a regionalisation process would build on an endeavour which comes *from within* the region to increase, suggested by actors *from below*, the region's cooperation for a more *inward-directed* regional economic development.

This would naturally initially imply that South African economic actors would come to dominate the economic life of the region. But at the same time a regional economic and political integration in the longer term would provide Southern Africa with a position in the world economy that neither South Africa alone nor the individual countries are capable of achieving. Thus the region would be able to enter into an integration process, which could internationally strengthen the states' common position, at the same time as regional federative democratic development could create the preconditions for a cultural multiplicity and local self-determination.

Division of the state-nation

The preconditions for a politicised ethnicity which are developing in Mozambique have their roots in a historical inequality between three regions: southern, central and northern. The material preconditions for a possible sub-national conflict in Mozambique have changed since independence, through the unequal development from the colonial period being reinforced.

In pace with people in the centre and the north increasingly feeling that they are being treated unfairly by the central authorities' method of distributing public resources, the foundations have been laid for ethnic tensions to rise. In each of these three regions there are dominant ethnic groups who could form the nucleus of a new politicised ethnicity. Ndau in the centre and Macua in the north may become these dominant elements.

There is a risk that the state-nation, if it is not decentralised, will come to be perceived more and more as an ethnocratic state, i.e. a state controlled by Mozambicans from the southern parts of the country. A widespread feeling that there is an ethnic monopoly of power, which cannot be broken by other élites, increases the possibilities for protest movements built on ethnic grounds to grow and gain strength.

Mozambique is not yet on the way to being torn apart by ethnic conflicts. But there are enough signs that ethnic and regional tensions are growing. These may come to interact with local fragmentation, where widespread violence develops into a local war. A politicised ethnicity may gain strength and popular 'enthusiasm' so that local conflicts attain national significance. A political élite at provincial/regional level may exploit local dissatisfaction and attempt to develop political mobilisation on ethnic grounds. Separatist movements may grow from such a development, or set such irreconcilable demands for local/regional self-determination that they cannot be accommodated within the framework of the state-nation structure.

The military destabilisation of Mozambique and Renamo's progress have not thus far appeared to be an ethnic 'project'. Nevertheless, there is a historic background which could legitimise Renamo as an ethnic/separatist movement. Renamo has had two leaders, who both belong to the Ndau ethnic group. A very large number of its local commanders come from the same group, and the 'official' language in their bases has been Ndau. If the immediate future in Mozambique involves a development in the direction of the politicisation of ethnicity, there exists in a Ndau-Renamo a military capacity which few other ethnic groups can demonstrate.

The possibility should not be discounted that a Ndau-Renamo can be born from a failure in the democratisation process or that Renamo's leadership, when it is absorbed by Maputo's political and international environment, will not able to satisfy the needs of local and provincial commanders. In an internal planning document before the negotiations, Renamo demanded absolute control over the four central provinces (Manica, Sofala, Tete and Zambezia) during a two-year transition period between the ceasefire and the elections.[280]

These four provinces represent about 40 per cent of Mozambique's population and 42 per cent of its surface area. More than half the total export potential is located there, all tea plantations and factories, the Cahora Bassa power plant, four of Mozambique's sugar refineries, Beira port and the Beira corridor. This principle is also found in a press communiqué from Renamo's national council in April 1992. There it is demanded that Renamo should continue to administer after a ceasefire the areas which they also occupied before the ceasefire. The recent elections also showed considerable popular support in these areas. In fact, Renamo won the majority of votes in these provinces.[281]

In practice Renamo has also tried to implement this claim after the peace agreement, even if on a smaller scale than four provinces. The question of two different administrations in the country has long been an important bone of contention in the negotiations in Maputo after the peace agreement. Renamo has stubbornly maintained the right to continue to administer the areas which they considered they controlled on 4 October 1992.

Several of the potential political parties have a strong federative element in their policy. If Renamo, as a future political party, intends to mobilise its electoral base on the basis of a politicised Ndau identity in the central areas of the country, it will certainly follow that other political groupings will attempt to carry out a corresponding mobilisation in the north and the south.

This fragmentation of the country, which would result in deepened chaos and anarchy, may go so far that a national solution will no longer be possible. As late as the 1960s Malawi's President Banda made a claim to parts of Mozambique's territory. The border with Zimbabwe cuts right through Shona land. The southern areas of Mozambique have always been economically and geographically closely tied to South Africa. In a 'Bantustanisation' perspective, forms may be developed for incorporating southern Mozambique into Transvaal, which may contribute to the division of the country.

Micro-regionalism

Such a division of the nation into sub-national units does not imply that macro-regional cooperation will be ended. On the contrary, as difficulties arise in nation-building, local advantages can motivate the growth of regional cooperation between different so-called micro-regions in a larger macro-regional context.

Consolidation of the state-nation

The third of the three scenarios is based on the concept of the homogenous nation-state approaching a consolidated nation-state. Building a homogenous nation-state along the lines of European development has been the goal for a couple of generations of African leaders. This support for the nation-state as a principle for political organisation has been common to both socialist-orientated regimes and conservative nationalists. At the heart of this common attitude in African élites there is a perception of African culture and older African forms of management as being inimical to progress. African society must be modernised in order for it to be developed, and the European nation-state has become an important part of the pattern for modernisation.

For large numbers of the national domestic élite within the Mozambican administration the nation-building project is still alive. For them it is a question of finding a route between free market forces and rigid state planning, at the same time as the state-nation is being developed into the political unit within which both the economy and a democratic political system can be accommodated. Successful implementation of the adjustment programme requires that central political and economic institutions function over the whole country. The economy requires national coverage in order to obtain sufficient strength.

Within the very broad group of politicians and state functionaries who still support the idea of consolidating the state-nation and providing it with a democratic political content, there are several different opinions on the way in which this should be done. One point of view follows the relatively strict principle that the national overall interest is superior to local special interests. A second point of view could be described as an administrative decentralisation. Such a policy would mean that provincially and locally elected assemblies would have expanded authority and opportunities to administer the resources placed at their disposal according to a decision on national distribution at central level. Today provinces and districts are in principle only executors of central decisions and prioritisations. A third point of view is represented mainly at provincial level, and it is characterised by a demand for a relatively far-reaching self-determination for the provinces. How close this would be to a federative state is not clear.

The possible future organisation of a more homogenous state-nation may combine a nationally rooted democratic development and a far-reaching political and economic decentralisation. If provinces and regions can also grant a high degree of cultural self-determination it may also be possible successfully to recreate the legitimacy of the nation-state project at grassroots level.

A precondition for the consolidation of the state-nation is that the state is given adequate resources, both for developing those institutions and those actors necessary for a market economy to function, and to be able to supply the utilities required for a new political system to have any credibility in the eyes of the population. In order to manage this, Mozambique's political élite will need extensive support from the international aid donors.

This vision of the future requires consolidation of demobilisation and peaceful development. It also requires an institutional framework for political democratisation and the development of the institutions of a market economy. The realisation of this scenario depends on the possibilities for supplementing the implementation of the economic and social recovery programme with a more comprehensive plan for national reconstruction. Stable economic development could create a domestic base for those Mozambicans who have business ambitions and would reduce the need for 'Mozambicanness' to subordinate itself to foreign interests. Individual development ambitions would thus come instead to benefit the nation-state project.

In the final chapter we will analyse in more detail the preconditions for bringing about such development.

11

Searching for a Way Out

The main remedies for the Mozambican crisis have been the introduction of a market economy and democratisation in the form of multi-
party elections. The outcome of the recent elections, with a reasonably
clear victory for President Joaquim Chissano and a seemingly comfortable majority in parliament for the Frelimo party, may be interpreted
as a sign that the country is well on the way to overcoming its problems.
However, a closer look at the voting patterns reveals some disturbing
rifts which should give cause for concern.

First, in the regional distribution of votes Frelimo has a clear majority
in the three southernmost provinces and in the extreme north, which
constituted the main arena for Frelimo's war of liberation against the
Portuguese of 1964–75. In the rest of the country – covering around 60
per cent of the population – Renamo won a comfortable victory. The
central provinces of Fofala and Manica, in particular, showed a huge
majority for Renamo. There is thus clear evidence of regionally and
ethnically based voting behaviour.

There are sharp differences in voting behaviour within areas with a
large Frelimo majority. Two polling stations in the same local area
(*localidade*) may show, for example, 60 per cent voting for Frelimo in
some villages and 5 per cent in neighbouring villages. Here we are
dealing not with ethnic voting but with socio-economic factors and
local power struggles. Those who feel excluded from the Frelimo society's benefits vote for Renamo, perhaps more as a protest against local
power abuse and exclusion than as a demonstration of belief in Renamo.
This tendency is also reflected in a comparison between rural and
urban areas. When the election results of towns and rural areas are
analysed, there is a marked difference. Renamo's strength is reinforced
as soon as rural areas are separated from urban areas.

The general conclusion to be drawn from this short analysis is that
Mozambican society is still not free from future tension, instability and
violence. Any search for a way out must take this into account.

The need for reconciliation

The peace that was achieved after the war of destabilisation, with its imposed elections, is coming, like the war, to have special characteristics. A 'destabilisation peace' is not just a zero-sum game where the winner takes all. If the goal of destabilisation is not victory but change, then it follows that the peace does not need to designate any victor, despite the fact that Chissano was re-elected president and Frelimo got 129 of the parliament's 250 seats.

The negotiations between Mozambique's government and Renamo, which went on for two years before a peace agreement could be concluded in 1992, were characterised by two different circumstances. One was the problem that arose from Renamo's background, in that it was a purely military organisation long before it began to acquire any political content. The second was that different external actors could not agree on when destabilisation was no longer required but was becoming counter-productive.

Thus there were two parallel processes going on. One took place within the framework of the negotiations that later continued with varying intensity in Maputo under UN supervision. Renamo's participation in this process was probably pursued with the same strategic views that earlier characterised the so-called military alternative and Renamo's operational activity, which was largely managed by intelligence organisations, security services and the military. Within this sphere questions about the future for Renamo's leaders also were to be decided at different levels.

At the same time extensive work was going on to enable Renamo to present itself as a political organisation in Mozambique's first free elections. This involved many complications. One was the fact that those who were now joining Renamo had often had nothing to do with its activities during the war years. These politicians in the making are facing, mainly at local level, great suspicion on the part of Renamo's military commanders. The emergence and growth of a political party in Renamo's name is consequently a process that essentially resembles the development of other alternative parties in Mozambique today. It is still unclear how those who were earlier part of Renamo's military structure will be included in the wave of new recruitment following the peace agreement.

The second process is the political, social and economic change that goes on every day in Mozambique. This extensive reorganisation of Mozambican society should not be confused with the negotiations between Renamo and the government. They naturally go hand in hand, not least because it is MNR which has largely triggered off the process of societal change. But at the same time the peace process has been hampered by the fact that Frelimo alone has carried out the political transformation in Mozambique, because this transformation has taken away the chance for other political parties to elaborate any political content in the election campaign. The political content of the peace agreement is thus non-existent.

Following the elections, the majority of actors who played a part in the destabilisation of Mozambique are convinced that the changes brought about by destabilisation are now irreversible. Accordingly the words reconciliation, policy of reconciliation and government of reconciliation are frequently used to describe events in today's Mozambique. However, the real reconciliation is occurring not in the form of changed relations between the former Frelimo government and Renamo, but in the daily lives of all Mozambicans. It is within this framework for the real reconciliation, the economic and political transformation, that the 'victors' of destabilisation can be found.

Frelimo's policy during the first decade of independence was naturally directed against the interests of private capital that the country inherited from the colonial period. Mozambicans who had seen an opportunity in independence to expand their economic activity were forced to retreat by Frelimo's policy, but they did not disappear, merely bided their time. The antagonisms between Frelimo's socialist policy and these would-be entrepreneurs gained new force and sustenance as destabilisation developed. Frelimo's conclusion was that a reconciliation with these forces would be a crucial signal to the external forces behind destabilisation.

Frelimo had another broad and deep conflict with the churches. The church is now also an important part of the reconciliation. The different churches are regaining their properties, which were nationalised on independence, and they are being urged to reassume their responsibility for parts of the education and health-care systems.

A third group with which Frelimo must be reconciled is those traditionally in power. At local level it is clear that many of those who had actively cooperated with Renamo have been returning to Frelimo-controlled areas during the last years of the war. Some have come within the framework for the law on amnesty issued by the government. Others are coming with pretensions of regaining some of the power taken from them on independence. There are two reasons behind their return.

Partly, it is clear that Frelimo's district administrators have begun to consult these people to an increasing extent about questions concerning local conditions, mainly in matters referring to land and settlement. The planned decentralisation of the political system is also making possible an increase in their influence. Neither is their participation today in traditional ceremonies leading to the same reactions among the local authorities as it did about ten years ago.

Also, those traditionally in power, many of them older, began to realise that peace would not give them any special advantages at local level if they continued with Renamo. An aged *cabo de terra* from the Mozambican interior will not come to be celebrated as a victor now when the war is over. He prefers the offer of new forms of cooperation with the government which Frelimo's constitutional reforms give him through the policy of reconciliation. It is these processes that constitute the real reconciliation. However, a real and thorough reconciliation cannot only include relations between Frelimo and economic entrepreneurs, small capitalists, those traditionally in power and the church. The most important force with which Frelimo must be reconciled is the mass of marginalised peasants and other impoverished people in the rural areas.

The economic and social disaster created by the war itself holds the seed of new social conflicts, which may trigger off a state of violence both in the rural areas and in the towns. A conventional peace, with a 'winner takes all' mentality, or a policy of reconciliation which is limited to urban interests, may mean that the present economic and social situation will develop into a real peasant-based class war. The antagonisms between town and country may be developed into a 'Pol Pot situation', where messianic peasant leaders mobilise against the towns' parasitic upper class. Such a war would come to be directed directly against the new social order being created after the end of destabilisation. Destabilisation may prove to be a sowing of dragon's teeth, if the policy of reconciliation does not also come to include the poorest of the poor in rural areas.

This perspective is closely connected to the way in which Renamo has functioned in local society over the years of destabilisation. Banditry, as the activity has always been called in Mozambique, has its own special socio-economic and socio-psychological pattern of development, connected not least to the way in which the recruitment process has been formulated and developed. This has created a new pattern for the exercise of violence in rural areas, which is concentrated particularly in the marginalised sections of the population. The development of the war has created an extensive lumpenproletariat, around which other socially marginalised groups may gather in an organised struggle for survival through theft, robbery and looting. Through the war a culture of violence and destructive social relations has gained a footing among the youth of the rural areas. This has created preconditions for an institutionalisation of banditry and lawlessness. Even if the military on both sides allow themselves to be demobilised, the social and psychological consequences of the war will remain. It is the poorest and least educated strata in the rural areas that have been dominant among Renamo's armed groups. The total marginalisation of the poorest peasants that the war entailed constitutes fertile ground for the development of a new wave of 'self-destabilisation' and lawlessness, which can be combated not by military or police means, but only by social and economic development.

Reformulation of the security concept

A reformulation of Mozambican security policy ought thus to build on a new concept, which takes into consideration all the aspirations for the future found within the whole of Mozambican society. It must build on an assessment of the differing security threats which different 'communities' consider important, not just on the military's or the central élite's way of perceiving the threat to national security.

One conclusion is that discussions on national security must be based to an increasing extent on the way the individual, group or political, economic and ethnic élites perceive a threat to their own security. Hence an analysis of the regional security complex of Southern Africa which takes its starting point in people's collective security and how this is affected not only by military security, but also by political security, economic security, societal security and ecological security provides a much broader pattern of conflict than a strictly military analysis.

A new pattern of the region's potential conflicts has emerged as a consequence of the fact that the apartheid system has been abolished and that neither Mozambique nor Angola threaten South Africa any longer with the idealogical exportation of socialist revolution. The fears of a transformation into a Bantustan through membership of CONSAS has been changed into a genuine interest in economic cooperation with a majority-ruled South Africa.

This leads us to the question of whether it is really only states that are the major actors in maintaining, or threatening, the security of citizens. In the post-bipolar world order we have quickly seen how states break apart, mainly due to internal weaknesses – a type of implosion. The state's legitimacy has been undermined for different reasons and in many cases it has failed to maintain citizens' collective and individual security, as well as their confidence in a long-term stability within the framework of existing borders. The growth of strong and broad territorially based opposition groups has long not been perceived as a security problem. The phenomenon of separatism has been regarded as being the preserve of certain marginal groups with special historical conditions in a few countries. Even if the security concept is extended more to societal sectors than the military, our contemporary history of sub-national conflicts in different parts of the world shows that regional security analysis must take into account as well sub-national actors and events.

Let us look a little more closely at the threat which South Africa experienced from Mozambique and see whether other actors can also be found here who were 'set free' when the ties of the earlier pattern of conflict disappeared. The security problem that characterised Southern Africa consisted of two different patterns of conflict, both the Cold War and the apartheid system. The Cold War's pattern of conflict has disappeared, at least temporarily. Despite majority rule the apartheid system's pattern of conflict remains – even if in a modified form. Today there is no threat from neighbouring countries. Neither is there any threat scenario internally in South Africa, as the ANC has renounced its armed struggle and taken power. The threat scenario which was earlier predominant in white South African society came from black leaders in neighbouring countries, of whom some were also communists. It was this threat scenario that created the build-up of military force. Today this scenario is gone at the same time as a new one has taken its place, consisting today of a national political threat and a sub-national threat of increased civil violence.

For a white South African, the threat in real terms is the same as 20 years ago. Black people will have equal rights and will be placed on an equal footing with whites, and because of their numbers they will sooner or later be able to exploit the 'right' of a majority to decide over a minority. The big difference lies in the fact that the threat is today not perceived as being as serious as in the 1970s.

The apartheid system chained many actors very tightly through clear race discrimination. South Africa made an attempt to develop a black middle class with economic interests in common with sections of the white population. As a consequence there is today an extensive black middle class, but it is nevertheless prevented from integrating fully into South African capitalism. Race barriers will certainly remain as invisible walls long after the apartheid system has disappeared from all South African legislation. This means that although apartheid has been abolished, the race-conditioned antagonisms in society still exist. They may come to take other forms – economic, social, cultural, etc.[282] There are antagonisms on both sides of the apartheid barrier, which may take off as the pattern of conflict based on the apartheid system has disappeared. We will here indicate a few components which may come to affect the situation after apartheid.

The violence 'between blacks' which has been troubling people in the black townships in South Africa is mainly a political violence, with many links to the former regime's police and security services.[283] But the limits of a spontaneous 'Fanonist'[284] violence, which grows from an increasingly desperate social and economic situation, are not always absolutely clear. Poverty and unemployment facilitate recruitment to political groups of violence, in both the ANC and Inkhata. It is by no means certain that such mobilisation cannot be developed and consolidated through an increased politicisation of ethnicity. This may thus constitute a base for formulating political and economic demands which cannot be satisfied within the framework of South African society's modern sector.

However, the new situation has meant that the vision of the 'whites" expected homogeneity has proved to be inaccurate and different views on the future for South Africa have been polarised. Militant conservative Boers may develop as a base for continued violence.

South Africa thus risks the new post-apartheid system being born bearing a new set of security problems, where both threat scenarios and actors differ from earlier concepts in analyses of security. This applies both to a broadening beyond state level to a more complex, and perhaps more abstract but deeply felt, security threat – for example social and cultural threats, a threat to identity and a moral system of norms – and to a change of level as increasing numbers of sub-national actors begin to challenge both each other and the state from within. These new security problems, which a majority-ruled South Africa may be expected to face, will naturally come to have a decisive influence on security policies in the whole region. The importance of demobilisation of the four potential ethnic armies which are, or have been, active in the region, and which are still included (wholly or partly) in one chain of command, appear increasingly important in this perspective. This refers to the white South African regular army (it may also be that different sections of the armed forces will prove to have differing loyalties in relation to the political system), it refers to Inkhata and the involvement of the police and military which has become known, and it refers to Renamo, whose South African umbilical cord has not yet been completely severed. It also refers to UNITA, whose resumed war in Angola has obviously been supported by South African interests. There is also the importance of the demobilisation of the black ethnic battalions which SADF has organised, and there are the 'homeland armies', the paramilitary forces whose leadership structure has been in the hands of South African officers – inside or outside active service – and former white mercenaries.[285] As long as the risk remains that different interest groups may come, in cooperation, to exploit some of these military units for continued destabilisation in the region, the conditions necessary for peaceful, stable development are limited.

Inclusive political participation

Frelimo's political leadership has worked for many years to create a homogenous nation from Rovuma in the north to Maputo in the south. This is regarded as being an important precondition for the whole state-building process in Mozambique.

Against the background of the economic, political and social circumstances in which the country presently finds itself, we have previously
recorded the problems in introducing and consolidating the nation-
state model as we know it in Europe.[286] The preconditions for correcting
these problems – the state's weak capacity and its lack of legitimacy –
will be crucial to the success of the current transition from war to
peace.

As long as the government, the state administration and the activities
of the public sector are perceived to be dominated by a political élite
from the southern areas of the country, regional and possibly ethnic
tensions and antagonisms will continue to grow. The present trend of
restricting participation in the political process to the élites within
Frelimo and Renamo contributes, furthermore, to reinforcing the feeling
of marginalisation among many social and economic interests in the
country.

A perception that is taking root that all élites must be given opportunities to participate in the political exercise of power and economic activity stems from the fact that in its first year at the beginning
of the 1960s, Frelimo had an internal structure that allowed different
élites to manifest themselves within the framework of the front's
policies.[287] By transforming itself into an avant-garde party, Frelimo
reduced the possibilities for pluralism. Decision-making was centralised,
the scope for ideological variations disappeared, traditions and cultural
patterns were called superstition and were opposed and Portuguese
became the only national language.

In this perspective Frelimo's 'anti-tribal' and 'anti-racist' struggle
appears ambiguous. At the same time as Frelimo wished to unite the
population and give all inhabitants the same rights, opportunities for
expressing different socio-cultural or ethnic traits disappeared. By creating a centralised decision-making system in a multi-ethnic society, which
was characterised by colonial severe regional imbalances, Frelimo contributed to creating preconditions for future ethnic antagonisms.

A concrete issue for Mozambique is whether growing regional
tensions imply a risk of increased politicisation of ethnicity and growing
ethnic antagonisms. Frelimo succeeded during the war of liberation in
mobilising broad support from all strata of the population. The criticism
now being heard is that certain of the country's ethnic groups have
been favoured by government policies. Both Frelimo and other presumptive political parties must therefore make up their mind whether,
and if so how, the Mozambican state will be restructured in order to
allow increased participation in the exercise of power by the different
alternative élites,[288] which hitherto have felt marginalised. Such increased participation would reduce the probability of politicisation in
an ethnic direction.

The main question seems to be whether the state will also continue to be a homogenous state with only a central decision-making centre, or whether some form of federation is preferable.[289] Experiences of federative states in the West are not relevant in this case, because federalism often does not build on ethnicity, but is rather based on administrative divisions. At the same time it is increasingly obvious that classic federalism is not enough to restrict the growth of sub-national conflicts. The preconditions for future political stability may instead come to depend on the extent to which other organisational forms and principles of legitimacy in the form of a 'multi-nation state project' can be developed.[290]

State power and alternative élites

There is no doubt that a restructuring of the functions of the state apparatus must provide opportunities for alternative élites to take part in the exercise of power in Mozambique. The new constitution's ban on ethnically-based parties is very much a double-edged sword. Apart from the fact that they do not work, such attempts at preventing ethnic mobilisation themselves constitute infringements of people's political rights. Every ethnic group should be able to mobilise 100 people in each province without any difficulty in order to satisfy the rule on national representation, as required for official party registration.

In Mozambique the former nationalist liberation movements were all formed on a regional base.[291] The merging of these movements through the emergence of Frelimo as the only nationalist movement in Mozambique restricted the scope for action of some of the élites which had previously been able to dominate their own region. The war of liberation's requirement for military and political efficiency further limited opportunities for regional special interests to accommodate themselves within the demand for consensus imposed by Frelimo's military-political leadership.

This consensus principle, which had been the basis for the military-political successes during the liberation struggle, came to guide government work after independence as well. In this way alternative regional, religious, ethnic and economic élites were marginalised if they did not subordinate themselves to the consensus principles within Frelimo's and the state apparatus' leadership.

In the present political and economic transformation process, criticism may become public and assume organisational expression through the formation of parties, private enterprises and NGOs, and through full freedom of religious activity. But through the socio-political development over the last 20 years these alternative élites still have a very fragile social base.

The party formations presently developing offer no alternative to the economic policy being operated by Frelimo. The economic policy being carried out is considered to be a precondition for the continued support of the international aid donors. Thus these new parties cannot mobilise any social base on the basis of economic group interests in society. Their only possibility for establishing themselves in political reality via democratic principles – support from the voter in elections – is to seek their own social base, i.e. their voters, according to principles other than different interests in the economic policy. It may well be that they will come to attempt mobilisation on an ethnic or regional basis.

Satisfaction of local needs

Both Frelimo's economic policy over the first ten years of independence and the present economic policy have contributed to creating material preconditions for the dissatisfaction in rural areas to increase.

However, that people in local society must largely rely on their own resources and experience for long-term survival and turn to the principles and norms of traditional society for local society's functions does not necessarily mean that their ethnic identity or loyalty has changed, either in content or in strength. In local society loyalty mainly applies first to family or lineage and the immediate environment, and the ethnic dimension has less significance for the way in which the population organises its production and available assets are distributed. The conflicts of interest that are developing *in local society* are thus mainly of a social or economic nature. They may involve conflicts about land, water or other production resources, or may refer to local political influence. Obviously, there are also antagonisms and conflicts that have their origin in society's economic and social differentiation, in short between rich and poor.

This means that we believe that a possible politicisation of ethnicity in Mozambique will mainly come to have its origin in the alternative élites' need to mobilise or strengthen their social base, in order to be able to compete with the dominant élites of state power. If we want to distinguish this process from the local development, this movement among the élites could be called the ethnification of politics. Thus we will see a marked difference in that the precondition for a politicisation of ethnicity is that there is dissatisfaction or deep-rooted problems in the local society limited to areas with such a high degree of ethnic homogeneity that it can form the basis for a broader mobilisation. The reason for local society 'allowing itself' to be mobilised politically, by forces looking for possibilities to 'ethnify' politics, on an ethnic basis is that the local society suffers from a lack of satisfaction of its basic human needs, material or immaterial.

Politicised ethnicity may arise as a defence reaction to marginalisation and subordination, where ethnicity becomes the lowest common denominator among larger groups of the population which can be mobilised in order to set demands in the ethnic group's name. It ought to be possible to counteract the growth of ethnic conflicts through the social integration of different élites at national level and by local societies being given better opportunities to function according to their own cultural pattern and local conditions. It must be remembered that a return to other strategies for long-term survival in local societies, where traditional patterns, values and people in power are given a larger role, does not necessarily lead to ethnicity being politicised.

The resolution of the sub-national problems in Mozambique does not require federalism in the first instance, but will be found in both *broad political inclusion at central level*, without the élites being pressured in election processes which finally build on the majority principle and may come to force them to ethnic mobilisation, and in *genuine decentralisation* which provides self-determination for the local society, together with guarantees in order for sufficient resources to be channelled from central to local level.

A decentralisation process in an administrative and political sense would provide local groups with opportunities for managing their own affairs. There is also the policy of reconciliation, which must at national level include all the different types of domestic élites in an integration which is not in the first instance political, or based on political parties, but social. The needs of the alternative élites are reflected in that no parties are formulating an economic policy that differs from Frelimo's. Their political needs thus refer not in the first instance to a different policy for distribution, but quite simply to becoming visible in society and participating without restrictions as actors in political and economic activity.

Rural development and economic rehabilitation

Mozambique, with a population of 16 million, is a young country in demographic terms, and it is getting younger still. The median age is around 17 years and the actual growth rate is reportedly close to 3 per cent.[292] Hence forecasts show that the population will increase by more than 50 per cent to around 20 million people during the remaining part of this century.

The majority of the population live in the countryside. However, the destabilisation of the rural areas during the 1980s caused an extensive stream of refugees, of whom around 10 per cent searched for social security in neighbouring countries, with some 30 per cent (4.5 million) seeking refuge in urban areas, principally in and around Maputo, Beira and Nampula. The processes for the resettlement and reintegration of the population have been strengthened as a result of the recent elections and peace agreement.

The majority of the peasantry is self-sufficient in an agricultural sector with low productivity. Although only a small part of the agricultural production (10–20 per cent) constitutes a surplus available for marketing, the agricultural sector remains the largest sector of the Mozambican economy, presently corresponding to about 35 per cent of gross output. A re-established rural economy with opportunities to take care of the peasants' production potential thus constitutes an absolutely crucial precondition for democratic development and the country's economic and political future.

A precondition for a normalisation of the rural economy is that local food production can be resumed. Opportunities for local production are a necessity if people are to be persuaded to move back to the rural areas. At the same time the resumption of subsistence in food at national level is the quickest way to improve the negative balance of trade. Increased domestic food production would quickly reduce the import requirement, at the same time as a return to the rural areas created preconditions for increased production of traditional export goods from agriculture, such as cashew nuts and cotton.[293] Another precondition for people to be stimulated to move back to their home areas in the countryside is that trade and communications, as well as education and health-care, can quickly be rehabilitated.

National planning for the reconstruction of the country has undergone two phases. The first phase was introduced as early as 1989, when the government selected 40 districts where the war was not more intense than there was capacity for increased food production. These districts would be included in a very broad programme for rehabilitation and development in prioritised districts (PDP). PDP was an attempt to concretise the political strategy, and means that disaster aid would be designed so that it could change over to rehabilitation and development work when the situation improved.

In the second phase the government developed a national reconstruction programme (PRN), which aims to cover the whole country. This programme is based on inventory work executed in each district and province and collated centrally.

With regard to identifying inputs within the programme, there have been two guiding principles. One is that inputs should be financed in the long term using local resources. This requires harsh prioritisation and strong decentralisation of the identification of needs. It is those most closely involved at local level in each district who will identify the needs that must be satisfied. The second is that the largest common resource the districts have is a large surplus workforce. This means that labour-intensive inputs ought to be prioritised. This also leads to those involved in the programme benefiting economically and socially.

The overall goal of the programme is to return rapidly to 1981 levels of food production and social services. Growth in marketed production is expected to be 13, 17 and 20 per cent respectively during the first three years of the programme. In the first year it is expected that growth will mainly involve improved trade functions. In the following years growth is expected to reflect the increased levels of production.

The plan for national reconstruction, which focuses entirely on rural development, contains three important components:

1. Creating national security. The rural areas are still militarised, and only a fraction of the 2 million mines known to have been planted have been removed. Maintaining law and order should become a task for an effective police force. The country's external defence should be taken care of by a professional army. The rehabilitation of the country's communications system, not least the road network, is extremely important for this process.

2. Increasing domestic production. This mainly involves increasing production in rural areas. The programme for the prioritised districts is the basis for this, even if there are many objections to supporting only those districts which have a potential for growth. It is rather in those districts where the security situation has been most difficult and where the preconditions for rapid rehabilitation are not so developed that support should be greatest in order to restore social security.

3. Re-integrating of internal refugees and demobilised soldiers. In total over 6 million Mozambicans need to return to their home areas. This will entail heavy costs and demands for coordination between short-term disaster aid and the more long-term programme for national reconstruction. Hoes and seed will be supplied, as well as food, so that the first harvest can be salvaged. Disputes about land matters must be resolved in order to create stability in agricultural development.

In order for it to be possible for the programme, in its detailed formulation, to build on the local population's social and material needs and identification of necessary measures, and thus facilitate a future mobilisation of resources, extensive work has been going on in the provinces and districts to adjust the programme's general guidelines to the rural population's actual current living conditions. Apart from a large mobilisation of local resources, the programme will come to require a massive increase in the flow of aid for its implementation. The National Reconstruction Plan can be seen as an inventory of the most striking needs at district level. Thus it will constitute a first step in a process of developing planning mechanisms, which will manage to take care of long-term post-war development. As from 1995 the PRN material will be integrated into the regular triennial plan of public investments (PTIP).

Distribution of land

The future management of local land distribution matters is a central component in Frelimo's attempt to create a new balance of power between the authorities in rural districts and the traditional power in the rural areas.[294] Traditionally, no private land ownership exists in the literal sense. Each farming family has a right of use which is orally confirmed and is inheritable.

The extensive population movements over the last ten years have affected the previous pattern of land use. However, this does not mean that millions of refugees do not know which land is theirs. Even the most urbanised civil servants and politicians in Maputo can actually differentiate between certain cocoa palms or cashew trees in the home province where the families' traditional lands are located – even if they have not been there during the last fifteen years. Restoring stability in the distribution and utilisation of land must be a high-priority task, which peace will entail, confronting the new migration in the rural areas.

From certain donor quarters there has been pressure on Mozambique's government to introduce the system of legal ratification, which the regulation on the Land Law prescribes, quickly. The reason behind this rush is naturally that many private farmers are pressing to obtain a permanent and formalised right of use for the lands they are exploiting. This long-term security is necessary in order for them to carry out the productivity-improving investments that many donors wish to support. The government's argument for not accelerating this process is that the settlement pattern must be given time to stabilise before land in the areas where disputes are expected can be allocated to individual users. A new and decentralised administrative and political system would be given an unfortunate beginning if the central power's last measure before decentralisation were for a land distribution fixed for ten years or so which was not legitimate in the eyes of local society.

This discussion principally concerns areas around larger towns and district centres, and around the state farms in the earlier Portuguese settler areas. Around the 'colonial farms' this matter is extremely sensitive, because the farmers have already been deprived of their lands twice, first by the Portuguese settlers and then by Fremilo as after independence their spontaneous land reform was destroyed when the state farms appropriated the land. To force a redistribution of land through a system of legal ratification in the present turbulent situation risks ignoring the 'rightful' user families, and will create more conflicts than it resolves.

Traditional peasant farming land in remote areas will not be entitled to a system of legal ratification. For these peasants there is another threat, which is dependent on the way in which the organised repatriation of refugees from neighbouring countries and larger refugee concentrations within Mozambique is implemented. If people are moved in large groups to areas where they are allocated land through an arbitrary process, conditions will be created for conflicts which will break out if and when the peasant farmers who 'repatriate' themselves return to their home areas. Land regulation must build on local principles of legitimacy.

Alternatives to the adjustment programme

A frequently forwarded view when the short-term effects for the population of the economic recovery programme are discussed, or when its possibilities for contributing to sustainable rural development are questioned, is that there is no other alternative to the programme.

It is argued that short-term measures must be adopted in order to increase export production and thereby correct the macro-economic imbalance. These measures require increased international aid. The preconditions for mobilising this aid are that structural adjustments are made according to the programme and criteria developed by the IMF and the World Bank.

It is further stressed that the IMF's task is to ensure the necessary macro-economic measures which, *inter alia*, permit debt repayment and thereby maintain credibility in the eyes of the international finance system. The design of the structural adjustment programme is adapted to what the IMF considers that the international aid donors are prepared to finance.

It is obvious that some kind of an economic adjustment is necessary in order to correct the macro-economic imbalances created for several reasons in Mozambique during the 1980s. This does not, however, necessarily imply that the adjustment programme should be designed in the first instance to satisfy the creditors' demands for debt repayment through increased exports. Any rehabilitation programme should primarily be directed towards creating preconditions for long-term sustainable rural development. However, such a design would require both extensive debt forgiveness and a future increase in the flow of aid.

The problem is that the IMF's and the World Bank's mandate, together with the required international resource mobilisation force them to concentrate to an increasing extent on the question of how to design the structural adjustment programme in order to achieve a macro-economic balance in as short a time as possible. In order for sustainable economic development in the long term to be possible, however, it is not a matter of simply restructuring the existing economy, as this study has previously indicated. In the case of Mozambique it is rather a matter of creating an economic structure which historically has never existed.

The structural adjustment programme is therefore starting at the wrong end. The problem does not only consist of the fact that the country implemented a series of monetary policy measures before the fiscal regulatory framework had been built as required for the measures to achieve the intended macro-economic effect.

The main problem is the predominant perception that the short-term goal (macro-economic balance) is a condition for achieving the long-term goal (structural transformation) and not the other way around. This has entailed too great a concentration on monetary policy measures at the expense of measures to correct the real restrictions of the economy and the sectoral efforts that need to be carried out. The tragic result is that liberalisation is increasingly destroying the domestic production structure, i.e. the measures for achieving the short-term goal are undermining the preconditions for both the short-term and the long-term programme goals.

It is for this reason that the domestic production structure and the country's economy must be expanded if the adjustment programme is to succeed. Mozambique's present economic base is simply too small for traditional macro-economic measures to have a chance of producing the intended result.

Against the background of Mozambique's specific features, the scope of the present rehabilitation programme is thus inadequate. The possibility of achieving a long-term economic balance, which historically has never existed, is more dependent on the growth of a domestic production base than on further cutbacks in public expenditure and living standards. Without a recovery in domestic production, it will not be possible to resolve the problem of poverty or the great imbalances in the state budget and the current account. Increased exports are no optimal short-term solution either. Greater effects on the macro-economic balance should be achieved by replacing food imports with domestic production.

The alternative to the current policy is instead to put the long-term goal of structural transformation first, as a condition for a future macro-economic balance. Hence instead of short-term orientated efforts to achieve a macro-economic balance through increased exports, the development plans should be *more inward-oriented*. The creation of a sustainable market economy requires a more expansive fiscal policy in order to *create the required demand*. The need for such a policy is strongly reinforced by the present peace process and the resettlement of the rural population, which puts insupportable pressure on the state budget under the present restrictions imposed by the IMF. Such a policy requires both debt forgiveness and increased regionally balanced investments in rural areas.

Through the Mozambican plan for national reconstruction, an alternative, or perhaps a supplement, to the economic and social recovery programme may be presented. With its emphasis on efforts within the real economy, it implies greater opportunities for long-term economic development. In order for the plan to be realised, however, it is not enough that the ceasefire and the peace agreement should be respected. An increased flow of aid will also be required from the international donors so that the financing of the plan can be guaranteed. Above all else, the country's current debt burden must be forgiven.

Required debt forgiveness

With its debt amounting to some $5,000 million, representing 400 per cent of its GDP, Mozambique is one of the most indebted countries by world standards.[295] Debt servicing amounts to some $550 million. After debt rescheduling, Mozambique *de facto* pays some $65 million per year, which is equivalent to around 25 per cent of its earnings from the export of goods and services.[296]

The external financing requirements for 1994 amount to some $1,500 million, including some $400 million in debt relief.[297] The requirement corresponds more or less to the same amount pledged by donors at the 1993 consultative group meeting.

From the very beginning, the economic and social rehabilitation programme was facing a race against time. The challenge consisted of creating conditions for increased growth which would permit the closure of the financial gap using the country's own resources, grants or at least concessional loans before the non-concessional ones have to be paid at the beginning of the year 2000.[298] In order to achieve this, the projections of the Bretton Woods institutions, formulated at the beginning of the 1990s, aimed at closing the gap around the year 2000 through an economic growth of 5 per cent a year.

With regard to Mozambique's limited production of raw materials, spare parts and capital goods, a production increase of 5 per cent per year means that imports must increase by as much in the foreseeable future. It was calculated, therefore, that imports of goods would increase from $0.9 billion in 1991 to $1.4 billion in 1994. In order to facilitate this, exports of goods and services must increase from $365 million in 1991 to $535 million in 1994, which can be compared with export revenues for 1993, which amounted to $370 million. The export increase is principally based on exports of minerals, non-traditional goods and on revenues from the transit trade and migrant labour.

As a consequence of current debt servicing which must be paid, the financial gap will increase further in the short term. The requirement for foreign financing will continue to amount to over $1 billion, a sum corresponding to 75 per cent of GDP.

It is the use of the imports and the preconditions for achieving a sufficiently rapid production increase which are crucial in determining whether the gap can later be closed. With regard to the deficiencies in the implementation of the rehabilitation programme, as previously discussed, it is doubtful whether such a production increase can come about. The undertakings made by the IMF in respect of the country's future financial resources also give cause for concern.

Over-optimistic prognoses

Exports which, apart from non-traditional exports with limited international and domestic outlets, mainly consist of coal, tea, shrimps and cotton, are expected to increase very rapidly over the next ten years. However, few of the conditions necessary for this export increase at present exist.

The prognoses made by the Bretton Woods institutions appear to have been oriented towards convincing bilateral donors to, *ex ante*, contribute financial resources for the implementation of the programme, rather than towards arriving at actions based on factual possibilities and realities. Hence, when comparing the different policy framework papers over time with the factual results obtained, the exaggerated optimism is striking.

This is typically the case for, *inter alia*, the development of exports as a means of closing the financial gap. At the beginning of the PRES, the export of coal was used as one golden solution for closing the gap; some years later, the development of non-traditional exports was portrayed as the solution, since simple calculations showed that coal exports in the order of magnitude of the prognosis were totally unrealistic.[299]

The IMF's assessments of anticipated export revenues from increased exports of cashew nuts, shrimps, cotton, tea and sugar are also on the optimistic side. No investments have so far been allocated to destroyed production plants or infrastructure, although this is essential if the calculated export quantities are to be achieved. At the same time, historical development on the world market shows that export prices have developed considerably less well than the IMF envisaged.[300]

There is also the fact that the export increase functions almost as a disincentive, as it is exposed to a form of international taxation. Improved export revenues imply, apart from the share of the export value that the exporting enterprise can dispose of itself, increased demands for debt repayment. The country cannot itself dispose freely of its export revenues because a certain percentage of the export revenues is tied to pay off debt servicing.

The IMF also reckons on a continued increased flow of aid. As has been made clear in earlier chapters, a large part of the aid flow into Mozambique is motivated by political reasons. The West's diplomatic and political support for development towards a majority-ruled South Africa has affected the extent of aid to those countries that suffered from the apartheid policy and military destabilisation. Also important is the regional cooperation and support for SADCC in order to reduce dependency on South Africa.

With a changed domestic political situation in South Africa, the aid flow to the frontline states will probably diminish. Several of the factors that motivated a high flow of aid will become weakened through the end of destabilisation and the abolition of apartheid. Competition from a majority-ruled South Africa for scarce international aid resources must also be taken into account.

To this should be added the developments in the Eastern bloc. The previously extensive aid from the East of around $150 million per year has ceased. It is also probable that the aid dependency that arose in the Eastern bloc after the break-up of the Soviet Union will come to draw on international aid resources at the expense of African countries. In other words, it appears highly improbable that the present flow of aid to Southern Africa will be sustained and even less probable that it will increase.

Current financing requirement

Table 11.1, which clarifies the external financing requirement in millions of dollars and which builds on the World Bank's prognoses for the period 1992–94, reveals the extent of the problem. As is evident, the financing requirement considerably exceeds the resources. The problem for Mozambique is that economic development has not allowed any repayment of debts. At the same time too few measures have been adopted to write these off. The debt renegotiations carried out have principally meant that interest costs have been capitalised and that the total debt has been accumulated, i.e. problems have only been deferred to the future.

However, estimates of the financial gaps made by the Bretton Woods institutions are spurious, as no detailed analysis of the size and composition of import demands over time has been carried out. Nevertheless, the present current account deficit and increasing debt servicing are drawing attention to the immediate need for a more accurate strategy to be formulated in order to be able to close the financial gap.

Table 11.1 Mozambique's external financing requirements, 1992–94 ($ million)

	1992	1993	1994
Current account deficit	-750	-820	-855
Debt service	-335	-330	-295
Deferments, build-up of reserves and other outflows	-105	-85	-35
External financing requirements	-1,190	-1,235	-1,195
Existing commitments/loans	155	110	80
Financing gap I	-1,035	-1,125	-1,115
Expected new commitments:			
Grants	530	550	565
Loans	90	115	135
External direct investments	35	35	40
Anticipated financing	655	700	740
Remaining financing gap	-380	-425	-375
Debt relief needed	380	425	375

Source: Calculations and grouping based on World Bank, April 1992.

The problems will become even greater in a few years time. The debt servicing payments will rise substantially in 1995 when the current debt rescheduling agreement with the Paris Club expires. From the year 2000, debt servicing will increase further as it will not be possible to reschedule the payment of arrears again.

The need for an immediate and total debt forgiveness is also shared by the World Bank. Mozambique is one of the world's poorest countries, with a per capita income of less than $100. More than 65 per cent of the population live in absolute poverty. The World Bank's calculations show that even according to the most optimistic scenario, with an annual growth of 6 per cent, by the year 2000 the country will only have achieved a per capita income corresponding to 90 per cent of the income for 1982.[301]

The World Bank's definitions of countries with great needs for actual debt relief include four conditions:

1. the debt's share of GDP should exceed 50 per cent;
2. the debt's share of exports should exceed 275 per cent;
3. debt servicing's share of exports should exceed 30 per cent, and;
4. interest payment's share of exports should exceed 20 per cent.[302]

Mozambique thus satisfies all the criteria set by the World bank for the world's most indebted countries, for whom a more extensive debt forgiveness should be seen as the only possible way for long-term sustainable economic development to be brought about. The alternative is a continued and never-ending inflow of aid, which is naturally both unrealistic and undesirable.

Discussions on other types of payments of arrears to the international finance institutions, other than those made through financing by bilateral donors, must be initiated promptly. With regard to the debts to the IMF, one course of action for such debt forgiveness could be that the IMF, in order to compensate itself for costs, sells off parts of its significant gold reserves. The debts to the World Bank could be written off by using the profits that the Bank has been able to assimilate through its lending activities during the 1980s.

Reorientation of aid

At the same time as Mozambique is in a class of its own as the world's most aid-dependent country, its need for international aid is insatiable. Because of the country's geopolitical position it has been afflicted by both the political turbulence and the climatic disturbances which have afflicted Southern Africa during the 1980s. The country lacks the resources to guarantee the population's survival. Enormous inputs will be needed to reintegrate the country's internal refugees into the rural economy in order to avoid continued political instability in the region when peace has been consolidated. From an international peace and development perspective, therefore, not only continued aid but also an increased inflow of aid is justified.

The increased aid dependency that this implies is the political price Mozambique must pay for its colonial inheritance and the regional and international power-political realities. The long-term preconditions for reducing this dependency are determined both by the extent to which the negative effects which aid has hitherto entailed can be avoided, and by whether international aid can contribute to bringing about long-term sustainable rural development.

Future challenges of aid

For a stable transition from war to peace and a long-term and sustainable rural development, a development model is required which allows more equal regional distribution, decentralised decision-making and local identification of need. In this way a better adjustment to African traditions, cultural patterns and popular participation can occur.

However, few of the conditions necessary for the emergence of an alternative, more territorially-directed, development strategy appear to exist. Ever since the 1960s, the orientation of international aid has rested on the African élite's view of the necessity for rapidly creating a nation-state. Aid has principally been channelled into countries with clearly expressed ambitions for bringing about economic growth and a fair distribution of societal resources, supported by forced modernisation. The strengthened homogenisation which occurred at international level regarding the goals/means for development, for which the Bretton Woods institutions were a mouthpiece during the 1980s, have increasingly reduced the economic and political scope for an alternative development route. Continued enforced modernisation constitutes the predominant paradigm for the majority of actors with political impact, both within and outside the country. International support for modernisation has been dependent for its implementation on, and has strengthened, the limited state élite in Maputo. At the same time few demands have been made for essential regional distribution. Through its reliance on enforced modernisation, aid has contributed to creating an élite which has increasingly distanced itself from the population. The aid has, for understandable reasons, been too centrally orientated and directed more towards economic growth than towards development and political legitimacy.

As a result of the difficulties of modernisation, the Mozambican state has successively failed in most of its legitimacy-creating functions. In this way the conditions necessary for the government's nation-building have been substantially diminished. The Mozambican state has not only failed thus far in providing individual security for its inhabitants or in providing an efficient and effective administration. It has also failed in its third function, namely providing the social safety net which the population expected after the end of the liberation struggle and the coming of independence. Such a provision is a precondition for the legitimacy of the state to be restored and for nation-building to be possible at all.

Aid policy must tone down its vision of the modernised nation-state project in order to become adjusted to a greater extent to multi-ethnic societies, sub-nations, which all have their own special traditions and cultural overtones. The role of aid should be to help to restore the state's legitimacy so that a multi-nation state can be allowed to develop. Aid should therefore in future aim to provide the Mozambican state with such resources that its social undertakings can also be fulfilled. This requires that aid begins to move away from enforced modernisation as the only axiom for development and look more actively for alternative ways of improving the population's living conditions.

Such a search is not a matter of questioning the necessity of modernisation. Study of the peasants' slash-and-burn production methods show clearly the limitations of traditional farming. Long-term rural development therefore requires that the peasant farmers' productivity and purchasing power be improved. Agriculture thus needs to be modernised in one way or another. The same need for modernisation also exists within the industrial sector, not least to facilitate the growth of as energy-efficient and environment-friendly production as possible. This is a matter rather of finding criteria for identifying the extent of modernisation, its direction and the pace at which it should be implemented. How aid should contribute in the longer term to creating this situation, in which Western modernisation can supplement the traditional patterns and cultural customs of African society, will become an increasingly urgent question, which future aid planning must consider.

The future design of aid

The design of future bilateral grant aid to Mozambique ought to have as its overall long-term goal to contribute to a sustainable economic rural development. In the short term aid should be designed so that it contributes as far as possible to the population's survival and ensures that social chaos does not arise. The aid should further be designed so that its short-term inputs do not counteract its long-term goals. It is against the background of these starting points that the direction of future aid should be formulated.

The intention of the aid should be to contribute to more tolerable living conditions for the poorest and most oppressed, i.e. poverty alleviation. The poverty alleviation needed will require a significant shift in expenditures towards social sectors. However, bearing in mind the limited ability of the government to increase revenues, implying severe constraints in the recurrent budget, it is indeed unlikely that the government will be able to take on such a reorientation in future budget allocations, unless it receives extensive support from the donor community.

In the same way that it is difficult to imagine any long-term poverty alleviation without economic growth, it is not possible in the case of Mozambique to foresee any sustained economic growth without poverty alleviation. Hence the two factors are intertwined. In order for the population to resettle in the countryside, thus increasing agricultural production, the social infrastructure needs to be rehabilitated, giving the peasantry access not only to water, but also to health-care and education. Without such a rehabilitation the process of resettlement will be halted, and the recreation of security and social order delayed.

Undoubtedly, the urban population – which drastically increased with refugees escaping from insecurity in the rural areas – has suffered from reduced subsidies, few employment opportunities and low real wages. Special programmes, supporting around 50,000 families located in 13 different urban zones, have been established during the last few years. The impact of these efforts has still to be evaluated. However, sustainable poverty reduction can only be achieved if conditions are created in the countryside which make it possible and feasible for the recently urbanised population to resettle.

Accordingly, poverty reduction in Mozambique has to be primarily directed towards the rural population. With the population's resettlement, social differentiation has been reinforced. Returning peasants without access to land are forced to provide cheap labour for those with access to land at income levels far below the level of sustainable reproduction.

Thus poverty alleviation needs to focus on increased employment, income and purchasing power for the majority of the peasantry. The physical and social infrastructure must be rehabilitated, and support given to a strengthened commercial network providing peasantry with land, outlets and incentives for agricultural surplus production. Accordingly, demands and markets have to be created in rural areas. It is unlikely that the emerging market forces will have the long-term perspectives required for this development to take place.

One precondition for international aid to benefit the poor rural population to an increasing degree and contribute to long-term sustainable economic rural development is, however, that its present one-sided emphasis on economic adjustment and support for the modern sectors is toned down. It is in fact correct that long-term rural development also requires support for both macro-economic adjustment and development of the modern sector. A macro-economic balance is a necessary, if far from sufficient, condition for stable prices and trading conditions in the same way that the exchange between town and country requires a functioning road network, a credit system and a capable central administration. However, as has been made clear, the economic actors of the market are not at present channelling any resources to the rural areas to increase the peasants' productivity and thereby create the still non-existent domestic market. These measures must be adopted by the state with the help of international aid. However, neither the present design of the economic adjustment programme nor its implementation allow any scope for this. A free-market allocation of foreign currency implies continued imports in order to satisfy the little domestic demand existing already, and this presently exists chiefly in the towns.

Besides considerable increases and reallocations in government expenditure to the benefit of the rural population, poverty alleviation underlines the need for a reorientation of aid and the implementation of a more inward-looking strategy. Relief aid has to be phased out and integrated with prevailing plans for national reconstruction, giving priority to local food production and long-term development. Hence the prevailing tendency within the Bretton Woods institutions to play

SEARCHING FOR A WAY OUT

down the importance of self-sufficiency in food production as long as food security can be achieved should be questioned. In fact, such an attitude will further hamper sustained growth in the long term, as a consequence of lost dynamics and interaction between agricultural food production, industrial processing and internal trade.

Aid channels

The preconditions for international aid reaching the poor target groups in rural areas in the short term and contributing to sustainable rural development in the long term have long been restricted by the prevailing security situation. To too great an extent the direction and use of aid is identified and planned in the capital, Maputo.

However, as has been made uncomfortably clear, the Mozambican state administration is starting to become increasingly paralysed and risks collapse. A *laissez-faire* mentality and corruption are spreading within the administration. The aid donors' endeavours to bypass the Mozambican administration at central level, and carry out aid-related activities in as close cooperation as possible with the target groups at local level, has directed interest towards the possibility of different foreign NGOs increasing their aid activity. However, as previously stated, the solution does not lie in channelling increasing resources to NGOs in the hope that they will build up their own structures, parallel to but separate from the state. It is far from certain that a better identification of need and use of resources can be achieved through increased resources to these organisations. In too many cases the organisations' independent activity at local level has distanced itself from the local population's need and thereby contributed further to diminishing the population's confidence in the local administration. It is thus important for bilateral aid to find new channels within the central administration in order to reach the local administration and the needy target groups.

Aid must not only be more equally regionally distributed, but also be decentralised in order to get as close to the target groups as possible. A more equal distribution of power requires, quite simply, a decentralisation of decision-making and financial resources. Important questions are whether there is the administrative capability at central level needed in order to decentralise. Above all, there is the question of whether there are sufficient resources to decentralise. At the same time the local identification of need implies a great challenge for aid. Hitherto aid has been based on identification of need carried out together with central structures and authorities. But a continued identification of need in this way thus runs the risk of distancing itself increasingly from the reality. These procedures must therefore be re-examined if aid is to be of maximum benefit to the local population. Aid requirements can no longer be solely identified in consultation with authorities at central level, but must also be based on the needs of the target groups, adjusted to the people's cultural patterns and traditional habits.

The fundamental question of ownership

As previously stated, the international aid donors have come to take over an increasingly large part of aid planning and the implementation of different aid activities. The international flow of aid's extreme importance for the Mozambican economy has seriously reduced the country's control of influence over its own development (ownership). The situation has got worse because the different aid donors have had difficulties among themselves in finding forms for coordination and uniform methods for implementation, result evaluation and reporting. The government has been forced to attend more and more meetings, in which it tends to participate more and more as a passive observer because, quite simply, it no longer has any time for its own thinking.

In order for the country to achieve the best possible result from the aid and, in the longer term, to be able to reduce its aid dependency, immediate measures must be taken to correct this situation. The question of 'ownership' and the importance of getting the government 'back into the driving seat' has also begun to be discussed at the donor meetings as a result of the lack of efficiency and other palpable results in the use of aid resources.

Decentralised aid, based on local participation in the identification of need and in planning and implementation, is therefore a necessary precondition for increased 'ownership'. At the same time this measure is not enough. The importance of coordination of aid-related activities among the various donors cannot be over-emphasised. This refers not only to methods for implementation and reporting routines. It chiefly refers to formulation of policy, methods of approach, and regional and sectoral distribution. Different donors within the same sector cannot continue to use different policies, often within different geographical areas. A uniform policy must thus be developed for every sector.

The responsibility for formulating such a sector policy lies with the Mozambican government. Completely regardless of aid dependency, the country's leadership must begin to say 'no thank-you' to aid if the donors do not subordinate themselves to the guidelines the government has developed. However, donors can do a great deal to allow, through capacity-building, the empowerment of institutions and nationals which is a precondition for this.

Future challenges

Frelimo's attempt rapidly to modernise Mozambican society did not pay sufficient attention to the popular legitimacy of traditional society. The state-nation building project never found any nation for its state. The external forces that Frelimo challenged with its development strategy succeeded in their economic and military destabilisation through exploiting the widening economic and social differences to which the rural policy gave rise.

The future for Mozambique is uncertain. There is a risk that the country will continue to be subordinate to foreign capital interests and/or that its colonial borders will be broken up. In order for the fragile state-nation to be consolidated, the economic adjustment programme must be redesigned. Rural development must take precedence over efforts to increase exports and debt repayments. This is also necessary if continued violence is to be avoided in the rural areas. There is also a political need to establish conditions for decentralised decision-making and a democratic distribution of power.

The great challenge for international aid to Mozambique therefore lies in finding a formulation such that modernisation, which the aid must of necessity continue to represent, can conform with African cultural reality at local level. The key concept in such aid is decentralisation and local identification of need, with the aim of increasing popular participation and strengthening the democratic development process.

12

Instead of a Conclusion

Introduction

As has been made clear in this study, the implementation of a national development strategy is not a socially neutral process. It affects and is affected by the political and economic development of the power structure at local level.

At the same time the study has showed that a development history analysis cannot be based only on the strategy's national roots. Because of increasing internationalisation, the analysis must take into account the globalisation of the development process. During the 1980s the nation-state's function has been increasingly reduced to being a filter, whose ability to filter off or reform external influence fluctuates.

The more radical the societal transformation aimed for by the strategy, the greater the need for internal capability and political strength as a protection against the influence of the the rest of the world. The formulation of a foreign and national security policy is thus important. A radical foreign policy reduces the filter's ability to withstand external pressure. In a certain specific historical context a radical foreign policy can actually completely undermine the nation-state's ability to filter the external influence to which the country becomes exposed.

Mozambique is a striking example of this. Frelimo's vision of independent socialist development, which aimed substantially to improve living conditions for the majority of the rural population within the decade, is contrasted today with a reality where the majority of people live in conditions worse than those of the colonial era, with its forced labour and racist degradation.

Against this background the present study had two aims. The first was to identify and describe some of the external and internal factors, which together and in interaction affected the implementation of the Mozambican development strategy and the results achieved. The second aim was also to create a model, within which a development history can be described in a way which takes into consideration the complex network of such interaction between external and internal factors, over time.

The simplification of reality that would be entailed in limiting the work to entering historical events together in boxes, even if at different levels, naturally has serious limitations. The result risks becoming an over-statistical description of an historical development. In this study we have attempted to avoid this by directing attention towards the connections between the historical events described in the boxes at different levels.

Our work has, as indicated in the introduction, been limited to indicating this interaction, based on empirical experiences, and discussing the different channels and methods through which it occurs. The work does not make any claim to attempt to measure the strength of the various connections or to deduce the factors which have had the greatest influence on the development of events. The arrows in the figures should be seen as symbols of interactions between levels rather than as illustrations of demonstrable causal connections.

In this section we will attempt to clarify parts of the complex web of factors in this interaction which have been described in different sections of this study and which reflect important elements of Mozambican development history. We will attempt to do this on the one hand by briefly summarising some of the vertical and horizontal links indicated and on the other by completing earlier figures by introducing, in Figure 4, a number of arrows which each represent one example of this interaction. The concluding text therefore refers continuously to the numbering of the arrows in the figure. As indicated in the introduction, the aim of the figures and text is principally to reveal the complexities and difficulties and to attempt to concretise and illustrate the multiplicity of existing connections.

Starting position

The starting position for Frelimo's vision and the design of its development strategy was politically favourable. The USA had lost the Vietnam war and the non-aligned movement had set demands for a new international economic order. Internationally there was scope for development strategies where the state's role and the necessity for modernisation were emphasised (1). Regionally, Southern Africa was characterised by the advances of the colonial liberation struggle. As distinct from South Africa's relations with Angola, the Vorster regime was seeking economic cooperation with Mozambique instead of confrontation (2). As a consequence of President Carter's *détente* policy and demands for human rights, the regime in South Africa was also exposed to international pressure to reform the apartheid system (3).

The economic starting position was considerably less favourable. The country's economy on independence was characterised by an extreme

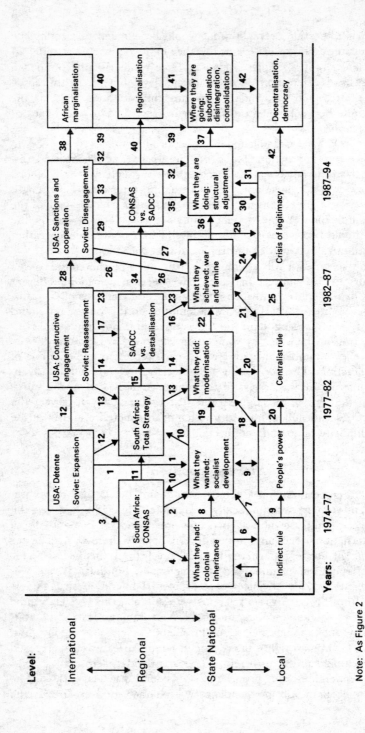

Figure 4 Interaction between different levels

Note: As Figure 2

need for service revenues from neighbouring countries (especially South Africa) in order to be able to keep the chronic deficit in the balance of trade, which characterised the country during the colonial era, at a fairly reasonable level (4). Productivity within agriculture was very low. This referred not only to the traditional sector, where slash-and-burn constituted the predominant mode of production, but also to the modern sector, where the workforce recruited by force held back any motive for labour-saving measures (5). There was also the fact that both the administrative and the productive sectors lacked educated personnel, since the majority of the population had been denied the right to education and management posts during the colonial era (6). The effects of this were evident not least in agriculture, where the majority of Portuguese farmers and traders left the country at the time of independence. Farms were abandoned and the urban population's food supplies were seriously threatened (7).

The positive political environment, together with the difficult economic starting position, formed the background to design of the country's development strategy. Traditional modes of production within agriculture would be changed and forced labour abolished so that productivity and purchasing power among the rural population, which a lasting economic development required, could be brought about. Abandoned farms would be taken over and become the hub of the modernisation of rural areas which Frelimo considered necessary to break down the distorted structures of the colonial era and facilitate the production increase required to cover the chronic deficit in the balance of trade (8). Colonial power structures and institutions would be demolished, as well as the traditional power structure which characterised rural areas. This applied not least to the removal of those traditionally in power, who were exploited for the colonial power's indirect rule and would be replaced after independence by the people's power which developed during the liberation struggle (9).

Foreign policy became equally radical. In order for economic development to come about, a regional environment at peace was required. Black majority-ruled development, not just in Rhodesia but also in South Africa, was considered to be a precondition for this. The analysis implied extensive political support for ZANU and the ANC (10).

Horizontal and vertical links in interaction

The country's radical development strategy, in combination with its radical foreign policy, never coped with the increased pressure from the outside world, whose political make-up changed drastically during the beginning of the 1980s.

As a consequence of changes in domestic policy and the intensification of the struggle against apartheid which the South African government was experiencing at regional level, not least due to Mozambique's radical domestic and foreign policies (10), President Botha had some years previously replaced Prime Minister Vorster as the country's political leader and launched his 'Total Strategy' (11). In the USA President Reagan took over a changed view of both regional conflicts and the preconditions for development in the Third World. President Carter's *détente* policy was considered to have provided too much scope for Soviet expansion in the Third World (12). Regional conflicts were now suddenly analysed in terms of East–West conflicts where communism should be actively opposed wherever it spread (13). Development theory toned down the role of the state and development planning in favour of market forces and liberal domestic and foreign trade. Hopes for vastly increased aid in the form of massive transfers of resources which would facilitate the implementation of desirable modernisation were dashed completely. The situation was rather the reverse – the costs of modernisation increased dramatically during the second half of the 1970s and at the beginning of the 1980s, first as a result of greatly increased international oil prices and then as a result of increased interest costs for the loans taken up (14).

In connection with Zimbabwe's independence and the fact that the frontline states took the initiative in 1980 to form the regional cooperation organisation, SADCC, in order to reduce the region's dependence on South Africa, the apartheid regime's military and economic destabilisation of Mozambique took off on a large scale (15). This destabilisation forced millions of peasants to flee and in the long run destroyed the economic and security preconditions for the implementation of the strategy (16).

At the same time SADCC cooperation did not develop as quickly as the frontline states' leaders had hoped. The anticipated service revenues from the regional transit traffic failed to appear, despite considerable investments in the transport infrastructure in Mozambique in order to steer back the flow of goods from the South African transport network. It was not only the South African military destabilisation which destroyed the preconditions for this. As a consequence of the structural transformation of the international transport trade and the introduction of integrated door-to-door transportation, the region's commercial actors still preferred continued cooperation with South Africa because Mozambique could not offer the necessary international network and information systems (17).

Over the period Frelimo's domestic policy problems had increased as a result of forced modernisation and allied large-scale investments. The classic conflict between popular mobilisation, on the one hand,

and short-term sacrifices for more long-term accumulation on the other, increased the political tensions. The party's alliance with the peasants was abandoned and people's power was sacrificed at the altar of the rate of growth (18).

The shortage of a skilled labour force, as well as political and social tensions, meant that agricultural production within the modern sector was not developed as expected. Frelimo's vision of rural socialisation, with communal villages and producer cooperatives, did not pay enough attention either to the rural population's production preconditions or to its cultural customs and settlement pattern (19). Frelimo's transformation from a liberation front to a Marxist-Leninist avant-garde party, together with the centrally managed planning, which was considered to be a precondition for the implementation of modernisation, meant that large numbers of the rural population questioned Frelimo's legitimacy (20).

Falling export revenues, weakening service revenues and increased expenditure on oil imports, together with rising interest costs, decreased the country's ability to provide the peasants with the incentive goods they wanted in exchange for their participation in the production of agricultural surpluses. The shortage of food became acute in connection with the drought which struck the region at the beginning of the 1980s (21). As one stage in the South African economic destabilisation, the number of migrant workers from Mozambique was simultaneously dramatically reduced. As well as reduced service revenues, food supplies for the families of migrant workers, who were suffering from the drought, diminished further (22). The conditions imposed for receiving international emergency relief reduced the state authorities' role at both central and local levels (23).

Unsatisfied material basic needs, together with increasing thefts and constant rumours of corruption, increasingly undermined the legitimacy of central power. The state failed to satisfy the rural population's expectations of what political independence and liberation from Portuguese colonialism would entail (24).

The problems were not just material ones. The political analysis which formed the basis for the country's national security policy had proved to be incorrect. The security threat did not consist of any conventional attack, which the Mozambican army had been trained to repel. The security threat came from the low-intensity destabilisation which South Africa set in motion, through Renamo, with the help of kidnapped poor children and youths from the rural areas. The enemy's tool was internal and created bewilderment and paralysis among the rural population. Frelimo's inability to guarantee the population daily food and military security aggravated the legitimacy crisis both in the rural areas and in the towns (25).

Frelimo's mistakes

As already explained, the attempts to modernise Mozambican society did not pay sufficient attention to the popular legitimacy of traditional society. External destabilisation found a route for itself through the widening economic and social differences to which the rural policy gave rise. A freak of nature increased the burden.

The present analysis of development history has consciously avoided any detailed discussion of the extent to which the difference between the vision on which the development strategy built, and the reality which it proved to create, depends on Frelimo's mistakes. It is natural that there are many opinions on this matter.

With regard to domestic policy, one can seize on and criticise the forced modernisation, the misunderstanding of the role of traditional society, and Frelimo's transformation into a Marxist avant-garde party. With regard to foreign policy, with hindsight one can question the analysis which formed the basis for international indebtedness, the economic and military preconditions which lay behind the formulation of the country's foreign and security policies and the background against which Frelimo based its development of aid cooperation with the Eastern bloc and the Soviet Union to the extent that it *de facto* did.

One question that could be posed, with an answer at hand, is whether Frelimo ought to have chosen another route. The question is posed against the background of the hypotheses that the domestic power base at the time of liberation could have allowed a more market-orientated and less capital-intensive development strategy, with a less challenging foreign policy, and that South Africa would have allowed a more comprehensive non-aggression treaty.

In some sense the study shows that this is the route which Frelimo has taken today, but with a significantly worse starting position and with fewer of the conditions necessary for success.

Changed political alliances

As this book has shown, Frelimo was forced, after it was refused membership of the Eastern bloc cooperation organisation COMECON in 1982, to reformulate its development strategy and to seek new political alliances (26). The Western powers later became new partners in co-operation as Frelimo carried out necessary domestic and foreign policy changes. The country's economy gradually became liberalised and more market-oriented, in accordance with the design of the structural adjustment programme that the Western powers considered necessary in order to achieve a macro-economic balance (27). As a result of political developments in Eastern Europe, aid cooperation with the former socialist countries later decreased dramatically (28).

However, there are several problems with the design and implementation of the structural adjustment programme developed in cooperation with the World Bank and the IMF, which was formulated according to the conditions prevailing at both international and domestic levels. In order for increased exports and the liberalisation of foreign trade to produce the required results, a different international context is needed. Various trade restrictions in the West, together with international food subsidies, are creating serious obstacles to development, not least at local level where peasant farmers have to be motivated to increase agricultural production for sale (29).

The market forces and domestic economic actors who were expected to bring about economic development in the long term are allocating their investments according to short-term criteria for profitability, which in turn depend on existing domestic demand (30). Far too few economic actors are interested in the more long-term investments (31) required if the distorted rural structures are to be transformed and the rural population's productivity and purchasing power increased, enabling an expansion of the domestic market.

As a consequence of the country's enormous dependence on aid, however, the government does not itself decide where and to what extent these public investments should be made. These decisions are controlled by the special interests of the different donors, and channelled in particular to the modern sector in order to increase the export earnings needed for debt repayment (32).

At the same time, political reform in South Africa has been initiated following internal social instability and international pressures (33). The new South African government strove to maintain its regional dominance through increased bilateral economic cooperation (34), at the same time as South African commercial interests had begun to make some investments in Mozambique, principally in agriculture and trade (35).

Uncertain future

The future for Mozambique is extremely uncertain. Structural adjustments have been implemented in an international situation characterised by different trade restrictions, protectionism and low demand for Mozambique's traditional export goods. There is a strong possibility that the single-minded concentration on increased export production will not succeed in the short term in creating a macro-economic balance, with a resulting permanent dependency on aid (36).

In the long term the structural adjustment programme risks facing the same fate as Portugal's development strategies during the colonial era and which Frelimo's attempt at enforced modernisation met after the country's independence. Insufficient investments in increasing the productivity and purchasing power of the rural population limit the expansion of the domestic market and thus the preconditions for long-term sustainable economic rural development (37).

At the same time it is extremely uncertain whether the present capital flow to Southern Africa can be maintained. As a consequence of international developments, there are signs to indicate that the African continent will become further marginalised in its entirety and will play an increasingly subordinate role in the world economy (38). In the case of Mozambique, against the background of the country's weak financial strength, such a development would entail further strains for attempts to consolidate the state-nation and facilitate peaceful and socially stable long-term economic development (39).

This trend towards the marginalisation of Africa, however, may come to force a vitalisation of regional cooperation (40). Strengthened co-operation at regional level may partly compensate for a reduction in the international exchange of commodities and thus become an important precondition for the state-nation project being consolidated (41). Other preconditions depend on the regime's ability to decentralise decision-making so that a division of power can be brought about which allows alternative elites to become politically visible at both central and local levels (42).

Mozambican development history

The present work lacks any means of assessing the extent to which Mozambican development history after the country's independence has been shaped by political errors; a fuller analysis could have provided this. The aim of this study has been to describe in close detail the given historical and foreign policy context which explains, at least in part, why Frelimo acted as it did.

The study has also attempted to summarise existing experiences and the lessons which can be drawn for the future with regard to attempts at correcting the ongoing disintegration and consolidating the nation-state project. It has discussed the need for a more territorially directed development strategy, where regional distribution and decentralised decision-making, together with local identification of need, are necessary for it to be possible to modernise society in peace and in harmony with local traditions and cultural customs.

We hope that through the present work we have contributed to the description of Mozambique's development history by recording our understanding from our perspective of the development of events. However, our contribution, written by two foreigners, has its limitations.

The observations we have made are based on our own understanding of the sources to which we have had access and those parts of the Mozambican reality with which we came into contact and were capable of understanding. It is very important that our interpretation should be supplemented and corrected by all Mozambicans who, through their different roles and at all levels in the Mozambican social hierarchy, have formed their own perspective and their own understanding of the development the country has undergone.

It is, of course, only Mozambicans themselves who have the necessary knowledge to be able to describe their country's development history. It is also important that this should be done so that the new generation which is growing up can obtain an understanding of the many factors which, in different ways, have shaped the country's fate. Through our study we hope that we have contributed to this work becoming a reality.

Notes

Introduction

1. One exception was naturally *The Struggle for Mozambique*, written by the first president, Eduardo Mondlane and published in 1969. This also applies to the exposure of the massacre by colonial troops in Wiriyamu village by the British priest Adrian Hastings (Hastings, 1974), as well as John Paul's *Memories of a Revolution* (1975). Paul sheds light not least on the Catholic Church's colonial position at local level during Frelimo's war of liberation, 1964–75.

2. In this tradition we include, for example, Munslow, 1983; Hanlon, 1984; Isaacman and Isaacman, 1983; Seidman, 1985; Johnson and Martin, 1986; Hanlon, 1986b. However, there are exceptions amongst authors who wrote earlier about Mozambique. This applies to, for example, T.H. Henriksen (1979) and L. Vail and L. White (1981), who described Frelimo's choice of strategy during the first few years after independence from a more liberal stance.

3. Amongst the few exceptions is Rudebeck's 1990 report from field work in Frelimo's former liberated areas in Cabo Delgado.

4. Geffray and Pedersen, 1985 and 1986; Geffray, 1991.

5. Rhodesia's former security chief, Ken Flower (Flower, 1987) has taken the responsibility for having created Renamo. Former mercenaries appear to have a need to justify their actions. These include, for example, Cole, 1984 and 1986b and Reid-Daly, 1983; both these are 'adventure-oriented' reports on how Rhodesian special units worked with Renamo.

6. Fauvet and Gomes, 1979, Fauvet, 1984 and 1985, Nilsson, 1990 and 1991, as well as Vines, 1991. In this connection Gersony, 1988, should also be mentioned, a report on Renamo's violent practices in rural areas, ordered by the U.S. State Department.

7. One exception is Hoile, 1992, written by David Hoile, who is an 'executive director' for a lobbying organisation for Renamo in London – Mozambique Institute. Another is Sibyl W. Cline, who wrote a pamphlet published in the USA with the title Renamo em Defesa da Democracia en Moçambique (Renamo in the defence of democracy in Mozambique) (Cline, 1989). Sibyl Cline's pamphlet was edited and published by Ray Cline.

8. One example is Griffin (1989), who formulates six different types of strategy: monetary, the open economy, industrialisation, the green revolution, redistribution strategies and socialist strategies. Different countries' strategies can then be arranged in such groupings and the outcome of the strategies

evaluated, for example against normative indicators such as levels of investment, economic growth, social justice or democratic development.

9. The macro-region concept is used in the sense of a group of states, i.e. as a term for the region of Southern Africa. The micro-region concept is also used in the paper to denote sub-national regions, i.e. parts of the territory of Mozambique.

1. Colonial Legacy

10. The description of the early history of Mozambique is based mainly on História de Moçambique, Vols 1–2, and Serra, 1986. Shorter summaries in English are found in Munslow, 1983 and Isaacman and Isaacman, 1983, for example.

11. Munslow, 1983, p. 24.

12. Historical perception in central Mozambique maintains that the last emperor of the Gaza empire, Gungunhana, was actually the love-child of his father and a Shona princess. This should have contributed to the expansion of the Gaza empire which built on an alliance between the dominant people of the Gaza empire, the Changana and parts of the Shona population, of which the N'dau ethnic group in central Mozambique is a part.

13. Railway construction occurred in cooperation with the Boers and the Portuguese, against the wish of the English. The latter tried to maintain Transvaal's, and therefore the Boers', transport dependence on English-controlled Durban.

14. See Liesegang, 1986, for a description of some of the Gaza empire's diplomatic activities.

15. An illustration of this is the agreement between the Portuguese government and the Compania de Moçambique, which stipulated that the Portuguese state, in exchange for concessions, would receive 7.5 per cent of the net profit and 10 per cent of the annual bonus on the company's shares (História de Moçambique, p. 174).

16. O Mineiro Moçambicano, p. 26.

17. The export of cotton from Mozambique to Portugal increased from 160 tons in 1931 to 29,000 tons in 1946. Compulsory cultivation of cotton was introduced in 1938 (Isaacman and Isaacman, 1983, p. 45). During the same period the value of Mozambique's imports of cotton cloth from Portugal increased fiftyfold (Nogueira da Costa, 1986, p. 61). In 1964 cotton cloth and wine were Mozambique's largest imports from Portugal in terms of value (Nogueira da Costa, 1986, p. 61).

18. Informação Estatística, 1975–84.

19. Isaacman and Isaacman, 1983, pp. 41–6 and Munslow, 1983, pp. 34–7.

20. This can be compared with 65,000 employed in the Ivory Coast and 130,000 in Kenya during the same period. A survey of Mozambique's industrial sector at the time of independence can be found in Torp, 1979.

21. It is important to differentiate between types of agriculture in a Mozambican context. One main difference is between peasant production for subsistence, using only family labour, and a small number of emerging farmers who employ seasonal workers. Some distinctions should also be made within the

category of subsistence farmers, since their production requirements differ. A number of peasants already make use of 'inputs' and technical aids and also occasional hired labour. This share possibly amounts to 4–5 per cent. There are also farmers who are totally dependent on their own cattle (approximately 3 per cent) and there are a number of farmers (perhaps 10 per cent) who base their survival on so-called permanent crops (mainly sugar-cane, bananas, cocoa nuts, cashew nuts and mafurra). But the overwhelming majority of the rural population use traditional slash-and-burn methods with an extremely undeveloped method of agriculture, where no form of 'input' in the form of processed seed or fertiliser is used.

22. See for example Wuyts, 1978 and Mackintosh, 1983.

23. Calculations regarding the capacity and production potential of family agriculture show the slight possibilities for production for sale produced by slash-and-burn. While each farming family on average needs 1,100 kg of maize per year for its own maintenance, the average production quantity per family amounts to 1,200–1,500 kg. After deductions for losses during grinding and sowing, approximately 200 kg, a theoretical quantity of up to 200 kg of maize remains for sale per family per year (i.e. 10–20 per cent of the family's total production). With regard to the rural population and settlement structure, the theoretically possible marketed total quantity from the family sector may be calculated as being in the order of magnitude of 150,000–200,000 tons. This is double the amount that was usually marketed during the 'good years' of the colonial era.

24. Pereira Leite, 1990.

25. Pereira Leite, 1990.

26. Wuyts, 1989, p. 87.

27. The trade system was dominated by two different groups, both business capital of Asian origin and Portuguese in rural areas who often combined business activity with their own agricultural production. This gave them a comparative advantage compared with Asians, who seldom engaged in agricultural production. See, for example, Mackintosh, 1983.

28. See, for example, Adam and Gentili, 1983.

29. Isaacman and Isaacman, 1983, pp. 51–2.

30. Nationalists from southern and central parts of Mozambique founded UDENAMO (União Democrática Nacional de Moçambique) in the then Rhodesia. UNAMI (União Nacional Africana de Moçambique Independente) obtained its chief support amongst Mozambicans from the Tete and Zambezia provinces who worked in Malawi. With inspiration from Tanzania and Kenya, MANU (Maconde African National Union) was founded by migrant workers, mainly from the northern province of Cabo Delgado. In MANU the backbone came from amongst the farmers who had tried to establish their own forms of cotton production. See, for example, Munslow, 1983, pp. 79–80. Frelimo's own description of this process can be found, *inter alia*, in Machel, 1975, pp. 199–207.

31. 'The Mozambican people's struggle at its current stage has three aspects. It is an anti-colonial struggle aimed at destroying the colonial-fascist state; an anti-imperialist struggle aimed at destroying the control by multinational companies and ending imperialism's use of our country as a launching pad for aggression against progressive African regimes and protection of the bastions of

racism and fascism; finally it is a struggle aimed at destroying the system of exploitation of man by man and replacing it with a new social order at the service of the labouring masses of the people. These varying aspects of our struggle are a real factor in our day-to-day fighting: the enemy troops we are fighting are armed by the imperialist powers, notably the United States, Federal Germany, France and the United Kingdom. We face, in addition to the Portuguese colonial army, the armed forces of Rhodesia and South Africa which are equipped by the same powers ... The facts provide ample testimony that maintenance of the colonial war is closely tied to the military, financial and technical assistance of NATO.' Machel, 1974, quoted in its entirety in Munslow, 1985, pp. 34ff.

32. The Lusaka Agreement was signed by the Portuguese government and Frelimo on 7 September 1974. The agreement meant that Portugal handed over political power in Mozambique to Frelimo.

33. These figures are the result of a calculation based on areas Frelimo regards as being liberated in 1974 and the population figures for respective districts based on a population census of 1980. The liberated areas are made clear in the *Atlas Geograficó*, Vol. 1, p. 46 and population figures at district level have been published in a series of publications from Conselho Coordenador do Recensamento.

34. Descriptions of this fundamental opposition may be found in several sources. Frelimo's victorious wing has described it, *inter alia*, in the central committee's report to the third congress (Frelimo, 1977). There are factually similar descriptions in Munslow, 1983, and Isaacman and Isaacman, 1983.

35. Frelimo's attitude was not only based on the fact that the availability of consumer goods was important for political mobilisation of the population. Collective transportation on foot organised by Frelimo would also make possible transportation of weapons and ammunition to its liberation fighters. It was considered inappropriate to hand over these commercial activities to private business.

36. *AIM Information Bulletin* No. 84, June 1983.

37. At least two people who actively participated in this process in 1974 can now be found as leaders of new political parties in today's Mozambique. This applies to Maximo Dias, who now leads a party called MONAMO, and Domingos Arouca, who leads a party called FUMO. An examination of the Beira newspaper *Noticías da Beira* between 25 April 1974 and 7 September 1974 indicates that at least 27 new parties started up and disappeared from the political scene over slightly more than four months. It is estimated that approximately 50 new parties were formed and disbanded in the country during this period.

38. There were actually six, because undertakers' activities were also nationalised. The motivation for this was that the dead should not be a trade commodity and that all people should have the right to a decent burial.

39. This lack of knowledge affected different areas of the peasants' activities. There was insufficient knowledge of the peasants' production methods, technology and distribution of production resources. Information on production levels and rates of growth was unreliable. Statistics were based on marketing within the official market. Moreover there were difficulties with the conceptual perception of the rural economy and the close connection between production and

marketing. Knowledge of these matters is still very limited. Remarkably few studies have been carried out with reference to prevailing living and production conditions in rural areas or the effect of the traditional socio-cultural pattern on production for sale and own consumption respectively. Amongst the few exceptions is some research carried out after independence at the Centro dos Estudos Africanos in Maputo.

40. Plans from the end of the 1970s indicated that in 1990 ten large state farms would include one million hectares and represent 75 per cent of all agricultural production (Isaacman and Isaacman, 1983, p. 152).

41. During the later years of the colonial period, the Portuguese state carried out extensive investigatory and planning work to develop the Mozambican economy and production capacity. This work was reflected in, *inter alia*, the so-called promotion plans. In Portuguese they are called *Planos de Fomento*. Their function in the colonial planning process is elucidated in Darch, 1983. Three such plans were developed, the first for the period 1953–58, the second for 1959–64, with an extension to 1965–67, while the third complete plan referred to the period 1968–73. Work on the fourth plan for the period 1974–79 was broken off on independence. There was also a special institute, which worked on development plans for the whole of the Zambezi river's long valley through Mozambique. When, after independence, Mozambique's new government began to initiate discussions and negotiations with prospective aid donors, all this Portuguese investigation material was made available. The technical descriptions in this investigation work were the basis of a very large proportion of the projects formulated together with the aid donors. In practice many projects were actually a direct continuation of the Portuguese plans available in the archives. For example, there were well advanced plans for both the huge dams in Maputo province – Pequenos Libombos and Corrumana (Directivas Economicas e Socias, Frelimo's 3rd party congress, 1977).

2. The International Setting and the Regional Constraints

42. West European decolonisation was in the USA's interest. In this way the USA could increase its influence over a continent which until then had been reserved by Europeans. This was one of the explanations for the view that 'anticolonial revolutions could be and indeed were reconciled with the American vision of a global economy under American leadership'. See Bender et al., 1985.

43. Brzezinski's influence over the West's attitude became important during the 1970s. This not only referred to his role as national security adviser to President Carter, but was also chiefly a result of his role of chief ideologist for the Trilateral Commission. For an interesting account of the concepts that impressed Brzezinski, see Brzezinski, 1963.

44. Brzezinski, 1963, p. 205.

45. Brzezinski, 1963, p. 208.

46. Many were also in Europe. Some had the task of mobilising international support for the liberation struggle. Several others from the Mozambican black élite sympathetic to Frelimo studied in the USA. Many remained in exile after independence.

47. The country's late president, Samora Machel, was one of the first to be sent to Algeria. There he was greatly influenced by the experiences of the Algerian revolutionaries, not least with reference to the organisation and military strategy of the struggle for liberation. See Munslow, 1985, pp. xiii ff.

48. According to the dependency school the Marxist, like the liberal, development analysis was erroneous. Capitalism in the Third World was not progressive (as no domestic bourgeoisie was allowed to develop). The Third World's (i.e. the periphery's) subordination to industrialised nations (i.e. the centre) and the traditional division of labour which characterised this relationship, made development impossible. As a consequence of the unequal exchange and the rules of the game applying on the world market, the purchasing power in rural areas was low. As a consequence of this low purchasing power in rural areas, private capital turned to the sectors where there was already demand, which would maintain the distorted and disconnected production structures which were a result of the colonial era and thus reinforce the Third World's position in the world market as mainly a supplier of raw materials. A good examination of the spread of the dependency school to the African continent and to Tanzania is given in Blomström and Hettne, 1984.

49. The new strategy, which intended to reawaken African socialism, was presented by Nyerere at the beginning of 1967 in the so-called Arusha declaration.

50. Blomström and Hettne, 1984, also give a description of the intellectual climate that prevailed on 'the Hill', as the University of Dar-es-Salaam was called. A series of Western and dependency theory inspired researchers, and teachers were frequently visiting scholars. During these years a firm friendship was established between several of these researchers and Frelimo's leadership. Caribbean researchers, such as Walter Rodney and Clive Thomas, also came to make their mark on the Tanzanian development strategy. Clive Thomas in particular is considered to have played a very important role in the formulation of the country's industrialisation strategy during the 1970s. He had taken the theories behind the industrialising industries from the French growth economist, Gerard Destanne de Bernis, who in turn, at the request of the Algerian government, had developed Algeria's industrialisation strategy towards the end of the 1960s.

51. Destanne de Bernis is presently the head of the Perroux Institute in Paris. For his economic growth theories and industrialisation strategies, see de Bernis, 1970. Work on formulating the ambitious planning model which was regarded as being required for Algeria's long-term development was performed by a group of experts from GOSPLAN, under the guidance of the Polish planning expert, M. Bobrowski.

52. The theory of 'non-capitalist development' is based on that development towards socialism in the Third World *de facto* being possible without these countries first having to pass through the capitalist stage. However, according to advocates of this theory, neither the domestic bourgeoisie nor the working class is sufficiently strong to be able to initiate progressive development of productive forces alone. This development can only be brought about through a broad class alliance.

53. America realised relatively early that Mozambique should be given an-

other type of attention than Angola. It was perceived not least that the Soviet Union made a clear distinction with reference to military engagement in Angola and Mozambique respectively. The Soviets hesitated for a long time before supplying anti-aircraft missiles to Mozambique for defence against Rhodesian air attacks. Mozambique first received such supplies in the final stages of the war against Rhodesia in 1979. Soviet military support never reached the same levels as for Angola. Soviet military advisers located in Mozambique also made a disastrously wrong assessment of the South African military strategy. Both training and military supplies built on the assumption that South Africa would attack Mozambique in the same way as it had Angola. It was possibly this incorrect analysis that prompted Samora Machel's challenge to the South African military in his so-called 'Que venham' (Let them come!) speech in February 1981. There was probably an air-defence system around Maputo then and troops directed against conventional land attacks against Maputo province. But as Machel stated several years later, they never came. They sent bandits instead.

54. Instead the Carter administration concentrated on building up preconditions for so-called low-intensity warfare, i.e. logistical and military support for domestic opposition groups which the American government regarded as being worth supporting. The build-up of an American so-called 'Rapid Deployment Force' during this period formed an important stage of this American low intensity strategy to maintain its role as protector of the world order. See e.g. Klare, 1982.

55. A good account of the role of international social democracy during this period is given in Bushin, 1989.

56. The quotation is taken from Brown, Carolyn 'Apartheid and Trilateralism: Partners in Southern Africa', p. 365 in Sklar, 1980.

57. This financial assistance was interpreted by the Third World as a historically legitimate repayment of part of the transfer of value made to the North during the colonial era. The visit by the Swedish Prime Minister, Torbjörn Fälldin, to Mozambique in 1978 illustrates the prevailing international favourable attitudes towards developmental efforts in the Third World. The year after Frelimo was transformed into a Marxist-Leninist avant-garde party, not just friends from the East or international social democracy, but also representatives of more conservative-oriented governments in the West came to visit and promised increased aid.

58. John Vorster was elected as prime minister in 1966 after serving for several years as the country's minister of justice. He had limited experience of foreign policy but had a clear conception of domestic policy measures needed in order to consolidate and preserve the policy of apartheid. However, Prime Minister Vorster realised during his various visits to black Africa the need to formulate a foreign policy of *détente*; he needed to increase his international legitimacy in order to be able to consolidate his domestic apartheid policy. Accordingly he met with Kissinger three times during 1976 to discuss the preconditions for a negotiated settlement in Rhodesia and he actively participated, if secretly, in discussions between Ian Smith and Kenneth Kaunda.

59. In 1961, in response to increased domestic pressure, the ANC created its armed wing, Umkhonto we Sizwe, and supplemented its political opposition with different forms of sabotage and armed action. But large numbers of the

ANC's underground leadership were imprisoned in 1963, which greatly reduced the ANC's capacity to maintain its political and military threat.

60. According to the South African social researcher Geldenhuys, the decision to invade Angola was taken after strong pressure from the Ministry of Defence where P.W. Botha was minister. Both the Ministry of Foreign Affairs and the Bureau of State Security received the first accounts of the invasion through protests which the Portuguese ambassador presented to the Ministry of Foreign Affairs in Pretoria. See further Geldenhuys, 1984.

61. The military, or parts of the military at least, were prepared to intervene in Mozambique in support of the coup attempt which was staged on 7 September 1974 through occupation of the radio station in Maputo. On the same date an agreement was signed between Portugal and Frelimo, which gave power to Frelimo in an independent Mozambique. However, the then head of the civil security service, BOSS, van den Berg, opposed military intervention in Mozambique. It is in this context important to understand that the usual concept that the South African government and state leadership is a politically homogenous group, in which the prime minister has total control over different power groupings, including the police and the military, is very simplistic. For example, the development of a united security strategy to defend the apartheid system at the beginning of the 1970s was hindered by difficult internal antagonisms in the South African government. Not until P.W. Botha came to power in September 1978 was a united total strategy for South Africa's security problems developed. Until then Prime Minister Vorster strongly resisted and set BOSS to watch over the military establishment and its leader P.W. Botha. The sphere of state security was paralysed by internal antagonisms and was unable to fulfil its obligations (Cawthra, 1986, pp. 26–7). The same type of internal antagonisms also arose in the middle of the 1980s. In at least one case the military bugged a room where the South African Foreign Minister Roelof Botha held talks with the Mozambican minister Jacinto Veloso (the Gorongosa documents).

62. The treaty was referred to in the Portuguese press during November 1974 but was not made public (*O Século*, 7 November 1974 and *A Captital*, 23 November 1974). The existence of the treaty was confirmed by the country's former security minister, Sergio Vieira during a seminar organised by the Instituto Superior de Relações Internacionais (ISRI) in Maputo, December 1992, 'Moçambique Pós Guerra – Desafios e Realidades'.

63. See First and Davies, 1980. The authors' interpretation of a unilateral decision on reductions on the part of South Africa is, however, controversial. It is true that the South Africans wished to make an example of the effects of dependency. But at the same time the Frelimo leadership wanted to take home some of the migrant workers. They were seen as the only ones who were trained and who would be able to take over the leadership for the mechanisation of Mozambican agriculture facing the country.

64. Brzezinski, 1983, p. 141 ff.

65. Vorster had a firm social base amongst white small farmers, small enterprise and the white working class (Cawthra, 1986, pp. 26–7). His vision did not include the need for changes in the system. At the same time he also had no clear, aggressive, military strategy in relation to neighbouring countries, partly because it was not necessary before 1975, and partly because he saw internal defence as being most important.

66. Cawthra, 1986, pp. 26-7.

67. The Rhodesian unilateral declaration of independence in 1965, under the leadership of Ian Smith, led to international protests. The United Nations took a decision to boycott the illegal regime in Rhodesia. Independent Mozambique became one of the few countries in the world that followed the UN's recommendations for a total boycott of Rhodesia. In March 1976, less than one year after independence, Mozambique closed its borders with Rhodesia, which stopped all railway traffic on the Limpopo line from Maputo and Beira to Rhodesia. Mozambique's estimated loss of revenues during the period from closure to Zimbabwean independence is estimated to be around $550 million (Johnson and Martin, 1986, p. 17).

68. Through independence the ANC was also offered a political and diplomatic centre in Mozambique. It is not improbable that the constant accusations from Pretoria that several of the armed actions which the ANC carried out within South Africa were planned and carried out from Mozambican territory had a basis in fact. However, Frelimo never confirmed this officially, if they even had knowledge of it. The Mozambican border with South Africa is lengthy, sparsely populated and difficult to monitor.

69. The concept 'constructive engagement' itself was first used by Chester Crocker in 1980 in an article in *Foreign Affairs*, Winter 1986–88, Crocker, 1992, p. 75.

70. For a comprehensive study of the elaboration and implementation of US 'constructive engagement' in Southern Africa and the role of linking Namibian independence with the withdrawal of Cuban troops from Angola, see Crocker, 1992.

71. The importance of non-alignment shall not be understood from the need for balancing between West and East which characterised many countries in the Third World. For Mozambique, balancing between the Soviets and China was more important. Ideologically speaking, some of Frelimo's leadership were close to China. Both the writings of Mao Tse Tung and General Giap's theories on the civil war in Vietnam had made a great impression on Samora Machel (see Munslow, 1985, p. xiii). At the same time the Soviet Union was an important political ally and represented expectations of extensive military and technical assistance cooperation. Mozambican diplomatic capabilities were tested during the Rhodesia conflict, where Sino-Soviet rivalry for African influence was very obvious. But Frelimo remained, despite pressure from the East, nearer to ZANU and Mugabe, who received support from China, while the Soviet Union mainly directed its support to N'Komo and ZAPU. Support for the ANC constitutes another example of the independence of Mozambican foreign policy *vis-à-vis* the Soviets and China. While the ANC was the Soviet Union's ally, China gave its support above all to PAC.

72. 'We give total solidarity and support to the nationalist forces who in Rhodesia, South Africa and Namibia are fighting against the Salisbury and Pretoria regimes. The national liberation struggle of the Southern African peoples has direct and immediate impact on our own fight, and explains the close ties between us. The current intensification of the armed struggle for national liberation in Rhodesia, thanks to the successes achieved in search for unity, will force the racist aggressors in the Salisbury regime to diminish their

support to the Portuguese colonial war. The expansion of the fighting will create
better conditions for our own people's struggle. Development, under ANC
leadership, of the challenge and mobilisation of the people in South Africa is
gradually creating conditions for higher forms of the struggle at the very heart
of the racist empire. In this context too, the legitimate armed struggle by the
Namibian people under SWAPO's leadership against racist annexation and for
national liberation has diminished the Pretoria regime's aggressive capabilities
and presented more favourable conditions for our people's struggle and victory.'
Machel 1974, reproduced in Munslow, 1985, p. 68.

73. In May 1979, the same year as South Africa reintroduced the CONSAS
concept, in an attempt to retain its regional dominance, the five Frontline States
(Angola, Botswana, Mozambique, Tanzania and Zambia) decided to initiate
alternative regional cooperation under the term Southern African Development
Coordination Conference (SADCC). This decision was followed by a new conference in Arusha, Tanzania, in July of the same year, where potential aid donors
were also invited to take part. Both 'organisations' (i.e. CONSAS and SADCC)
were dependent on independent Zimbabwe's cooperation. As well as being the
region's most developed country after South Africa, Zimbabwe was situated in
the centre of the region and thus constituted an important transit country for all
inter-continental transportation. The South Africans hoped for a long time that
independent Zimbabwe would be led by Bishop Muzorewa, who expressed his
support for CONSAS, while the Frontline States in their struggle against the
white minority regime in South Africa were dependent on support from the
Patriotic Front – the political alliance between ZANU and ZAPU. Through
ZANU's election victory in 1980 and Zimbabwe's continuing connection with
the Frontline States, it was possible for SADCC to be formally established in
April 1980. The preconditions for CONSAS were completely undermined – for
the time being at least.

74. The Nordic countries together played an important role in financing
SADCC's investment programme. At the end of the 1980s they were responsible
for approximately one-quarter of total international support to SADCC. This
can be compared with the Nordic countries' total bilateral aid to the separate
frontline states, which amounted to one-third of their total inflow of aid during
the same period. See Østergaard, 1989.

75. Different perceptions of the background to the formation of SADCC
prevail. Some commentators feel that in fact it was the West which took the
initiative for the formation of SADCC in order to tie the frontline states more
closely together by maintaining the colonial transport system, thus preventing
increased Soviet influence in the region. To support this interpretation the fact
that SADCC's international financing finally came from the West is often cited.
The Soviet Union has never contributed to the organisation's finances. Other
observers go further and stress the interest of the West and South Africa in
extending the organisation from only including the more openly radical frontline
states to also including more traditionally cooperative countries, e.g. Malawi,
thus toning down SADCC's foreign policy profile. See, *inter alia*, Leys and
Tostensen, 1982. See also Amin et al., 1987.

76. We can here talk of double standards. Despite extensive foreign policy
condemnation of the apartheid regime, in which aid to the region's black

majority rule countries was also included as an important part, West European countries could not be prevented from allowing their commercial interests to continue trading with South Africa until more comprehensive international sanctions were introduced in 1986. No extra financial compensation was given for the costs incurred by the frontline states as a result of South African retaliations and its attempt to obstruct SADCC cooperation, when the Frontline States tried in practice to concretise the world's condemnation of the apartheid policy in South Africa. A further example of this double standard was the world's demand, expressed via the UN's recommendation, to isolate the Ian Smith regime in the then Rhodesia. As a consequence Mozambique closed its borders with the country in 1976, but was alone responsible for the effects this entailed.

3. The Turning Point: Vision and Reality

77. *Informação Estatística*, 1985.

78. Wuyts, 1989, p. 87. The breach occurred when South Africa changed the rules for the way in which the official gold price was determined. The price was now adjusted to the world market price and thus did not yield the extra profits which Portugal had been able to exploit, and in the same way as the new government in Mozambique had been able to do during the first two years of the country's independence.

79. *Informação Estatística*, 1985.

80. One example of this is the country's largest state farm complex in Chokwe, in the southern part of the country. Hermele describes the situation in the following way: 'However, by 1981 the harvests failed: of the 52,000 tons of rice planned, 26,000 tons were harvested. The total planned area, 16,000 hectares, had been planted, but the yield was only half of that expected, 1.6 tons/hectare as against the target 3.2 tons/hectare'; Hermele, 1988b, p. 50.

81. Saul, 1985.

82. Aid donors also contributed to this prioritisation. This is seen not least in the use of so-called import support. When during 1983 Mozambican decision-makers realised the importance of increased imports of consumer goods, there was great unwillingness on the part of the aid donors to finance them. The only exception amongst the donors was the Soviet Union, which fairly promptly made available significant quantities of consumer goods for rural areas. A number of international solidarity organisations also offered consumer goods, mainly clothing.

83. This situation gave rise to a number of paradoxes. In 1983 the population in the Changara district, in Tete province, was stricken by severe drought. At the same time other districts within the same province continued to comprise some of the country's few real granaries, for example the Angonia district on the border with Malawi. The food shortage in the country was acute. At the same time the farmers' surplus production in Angonia was smuggled over to Malawi as a result of the shortage of consumer goods. There international aid donors bought them up to air freight them back to Tete province and the starving people in Changara. Attempts to convince the aid donors of the pure transport economic benefits which would result from purchasing consumer goods for the farmers in Angonia instead was fruitless. In Inhambane province, in the southern

part of the country, the peasants' reduced interest in selling on the official market meant that they gave up picking a fruit called mafurra. The fruit is used for soap production. At the same time, six months beforehand production was halted in one of the country's largest soap factories which was also situated in Inhambane province, as a result of the shortage of raw materials. Amongst the consumer goods which the farmers desired most, apart from clothing, sugar and paraffin, was soap.

84. Saul, 1985, pp. 112ff.

85. John Saul himself describes the relationship between accumulation and mass consumption in the following way: 'far from being opposites, one of them – accumulation – can be driven forward precisely by finding outlets for production in meeting the growing requirements, the needs, of the mass of the population. An effective industrialisation strategy would thus base its 'expanded reproduction' on ever increasing exchanges between city and country, between industry and agriculture, with consumer goods and producer goods ... moving to the countryside. Collective saving geared to investment can then be seen as being drawn essentially, if not exclusively, from an expanding economic pool.' See Saul, 1985, pp. 125ff.

86. The Mozambican rural population, like a surprisingly large number of the country's political leadership, had themselves a very vague notion of the concrete implications of the concept of socialism. For the majority of the Mozambican rural population, Frelimo represented the force that would be able to satisfy the great expectations of the population for a better quality of life under black majority rule. In concrete terms this meant the abolition of forced labour and access to health-care, and education, fertile land and material goods which had been denied to the majority of the population during the colonial period. There was scant understanding of the production processes and the work that lay behind these facilities. Few had taken part in industrial work, but the majority had seen the stores from which the colonisers had unearthed their assets. The prevailing perception among large numbers of the population at the time of independence can most accurately be described in terms of a 'capitalist warehouse theory'. For many of the rural population, factories were an unknown concept. Things were not manufactured. They just were, as if they came tumbling down from the heavens or from some alien planet. This is partly explained by the Portuguese inability, or unwillingness, to expand the market. In several parts of the country money was not introduced as a means of exchange until well into the twentieth century.

87. Wuyts, 1989, p. 69.

88. At the beginning of the 1980s, however, the government attempted to establish a state enterprise for purchasing agricultural surplus production (AGRICOM) in order to supplement the remaining traders, not just to re-equip the colonial trade system but also to extend it to those farmers who lived outside the official economy. These measures should be seen against the background of political pressure for increased state intervention in trade in order to avoid the colonial era's exploitation of the peasants through an unjust price system. The government's aim was to allow private traders responsibility for purchasing at retail level, while AGRICOM's activity would be concentrated at the wholesale level. Despite these measures the trade network continued to decline throughout the 1980s.

4. External and Internal Factors in Interaction

89. A comprehensive explanation of this strategy is found in Kitson, 1969 and 1971. MNR's activity is explained in other books which describe activities amongst different types of special forces within Rhodesia's army. Reid-Daly, 1983, is an autobiography of the officer who started the first pseudo-terrorist units and later became the head of the Selous Scouts commando force. Cole, 1984 and 1986, builds on accounts from Rhodesian soldiers and mercenaries, who served in the Special Air Service (SAS) and operated in MNR's name. A third source is the former head of Rhodesia's security service, Ken Flower, who in his autobiography clarifies questions about this activity, Flower, 1987. Related descriptions of Renamo's history are found in Johnson and Martin, 1986, Vines, 1991, Fauvet, 1984 and 1985, and Fauvet and Gomes, 1979.

90. One of the leading Portuguese in this group was called Orlando Cristina. He had been in a responsible position within the special troops for guerrilla combat, which had been developed locally in Mozambique. They were known for their brutal rampage among the civilian population. Among these groups there were also people with experience of pseudo-terrorist activities.

91. See, for example, Johnson and Martin, 1986, p. 15.

92. See, for example, Tajú, 1990 and Jardim, 1976.

93. Cronje, Ling and Cronje, 1976, p. 236.

94. Guerra, 1988.

95. Cronje, Ling and Cronje, 1976, pp. 234–5.

96. Paulo Oliveira, Renamo's official representative in Lisbon, left Renamo in sensational circumstances at the beginning of 1988. He went to Mozambique and there he put himself at the disposal of the authorities. Information comes from his press conference in Maputo on 23 March 1988 and follow-up personal interviews.

97. One example is the head of the 'operations room' on the base in Phalaborwa, José Bento (*Africa Confidential*, Vol. 29, No. 24, 2 December 1988).

98. For example, the first general secretary of MNR, Orlando Cristina, obtained a small monthly salary from the Portuguese military counter-intelligence (Paulo Oliveira press conference in Maputo, 23 March 1988).

99. See, for example, *Africa Research Bulletin*, April 1–30, 1983 and *The Star*, 23 April 1983.

100. This former guerrilla was called Zeca Caliate. He deserted and surrendered to the Portuguese. He later worked during the war using Portuguese psychological warfare against Frelimo (Swift, 1975).

101. *Expresso*, Lisbon, 20 January 1983. Translation.

102. Information on this phase in Renamo's development comes, *inter alia*, from an interview with a defector from Renamo, Constantino Reis. The interview was published as Mozambique Agency News item No. 111284P. Orlando Cristina was murdered several years later, in April 1983, on a military base in South Africa. (See, for example, *The Star*, 22 April 1983, as well as the interview with Constantino Reis, who was present on the base in Walmerstadt when Cristina was shot.) The circumstances surrounding the murder were never explained. However there are indications that he was shot by infiltrating agents from Mozambique's security service. Accusations about this were made in connection with the murder (see, for example, *The Star*, 3 June 1983 and the interview

with Constantino Reis). If this is the case the Mozambicans concerned could have been an air-force officer, Adriano Bomba, who 'deserted' with a MIG-21 and landed inside South Africa, and his brother Boaventura Bomba, who later left Mozambique and joined MNR (*Africa Confidential*, Vol. 24, No. 7, 30 March 1983). Constantino Reis declared that he knew from a South African officer that they both 'were no longer in our world'. They have not been heard of since that occasion in 1983.

103. Some glimpses from their political history may serve to illustrate the state of relations between MNR's operational leadership and the exiled Mozambicans. Mahluza presented himself as MNR's foreign minister in an interview in *Die Welt*, 2 September 1982. He had belonged to Frelimo in the 1960s, but defected and approached MNR during the first half of the 1980s. Vilanculos was a former student, whom Frelimo had sent to study in the USA. He left Frelimo at the end of the 1960s and stayed on in the USA. Later on, in 1986, Vilanculos became involved in a public debate about whether he had a mandate to represent MNR in the USA or whether he had actually been expelled from MNR in 1983. Vilanculos and the MNR representative in then West Germany, Artur Janeiro de Fonseca, argued about this on the correspondence pages of the *Washington Times* (20 August, 1 September and 8 September 1986). Vilanculos argued that he was the legitimate representative, because he was supported, *inter alia*, by Franz-Joseph Strauss (*Washington Times*, 8 September 1986). Today neither Vilanculos, Mahluza or Fonseca remain in any publicly known function within Renamo. This type of friction has been a very commonly occurring phenomenon among Mozambican exiles who during the 1980s were involved internationally in MNR circles. There were also antagonisms among Americans who were involved in support for MNR, which occasionally became public. For example, during 1986–87 there was a fierce dispute between three American foundations, Free the Eagle Foundation, Heritage Foundation and Conservative Action Foundation, about who supported whom within MNR. See, for example, *Africa Confidential*, Vol. 28, No. 6, 18 March 1987 and *Wall Street Journal*, 20 January 1988.

104. See, for example, *Africa Confidential*, Vol. 24, No. 7, 30 March 1983, Fauvet, 1984 and 1985, and Nilsson, 1990.

105. At the interview mentioned, in spring 1988, Paulo Oliveira spoke about the South African brigadier Charles van Niekerk, who had personally installed a special fax machine using a military cipher system in Oliveira's flat in Lisbon. Charles van Niekerk had previously been linked to Portuguese forces in Angola and Mozambique and also participated in the formation of MNR in Rhodesia (*Africa Confidential*, Vol. 29, No. 24, 2 December 1988).

106. According to Paulo Oliveira this was a constant problem for Renamo's office in Lisbon.

107. In the current text the English abbreviation MNR and the Portuguese term Renamo (Resistência Nacional Moçambicana), as the organisation later came to be called, are used in turn.

108. In the former West Germany, where parts of the security service have maintained connections with MNR (this was asserted by a defector from MNR, Chanjunja Chivaca João, at a press conference in Maputo on 30 November 1988, and by Paulo Oliveira, at a press conference in Maputo on 23 March

1988. A connection is also suggested in *Foreign Report*, March 1986, where there is a report on German assistance to a faction among Mozambican exiles in West Germany who clashed about power over MNR. This is also described in *Africa Confidential* (Lisbon) in March 1986). In the USA, support for MNR was mainly concentrated in ultra-conservative circles, such as the Heritage Foundation, Free the Eagle and Conservative Action foundations (*Africa Confidential*, Vol. 28, No. 6, 18 March 1987 and *Wall Street Journal*, 20 January 1988). There was another support group based around the mercenary periodical *Soldier of Fortune*, which continuously organised journeys to MNR areas in Mozambique and published reports. The leading 'journalist' in this connection was a former mercenary in then Rhodesia (Cole, 1984 and *Soldier of Fortune*, May 1987), Robert Mackenzie (alias Bob McKenna). He was an American soldier in Vietnam, but was demobilised after being wounded. He continued his career as a mercenary in Rhodesia's Special Air Service (SAS), where he rose in the ranks to captain (*Soldier of Fortune*, May 1987). He participated both in attacks inside Mozambique and in MNR training (*Soldier of Fortune*, January 1988). After 1980 he moved to South Africa and again found employment as a mercenary in one of the South African army's special units, 1 Recce Regiment. Later on he served as a deputy in the Transkei Defence Force Special Forces regiment (*Soldier of Fortune*, May 1987). In these circles there were also figures such as the retired general John Singlaub, who was a colleague of Oliver North in the 'Irangate' scandal (*Africa Confidential*, Vol. 28, 16 December). All this type of activity around MNR in the USA was *de facto* a consequence of the strategy of the former head of the CIA, William Casey, of maintaining an extensive semi-private network for different forms of intelligence activity (*Africa Confidential*, Vol. 29, No. 24, 2 December 1988).

109. See, for example, *Africa Confidential*, Vol. 29, No. 24, 2 December 1988.
110. See, for example, *Africa Confidential*, Vol. 29, No. 18, 9 September 1988 and *Africa Confidential*, Vol. 29, No. 24, 2 December 1988.
111. *Africa Confidential*, Vol. 29, No. 24, 2 December 1988. An example of this is found in West Germany, where in 1986 a group of Mozambican exiles formed an organisation called CUNIMO. This gained support from both South Africa's Foreign Minister Pik Botha and Chester Crocker (*Foreign Report*, March 1986). The intention was to unite exiles in order to push aside the Portuguese who still remained in Renamo's leadership and who worked together with the South African military. In this way it was hoped that it would be possible to isolate the military and establish direct contacts with Dhlakama. But each time a new national council or other change in the leadership was presented publicly, it was followed by expulsions, the casting of suspicions or murder. All attempts by the followers of the economic alternative to gain a place in Renamo's leadership were unsuccessful. A nearly tragi-comical instance of this rivalry within the South African establishment as well occurred in October 1984. South Africa's foreign minister, Pik Botha, had successfully convinced Mozambique's government to talk to Renamo, with Botha as mediator. However, Pik Botha was not himself successful in bringing Renamo's then general secretary, the Portuguese citizen Evo Fernandes, or Afonso Dhlakama to the negotiating table. He was forced to ask the South African military for help. Documents published later show how the military thoroughly prepared Fernandes and Dhlakama for the

meetings with Pik Botha. They were also successful in 'bugging' the premises where Botha met with the Mozambican government delegation and they forwarded this information to Fernandes before his meeting with the Mozambican delegation (the Gorongosa documents).

112. An illustrative example is this short excerpt from an interview with a member of MNR who, on assignment in Inhambane province, boiled a baby before its mother's eyes: 'Question: Why did you do that? Answer: I don't know, it was the commander who decided that the baby should be boiled. Question: Who was the commander? Answer: He was called Commander Satan. Question: Was the water hot when you put the child in? Answer: The pot was already on and boiling food which the mother was preparing. The mother had left the child outside the house when she went in. She heard the child screaming, looked out and saw that the child had been stuffed into the pot. Question: Was it a big pot? Answer: The child was newborn and the pot was big, very big. It wasn't a clay pot but a big aluminium pot. Question: Did the child scream? Answer: No, it didn't scream when it was properly stuffed in and started to drown. It only cried when we took hold of it.' (From an interview with Alexandre Samson Seneta in Inhambane on 13 March 1989).

113. This is a common way among the Mozambican rural population of expressing their interpretation of the nation concept. People in rural areas, who do not speak Portuguese but only speak their local language, often use the Portuguese word 'nação' – nation – when referring to the government in Maputo. The nation is seen as something only found in Maputo.

114. *South Africa Destabilisation: The Economic Cost of Frontline Resistance to Apartheid* (UN Economic Commission for Africa), quoted in *Mozambiquefile* No. 160, November 1989.

115. *Anuário Estatístico* 1990, p. 146.

116. *Anuário Estatístico* 1990, p. 143.

117. *Children in the Frontline*, p. 20.

118. At the same time we can note that exports of products not reached by the war fell by a much lesser degree. The same applies to products which are clearly limited geographically and whose fall in production is directly linked to the time when the war reached the respective province or production area. This applies, for example, to tea exports, which did not begin to fall until 1983, when the war gained a foothold in Zambezia province where all the tea plantations and factories are located. Exports virtually ceased after 1986 when the factories were attacked and sabotaged. Cotton shows the same pattern, with decisive falls in production in 1984 when the war reached the important cotton province of Cabo Delgado and then the important cotton-producing areas in Zambezia province were occupied by Renamo. The clearest example to show that economic activities which were not reached by the war had a more positive development is that of shrimps. In round figures, exports of shrimps have remained constant throughout the 1980s.

119. Lázaro Kavandame was the most outspoken representative of the moderate tendency within Frelimo during the internal antagonisms of the 1960s. He later returned to Mozambique and cooperated with the Portuguese and was expelled from Frelimo (*Diário de Notícias*, 5 January 1973).

120. See, for example, *Guardian* 29 May 1983 and Steele, 1985.

121. In Portuguese *cortar a retaguarda*.

122. In Portuguese *leões da floresta*. This choice of words is not simply an expression for the fact that the soldiers would dominate the bush. It also implies a challenge to one of the most important symbols of spiritual power in the areas where Renamo had its heartland, i.e. the lion.

123. Zacarias, 1991.

124. We have borrowed the concept of a regional security complex from Buzan, 1991. In this context we understand by the concept a group of states whose security problems are sufficiently interlinked that their national security policies cannot be formulated independently of each other.

125. Angola, Mozambique, Botswana, Zambia and Tanzania.

126. In his book (Sørensen, 1991) Georg Sørensen has sought a possible causal connection between a regime's form (democratic regime, authoritarian growth regime, authoritarian state élite enrichment regime and authoritarian developmentalist regime) and the development which the respective regime can bring about. He finds that no clear connections can be established. His conclusions, as further developed in Sørensen, 1992, are that the connection should rather be sought within three aspects affecting a regime's opportunities to pursue the development strategy it has formulated. He calls them 'autonomy, capacity and statecraft'.

127. See also the discussion on Frelimo's two factions in Chapter 1.

128. In Mozambique the Portuguese word *ambicioso* has become a pejorative term for those who are regarded as striving for increased private advantages and privileges.

129. *Grupos dinamizadores* in Portuguese.

130. Frelimo, 1977, p. 63.

131. Frelimo, 1977, p. 63.

132. *Conselhos de produção* in Portuguese.

133. *Tempo*, 16 October 1977, p. 60.

134. See, for example, Serra, 1986, pp. 22–3.

135. Hanlon, 1984, pp. 135–6.

136. This is illustrated in a remarkable way by Hermele's case study of CAIL. See Hermele, 1988b.

137. *História de Moçambique*, Vol. 2, p. 223. As an illustration it may be added that in Inhambane province, whence many mineworkers came, wages were even lower. The relationship between wages in Inhambane and the mines in South Africa was 1:18.

138. This placing of administrators was also included in the Frelimo leadership's strategy to counteract 'tribal thinking'. This strategy also included using Portuguese as the official language. The use of local languages within the administration was regarded as reactionary.

139. A Portuguese compilation from 1970 (*Divisão Administrativa de Moçambique, por regedoria*) puts the number of *régulos* at 1,600. A probable estimate, based on our own studies in Inhambane province, indicates that each *régulo* had 12 *cabos de terra* within his area, which makes 19,200. There was another category under *cabos de terra*, which in southern Mozambique is called *nganakanas*. They were a sort of family patriarchy, with a certain responsibility towards a *cabo de terra*.

140. See, for example, Mondlane, 1969, pp. 163–7.

141. Mondlane, 1969.
142. Munslow, 1985, p. 57.
143. A public speech in Beira on 11 January 1980 (Munslow, 1985).
144. Munslow, 1985, pp. 77–8.
145. Munslow, 1985, p. 77.
146. Other common religions in Mozambique are Islam and Christianity, both Catholic and Protestant. After independence, religious worship was defined as a private activity, whose practice should only take place within the family. Public religious worship in different communion churches was no longer possible. Traditional religious worship, however, was not defined as religion in the same sense as the others. Its ceremonies, with connections with the soil's fertility and rainfall, were regarded as superstition. Because superstition is a sworn enemy of modernisation and rationalism, it should be combated.
147. This section builds partly on various periods of fieldwork, February–March 1989 and June 1991, in the Homoíne district of Inhambane province. During these periods interviews were carried out with internal refugees and former members of Renamo's armed groups. Earlier working visits of a couple of weeks each were made to the same areas in 1981, 1983, 1985 and 1986.
148. Personal interview with the Renamo commander who led Renamo groups for the first time into the northern province of Cabo Delgado, in Pemba, December 1989.
149. The table requires a brief explanation. The interview research was carried out so that different groups of these categories were found and interviewed about, *inter alia*, their situation before war broke out in the area. The indicators shown in the table have their basis in Inhambane province's economic geography. Cement houses are a very strong sign of a good economy. An improved house, between a hut and a cement house in terms of quality, most often consists of casting a cement floor in a house which is otherwise built of poles and clay. Access to land for rice-growing is another sign of relative prosperity. The province generally has little rainfall, but rice-growing can still occur in certain small river valleys which rarely dry out. Ownership of capital goods, such as a plough or a sewing machine, are other signs that a family has had adequate resources for a longer period in order to be able to make such long-term investments. These investments are often linked to incomes from migrant work in South Africa. It should also be noted that the average level of education varies between the different categories.
150. 1° Recenseamento Geral da População, 1980.
151. Minter, 1989, and Gersony, 1988, both point in this direction. However, neither Minter nor Gersony looked for any socio-economic information on their interviewees, but stopped with their accounts of how they were drawn in under Renamo's control for the first time. With the realisation that there is a socio-economic stratification, which coincides with how different categories of the rural population react to Renamo's activities, a new route for analysis of Renamo's recruitment and support in rural areas has been opened up.
152. Personal interview with Sr. Massalo, a nurse at the rural hospital in Homoíne, March 1989.
153. The Greek psychologist, Mika Haritos-Fatouros, has studied how torturers were trained in Greece during the junta period. Her study is referred to in the Swedish magazine *Psykolog Tidningen* [Psychology News] 9/92.

154. A discussion on ethnic antagonisms and politicised ethnicity in Mozambique requires a short background. Our use of the concept is based on three perceptions of ethnicity:

1. Ethnicity is never determined once and for all. It is determined historically and the common denominators which define group affiliations may change over time (Hettne, 1990b). Ethnicity may change in both its content and its form, for example in connection with migration and urbanisation. Earlier ethnic affinities may be dissolved and new ones formed. Earlier legitimate ethnic symbols and patterns of affinity can be referred to by political leaders in completely new historical situations. One example of this is population groups from certain areas in the countryside who re-gather in the suburbs of towns through immigration. Their ethnic affiliation may be expressed in the same terms as previously. But the towns' material reality shapes a new content: new language, new strategy for survival. Smaller groups can also be largely assimilated and thus change ethnic affiliation. Several ethnic groups of different origin can acquire common interests and develop new forms of group identity (Cohen, 1974).

2. Ethnicity is determined both objectively and subjectively. Objective factors include language, race, religion, common history and common territory. This thus involves factors which are also visible to outsiders and can be used to distinguish members of an ethnic group. But these objective factors are not uniquely decisive. When fixing the borders between different ethnic groups, the people's own subjective perceptions are decisive. Above all, in processes for change and where ethnicity is on the way to being politicised, subjective factors become prominent.

3. Politicised ethnicity means that an ethnic group appears as a political player, with group-specific political, economic and/or cultural demands. The political environment in which politicised ethnicity appears naturally has a decisive influence over how the politicised ethnic group is formed and defined. A politicised ethnic group can be directed against both other ethnic groups and against the state and institutions.

155. Mondlane, 1969.

156. The formation of a nation-state has historically followed two different paths: one in which the nation existed before the state, and one in which the state existed before the nation. The process by which a nation creates its own state we understand as a nation-state project. A state-nation project is a process where an existing state strives to create a nation within its own borders. The latter process applies to most African countries.

157. Babtista-Lundin, 1992.

158. Munslow, 1983 and Johnson and Martin, 1986.

159. From interviews with former members of Renamo's armed groups in Inhambane province, the names of 25 commanders have been identified. These were active in Inhambane province around 1988–89 and varied in rank from provincial commander to group chiefs. Of these 19 were Ndau, 4 Tsua, 1 Sena and 1 from Tete province. (Based on 78 interviews carried out in Inhambane, Homoíne and Maxixe during the period 15.2.89–17.3.89).

5. The End of Global Bipolarity and the Price of New Alliances

160. In the same year the World Bank's report was presented, which contributed to a great extent to the international perception of the increased need for a market-orientated economic policy in sub-Saharan Africa, 'Accelerated Development in Sub-Saharan Africa' (The Berg Report), Washington, 1981. The report attributed the continent's growing debt burden and reduced economic growth to the countries' domestic economic policies. The public sector was too large, ineffective and costly. An incorrect rate of exchange and currency policy had overprotected unprofitable domestic industry at the expense of agriculture. Farmers' producer prices were also far too low. This analysis largely came to form the basis for the different structural adjustment programmes which the World Bank and the IMF later drew up and whose implementation was set as a condition for continued international aid. The reason that most countries felt forced to implement the structural adjustment programmes, despite the domestic policy and the social turbulence that the austerity gave rise to, was the increasing debt burden and the countries' needs for food imports. Access to international credits presupposed that countries were carrying out a policy which could be approved by the Bretton Woods institutions.

161. A study of this discussion well worth reading is found in Valkenier, 1986.

162. One of the causes of Moscow's reluctant attitude to Mozambique during the second half of the 1970s was Frelimo's support for ZANU and Mugabe, who were regarded by the Soviet Union as being closest to China. Another reason was Mozambique's demand for non-alignment and total disinterest in satisfying the Soviet Union's wish to establish a naval base in Nacala, eastern Africa's best natural harbour. To the Soviet Union, Mozambique represented no larger strategic interest. Even if the extent of economic aid from the Soviet Union after Mozambique's independence meant that the country became one of Mozambique's most important aid donors, military assistance was limited.

163. The congress' position should be seen as a political shift in power from radical to conservative forces in Moscow. Whereas the former always had argued the importance of exploiting the enormous crisis, as they saw it, within capitalism for the purposes of a world revolution, they later pointed out the need to consolidate the advances made internally within the Soviet Union first. That the rejuvenated party leadership under Gorbachev took this stance should probably be understood against the background of efforts Gorbachev was forced to make in order to bring about the summit meeting with the American administration under Reagan's leadership in Reykjavik during the autumn of the same year. One demand from the Americans was that in order to discuss mainly matters of disarmament and the SDI programme which were so urgent for Moscow, the question of human rights and regional conflicts should be on the agenda and be resolved first. For a summarised examination of the Reykjavik meeting, see Mandelbaum and Talbott, 1987.

164. Roy Stacey, the US Deputy Assistant Secretary of State for African Affairs, quoted in Hanlon 1991, p. 47.

165. In August 1982 Frelimo's leadership realised that a radical shift in policy was necessary. At a Central Committee meeting in August 1982 a decision was taken on a shift in foreign policy. This bore the hallmarks of the then foreign

minister, Joaquim Chissano, and can be summarised as intending to create more friends and fewer enemies. Most important was becoming friends with the closest friends of the bitterest of enemies. The main targets of this diplomatic offensive were the USA and the former colonial power, Portugal. Other important targets were the EU countries. Samora Machel referred explicitly to this decision as one of the grounds for the N'komati agreement (*Tempo*, No. 2, 25 March 1984).

166.   It may appear remarkable that so little importance is generally given to the role of the former colonial power, Portugal, in this continued development in Mozambique. Portugal's role is, however, often perceived as being very limited. The very small extent of the country's aid cooperation is usually taken as a measure of this. The reason for the country's low profile is the political renewal the country went through after the military coup in April 1974. However, these assessments are not wholly correct. Behind the scenes Portugal plays a very important role in continued Mozambican development, for several reasons. First, the country has a direct link with the Portuguese colony in South Africa. Second, due to long tradition Portugal has always played the role of an intermediary between different international capital interests. During the colonial era it was an intermediary between British and South African interests. In the same way it is now trying to be an intermediary between American economic interests and the Portuguese-speaking areas of Africa. This is clearly evident from the meetings arranged over the last three years in Lisbon between representatives of the Mozambican government and spokesmen for the Trilateral Commission.

167.   Hanlon, 1991, p. 43.

168.   An extensive presentation of the institutional framework within which the distribution of emergency goods was organised is given in Ratilal, 1990.

169.   Hans Abrahamsson, at the request of the ministry for internal trade, took part in several of the Mozambican authorities' negotiations with CARE.

170.   Personal communication to Hans Abrahamsson.

171.   During the continued debate in the US Congress, not least during its later attempts to persuade Congress not only to finance Mozambique's essential reform policy but also to assist the Frelimo government with military assistance in order to end the war, the Reagan administration saw it as important to recall that 'Mozambique has played an important supportive role in US efforts to achieve a negotiated withdrawal of Cuban forces from Angola ... No country in southern Africa has worked more consistently than Mozambique with the United States to further the cause of peace and stability in southern Africa.'

172.   Probably this fact was also toned down during discussions in the US Congress. Indicative of this is the text of the agreement that exists between CARE and the American financiers, OFDA. While the agreement between CARE and the Mozambican government placed great emphasis on CARE's advisory and knowledge transfer role, CARE's agreement with OFDA stressed CARE's executive responsibility for the implementation of disaster relief distribution.

173.   There is an abundance of literature dealing with the American excess liquidity at the beginning of the 1970s, the growth of the Euro-dollar and the connection with the indebtedness of the Third World. For a comprehensive description see Gilpin, 1987. Joan Edelman Spero, in her capacity of Vice-MD of American Express, makes an important contribution to our understanding of

the functioning of the international currency market. See Spero, 1990. Among researchers who spent most time on the problem of international indebtedness is Cheryl Payer. See, *inter alia*, Payer, 1991.

174. The concept of 'indebted industrialisation' mainly refers to the so-called NIC countries, Brazil, Mexico and South Korea, but the concept is also used as a term for economic development in Portugal and South Africa. During the second half of the 1970s the concept became increasingly popular for an increasing number of countries in the Third World. See Körner, 1987.

175. IMF, 1991, Table 12.

176. The implementation by separate countries of the structural adjustment programmes drawn up by the IMF was taken by the international credit market and creditors as an indicator that the debtor was restructuring its economy to the extent required for re-establishing a credible capacity to repay. In this way the creditors' risks of losses were reduced. In connection with the deepening of the debt crisis on the African continent over the first half of the 1980s, international private lending diminished all the same. Since then increasing amounts of international borrowing, needed by increasing numbers of African countries, have been negotiated as public bilateral loans by separate states or by multilateral agencies. Western public creditors also demanded that borrowers implemented the IMF's structural adjustment programme. Gradually Western aid donors also came to impose similar demands for structural adjustments as a condition for continued aid cooperation. An economic policy in line with the IMF's and the World Bank's guidelines was regarded by the aid donors as a precondition for the aid to be of any use. In this way the IMF acquired an exceptional position of power which caused Tanzania's then president, Julius Nyerere, at his New Year's speech to the diplomatic corps in 1980, to pose the question 'When did the IMF become an International Ministry of Finance? When did nations agree to surrender to it their power of decision-making?' (quoted from *Development Dialogue*, 1980: 2). The IMF's powerful position was strengthened even more during the second half of the 1980s, as a result both of the deepening debt crisis and the fact that alternative creditors in the Eastern bloc dropped out of the arena after the break-up of the Soviet Union.

177. Mozambican membership of the IMF and the World Bank was a controversial matter for the boards of both institutions. The country's security problems were perceived by conservative forces in the USA and within the IMF's board as a civil war. In this way considerable difficulties could be expected with reference to the country's ability to repay loans to which the country's membership would entitle it. Mozambique's membership of the Bretton Woods institutions was made possible only by considerable diplomatic efforts on the part of the US State Department and the US government.

178. For the same internal political reasons as in the case of the support promised to Mozambique, the Reagan administration preferred to channel the promised economic resources to South Africa through the IMF.

179. This agreement created frustration and confusion among the frontline states and the ANC. Even if most of them realised Mozambique's precarious position, there was still doubt as to whether the South African government would comply with the agreement.

180. Frelimo's leadership's endeavours to build up bilateral relations with

South African capital interests can also be understood against the background of worsening opportunities for trade with the Soviet Union. Before economic and industrial development had achieved the desired regional cooperation within the framework of SADCC, Mozambique's need for supplementary foreign trade was very great. This was a result of the low complementarity prevailing in the region, where raw materials and agricultural products characterised the majority of the cooperating countries' exports, and Mozambique's import requirements for technology and capital goods for its economic development.

181. The first public advance for this diplomatic offensive was Samora Machel's round tour of Europe in October, 1983. He then visited Portugal for the first time, and most of the leading EU countries, including the EU headquarters in Brussels. This was followed a year later by Mozambique signing the EU's Lomé Convention.

182. Clough, p. 1070.

183. Gersony, Robert, 'Summary of Mozambican Refugee Accounts of principally conflict-related experience in Mozambique', April 1988, report submitted to Ambassador Jonathan Moore and Dr Chester A. Crocker, Assistant Secretary of African Affairs.

184. One ambition and goal which would later come to affect both the realism of the proposed measures and the opportunities for their implementation.

185. The US Congress more or less forced the administration to accept the 'comprehensive anti-apartheid act of 1986', with relevant sanctions, against its veto. At the same time demands were imposed on the ANC to end its terrorist activities, to break its links with the South African communist party and generally guarantee its support for peaceful democratic development in South Africa. No discussions were held on the negative effect of sanctions on the frontline states, the need for increased aid to compensate them and the need in that case to link this aid to increased military assistance in order for them to be able to withstand South African destabilisation.

186. According to press reports, President F.W. de Klerk confirmed in March 1993 something about which the world around had been speculating for a long time, namely that South Africa had developed its own nuclear weapons over the period. At the same time the president stated that the nuclear weapons had been phased out and destroyed some years previously. This insight into the country's ownership of nuclear weapons had naturally made its mark on the attitude of the USA and the Western powers to the country's future black majority rule as a result of the far-reaching consequences which any continued possession of nuclear weapons would have for the region's and the world's security policy.

187. In the foreword to Johnson and Martin, 'Destructive Engagement', Julius Nyerere points to the importance of the N'komati agreement seen from this perspective. The importance for the ANC of intensifying its political work inside South Africa has also been indicated by Mozambique. To a direct question which we ourselves posed to the country's then foreign minister and present president, Joaquim Chissano, on whether the N'komati agreement would make work more difficult for the ANC, the answer in a free translation was 'On the contrary – the more you are on the job, the more you get done.'

188. The antagonisms that arose in South Africa as a result of the N'komati

agreement again demonstrated the flaws in the perception that characterised the West's political assessment that the decision-making structure in South Africa was monolithic and that the prime minister should by and large be regarded as a dictator with full control and grasp of the country's internal and external affairs. Even if there is a great deal of evidence that the South African military flagrantly breached the N'komati agreement for a number of years, it is far from clear that these violations occurred with the knowledge or approval of the South African government. Much indicates that the South African government lacked the capability to ensure that the N'komati agreement was complied with in practice. It is evident that the military leadership was sceptical about the agreement. It is equally clear that several officers opposed the agreement. Several of these were originally Portuguese, who left Mozambique on independence.

189. South African companies completely shared Prime Minister Botha's description of the N'Komati agreement to South African domestic opinion as a very important stage in the endeavour for some form of 'constellation of Southern African states' under South African leadership. During negotiations on the agreement, extensive South African investments were also promised with the proviso that political differences of opinion could be resolved. Just one month after the agreement a contract was also concluded regarding Mozambican supplies of electrical power from Cabora Bassa to South Africa.

6. Stabilisation and Adjustment

190. In May 1985 the World Bank agreed on a set of loans worth $45 million, the first IDA credit, aiming to support the implementation of the programme (World Bank, 1985).

191. Government of Mozambique, 1987.

192. In June 1987 the IMF agreed on a $16 million structural adjustment facility and in August the World Bank opened a second rehabilitation credit amounting to $90 million (World Bank, 1987).

193. However, Mozambican attempts to make the creditors abandon their linkage of the interest rate level on bilateral loans to the growth of the floating commercial interest rate met with little sympathy. As a result of the influence of the domestic American restrictive monetary policy on the international finance market, the current commercial interest rate was high and was a great drain on the country's foreign currency reserves. At the end of 1988 only two creditors had reduced interest rates significantly, namely Italy (to 1.7 per cent) and the Soviet Union, which granted interest-free loans.

194. Apart from debts to the OECD countries, the bilateral debt also consists of loans from the former Soviet Union and the OPEC countries. It is not clear how and to whom debts to the former Eastern bloc will be repaid. A number of proposals have been drawn up for different types of buy-out and so-called 'swaps', where the creditors have the right to exchange a certain share of debts against domestic currency for local company purchases or investments. Mozambique has also renegotiated its debts to the OPEC countries, in several cases on better terms than had been obtained within the Paris Club. Mozambique's commercial debt has been relatively limited in relation to the bilateral debt and originally consisted mainly of due suppliers' credit. During the second half of

the 1980s, however, it grew rapidly as various foreign banks took over the debts and unpaid interest was capitalised and added to the debt capital. At the end of 1991 the commercial debt amounted to $274 million, of which $80 million comprised capitalised interest. At the same time a debt buy-back package was implemented whereby Mozambique repurchased more than half its commercial debts at a price of less than 10 per cent of their original value. However, several banks decided not to sell their claims despite the risk of never being paid for due interest or recovering their loans. They hoped instead to be able to use the claims to obtain real property in exchange – an exchange that would yield considerably more than the barely 10 per cent offered on repurchase.

195. Government of Mozambique, 1991b. See also World Bank, 1990b, 'Mozambique – Economic Policy Framework, 1990–92' which refers to the importance of including special economic measures for the socially most vulnerable population groups. The report, which was presented at the donor meeting in Paris in the spring of 1990, was followed in the autumn of the same year by a more detailed description of measures necessary to combat poverty. See World Bank, 1990c, 'Mozambique – Poverty Reduction Framework Paper'.

196. World Bank, 1985, Report No. P-4100-Moz, and World Bank, 1987, Report No. P-4608–Moz.

197. World Bank, 1993c.

198. IMF, 1993.

199. World Bank, 1993c.

200. World Bank, 1993a.

201. World Bank, 1993a.

202. World Bank, 1993a and IMF, 1993.

203. Fernandes, 1992.

204. The economic effects measured in foreign currency for destroyed materials have been estimated at approximately $250 million. Stephens, 1991, p. 130.

205. The value of lost freight revenues as a result of the stagnation has been estimated at approximately $350 million for the period 1982–89. Reduced volumes led to considerably larger losses. If Mozambique had been able to transport the regional quantity of goods for 1975 during the period 1982–89, currency revenues from transit traffic would have increased by around $1 billion. In other words, the total cost of destabilisation for Mozambique's transport system amounts to approximately $1.6 billion. There are also lost freight revenues during the period in which the Rhodesian border was closed, which amount to around $550 million according to the UN's calculations. Altogether this corresponds to about half the value of investments presently made in Mozambique within the framework of SADCC. From Table 6.3 the economic consequences of destabilisation with regard to transit revenues are made clear. It is interesting to note how freight revenues fell faster and by more than the quantity of goods. This is a result of another component in the South African transport strategy. Low-value goods are still sent across Mozambique, while high-value goods are increasingly transported via South Africa.

206. *Informação Estatística*, CNP, for different years. Bilateral and multilateral donors have exerted different forms of pressure on the government to reduce expenditure on defence. However, foreign military attachés have pointed out that the Mozambican defence budget as a whole is low in international terms

and is regarded as barely adequate for maintaining a regular army in peacetime – even less so in times of war. The defence costs' percentage share of the state budget and GDP should therefore principally be seen as a result of the country's far too limited economy.

207. IMF, 1991.
208. *Plano Económico e Social*, 1993.
209. World Bank, 1993a.
210. World Bank, 1993a.
211. *Plano Ecomónico e Social*, 1993.
212. World Bank, 1993c.
213. *Plano Económico e Social*, 1993.
214. *Plano Ecomónico e Social*, 1993.
215. World Bank, 1993c.
216. South Africa's regionally dominant role is shown clearly in the statistics. The country has, with its 36 million inhabitants, a GDP three times larger than the SADC members' total GDP, even though they have 77 million inhabitants. While GDP per capita in South Africa amounted to $1,729 in 1989, it was $308 for SADC's member countries taken as a whole. Agriculture was responsible for an unusually small share of GDP in both South Africa and SADC countries (6 per cent and 25 per cent respectively), while industry and the service industry were considerably more significant. Industrial production's share of GDP amounted to 44 per cent and 32 per cent respectively, while the service industry's share was 50 per cent and 43 per cent respectively. The total value of SADC's foreign trade in round figures is only half that of South Africa. The member countries' internal trade, i.e. their intra-regional trade within the framework of SADC cooperation, amounted to only 4–5 per cent of their foreign trade. International dependency is thus important for the whole region. Thus the trade pattern between South Africa and SADC is determined by the dominance of intercontinental exports of minerals and agricultural products for all the countries. These constitute over 60 per cent of export revenues. In this way only 7 per cent of SADC countries' total exports go to South Africa. Eighteen per cent of the SADC countries' imports come from South Africa. Of South Africa's exports only around 10 per cent goes to the region, while its imports from the region only amount to 3 per cent. However, it should not be immediately concluded that the SADC countries' dependency on South Africa is so much larger, rather the reverse. If we disregard South Africa's mineral exports, then as much as 20 per cent of South Africa's exports of goods from manufacturing industries go to the region. Furthermore, the economic mutual dependence between SADC and South Africa does not refer in the main to foreign trade. It is mainly within the service and transport sectors that the dependency is significant. A total of 40 per cent of the miners in South Africa come from the neighbouring countries, mainly Lesotho and Mozambique. Over 60 per cent of the region's intercontinental trade goes via South African ports at the same time as the transport corridors in southern Mozambique would imply significant cost savings for both South Africa's and the other countries' foreign trade. See further: Cardoso, 1992.

217. Government of Mozambique, 1993a.
218. World Bank, 1993c.

219. World Bank, 1993c.

220. Our own observations in the Montepeuz, Balama and Namuno districts show the same trend. Peasants are having to pay more for consumer goods calculated in kilos of maize sold.

221. *Children on the Frontline*, 1988.

222. Matthew, 1993

223. World Bank, 1993.

224. Available population statistics are unreliable. However, there is no doubt about the rapid growth in urbanisation. The urban population was estimated in 1970 to be 5.7 per cent of the total population, while in 1990 it was estimated to be nearly 30 per cent. See World Bank, 1990d.

225. World Bank, 1990d, p. 5.

226. *Plano Económico e Social*, 1993

227. Hermele, 1988a, World Bank, 1990d, Gebauer, 1991.

7. The Impact of International Aid

228. The figures presented are unreliable. They build on the donors' annual reports to UNDP. There are usually duplicate accounts for different years, as well as overvaluation of the aid resources provided. The figures presented by the Mozambican administration are significantly lower and for some years only amount to just under 50 per cent of what has been reported by UNDP. It is most often these lower figures which are used by the World Bank and the IMF. The variances are partly explained by some disaster, development and technical assistance aid still being channelled outside the state budget and not always being included in the Mozambican figures.

229. UNDP, 1992a.

230. However, Mozambican attempts to convert some of the support into joint ventures produced small results. One innovation during that period was the opportunity to send over 10,000 Mozambicans to work in East Germany. The aim was to educate Mozambican industrial workers in order to take over operations in industrial plants being built up in Mozambique at the time.

231. One of the reasons for the lack of countervalue payments is that many enterprises, like state authorities, quite simply lack the resources for this. Earlier subsidies have been abolished and debts still not repaid reduce the scope for new loans. This restrictive monetary and credit policy has reduced the possibilities and increased the costs for domestic borrowing for imports over and above what the enterprise itself can bear economically at the time. State authorities have had their budgets cut. The result has been a severe delay in exploitation of the financial resources that aid placed at their disposal and a large destruction of capital for the aid-financed goods remaining in ports in the case of recipients who lack the means to release them.

232. 'Department of Prevention and Combat of Natural Disasters'.

233. In this way the Ministry of Finance has expressed disquiet at the fact that the World Bank is employing foreign experts who have publicly expressed doubts about the programme's consistency and feasibility.

234. A concrete example is the various views of the state's role and the need for administrative capacity building. While the IMF and international creditors

put the main emphasis on deregulation and a free market economy, the World Bank and aid donors often stress the state's role as an instrument for economic control as a guarantee for the administrative and institutional framework which makes a market economy possible.

235. World Bank, 1993b.

236. Executive Summary, copy in the authors' archives.

237. The evaluation was carried out by the authors. The factual information in the text was gathered during the field work carried out during the spring of 1992. See Abrahamsson and Nilsson, 1992.

238. See, *inter alia*, VIAK, 1985, Berger, 1988, and Brennan and Lockwood, 1985.

239. Interview with Julius Schlotthauer, USAID manager, Maputo 9.4.1992, Abrahamsson and Nilsson, 1992.

240. Frequently the donors carry out their own identification of need and earmark their support to a certain local area. When the food aid then lands eight to ten months later the local supply situation has often changed.

241. Another reason why disaster support often drives out locally produced food is the existence of international food subsidies, together with demands from the international credit institutions that when Mozambique sets prices for its own food production it should use 'International Parity Prices', i.e. prices that are comparable with what it costs to import food. The background to these conditions is the fear that domestic farmers would otherwise be paid too little in relation to world market prices. However, prevailing international food subsidies mean that the world market price for grain is below actual production costs, even in countries with the highest efficiency. It is these subsidised prices that form the 'import value' of the food support intended for commercial sale through the trade network in Mozambique. Wholesale prices for imported maize in Mozambique are consequently determined by the subsidised world market prices with which few, or no, traders or peasants in Mozambique can compete. Low returns and extremely high transport costs make it impossible to supply domestically produced maize to the mills in Maputo and Beira at prices corresponding to the subsidised world market prices for grain. This means that the traditional low-yielding agriculture in Mozambique is being exposed to higher productivity requirements than the mechanised agriculture in Western Europe and North America. A Mozambican peasant farmer cannot compete with the imported maize without access to the same amount of subsidies. Local production can never reach the large ports at a price that can compete with the artificially low import prices. Besides, during the year 1992–93 large quantities of disaster relief food have been distributed in areas where there is no disaster situation. This maize is largely taken to the towns and sold at very low prices. In Manica, for example, maize was sold to consumers for 25 per cent of the world market price.

242. At local level competition sometimes arises between foreign organisations and the Mozambican administration. Conflicts have often been connected to situations where the Mozambican administration is attempting to avoid the negative effects of food distribution. In Changara district the administrator attempted to reduce the general free distribution of maize in favour of a higher degree of selective distribution. This resulted in a foreign voluntary organisation attempting to mobilise the population against the administrator. They main-

tained that it was 'he who did not want them to get any food'. Local tensions have direct repercussions on policy and democracy if the control over the population's survival, right down to individual level, gets into the hands of foreign religious organisations, for example, who demand participation in prayer meetings and religious activity for those who want some of the disaster support.

243. This leads us to make yet another observation. It often happens that disaster relief is distributed free in areas where some of the population have purchasing power, which comes from wages or other activities which are not as climate-dependent as grain. This applies, for example, in the Changara district in Tete province. Changara lies in an area with little rain which has a permanent grain deficit. The population lives on raising goats and cattle to some extent. Garlic is grown to a large extent along the riverbeds. This means that a large part of the population can maintain some purchasing power even in long periods of drought. Another example refers to the three southernmost provinces, Maputo, Gaza and Inhambane. Mozambican miners in South Africa send money home to their families and thus create the basis for a food market, which is neither climate- nor war-dependent. Making a selection among the population in disaster areas is naturally a hard task. Nonetheless, local authorities often make such selections based on their knowledge of local conditions. Different donors, however, have different attitudes to the value of such selections. A non-selective distribution of free maize to a rural population where there is purchasing power itself involves an extra contribution of resources, which immediately trickles back to the towns' informal sector. There the free maize supplements the commercial system's inadequate supplies. It can be sold at a yet lower price than the imported maize, because the donated maize has no 'production costs' at all. These circumstances surrounding donated maize also appear to obstruct local production. One example is free distribution to goat farmers with a certain purchasing power in Changara, which blocks supplies on the market in Tete from the maize-producing districts in the province – Angonia and Tsangano. At the same time as there is a surplus of maize in these districts, disaster relief maize is transported to the neighbouring districts of Chíuta, Macanga, Chifunde and Maravia. The peasant farmers who want to sell their surplus take their sacks instead for sale in Malawi.

8. State and Market in Distortion

244. The outline for a new constitution which was developed by Frelimo's Central Committee established in brief that the country's economy should be based on a market economy. This statement became the subject of intense debate at the subsequent People's Assembly. The Mozambican news bureau reported parts of this debate in the following way: 'The draft presented by the Central Committee stated baldly that the Mozambican economic order shall rest on a "market economy". But the governor of the Bank of Mozambique, Eneas Comiche, called for this to be removed, arguing that it was not normal to enshrine any specific economic model in a country's constitution. He pointed out that "there is no such thing as a pure market economy" and warned against expecting that "the simple play of market forces will result in equitable develop-

ment"', (Mozambique file No. 171). Eneas Comiche was the country's finance minister until the end of 1994.

245. One example of this is the World Bank's support for the municipal administration in Beira. Copies of the telex correspondence between the World Bank and the Mozambican authorities where these demands are explicitly made can be found in the authors' archives.

246. As stated earlier, savings are based almost exclusively on external sources of aid or revenues from service exports. Domestic savings are extremely low and have been negative for a couple of years. There are still no studies analysing how the restrictive monetary policy, in combination with continuous devaluations, is affecting the preconditions for increased domestic savings. It seems reasonable to assume a negative connection, i.e. that the credit restrictions, together with the price rises, are undermining the preconditions for both households' and enterprises' official savings within the banking system.

247. Sharpley, 1993. In November 1992 an EU mission highlighted the problems with the lack of access to credits. The banking system was seen to concentrate too much of its lending on short-term loans directed towards commerce (mainly imports of consumer goods with a high turnover rate). The productive sector's problems in gaining access to credits at a reasonable cost were reinforced during 1992 as a result of the new market-based system for distributing foreign currency. Payment of countervalue will now be made in connection with payment of foreign currency to the foreign supplier, i.e. before the goods leave the exporting country. The mission established that several export licences had been cancelled as a result of the banks' unwillingness to provide the necessary credits. The result has been a reduced exploitation of import support resources. The World Bank argues that it is not the monetary policy itself which is too restrictive, but that the problem lies rather in the lack of countervalue payments and that the countervalue payments actually made are largely tied by the donors. The Mozambican government is thereby denied an opportunity to make use of the countervalue funds in order to finance its own state budget or to raise the credit ceiling. (Internal PM circulated between the donor community and the World Bank in Maputo on account of the EU mission's report of 27.11.92. Copies can be found in the authors' archives.)

248. Matthew, 1993.

249. World Bank, 1993c.

250. In this way the government's opportunities to carry out a more expansive fiscal policy would increase. Credit restrictions, however, have meant that very few enterprises have any possibility of paying the countervalue. Delays have therefore arisen with reference to exploiting the international import support.

251. De Vylder, 1993.

252. For a general description of the negative influence of the international economy and world trade on separate countries' opportunities for economic recovery, see UNDP, 1992b.

253. No reliable studies to calculate the country's minimum import needs have yet been carried out. There is manifestly a risk that the unilateral endeavours for export-oriented development will draw attention away from measures which could reduce the need for imports. The macro-economic effects of increased food production on reduced food imports should be researched and

compared with the macro-economic effects that increasing exports are expected to entail.

254. The distinctions are borrowed from Karlström, 1991.

255. This concept is borrowed from Hydén, 1983.

256. Aid donors have done very little to help the country's authorities correct the administrative deficiencies which facilitate the misuse, for example, of disaster relief. The statement by USAID's site official in Maputo deserves to be re-examined in this context. The statement gives the impression that the American administration regarded the growing corruption as being something positive, because it contributed to undermining the administrative capacity of the Mozam-bican state, and to increasing the state's problem of legitimacy *vis-à-vis* the starving population.

257. Apart from selling stolen state property or smuggled goods, the informal sector offers very different types of services which should formally be supplied by the public administration. This ongoing individualisation and privatisation of public, collective consumption is beginning to be found in schools, health-care, transport and dispatch activity, and in the issue of different types of permits. Parents are forced to pay to have their children enrolled in schools, then they have to pay teachers for extra tuition every school year for the children to pass. It is today considered impossible to have an X-ray investigation carried out at the central hospital in Maputo without paying the staff extra. In order to obtain import goods from the ports, or through customs, extra payments to the person-nel involved are required, a sort of raised 'stamp duty', which helps people to survive in a pressured situation. The problem is not mainly economic in that the informal sector is coming to represent economic activities with ever higher added value than is either taxed or included in official economic statistics. Above all the problem is political. For the majority of people who are daily afflicted by this illegal system of distribution of essential goods and services, confidence in the public sector and the legitimacy of the state is naturally declining. The result tends to be a general moral disintegration where more are forced to take part in an unjust system in which individuals and family providers mainly lose out most themselves.

258. Disquiet concerning the ability of market forces to correct current im-perfections originate in the clear tendencies shown for private investments to move into areas where there is already demand and into speculation in urban trade and transport services. Even if this empirical basis is too inadequate for scientific testing by both the World Bank and our standpoint, the consultative studies made of the macro-economic effects of import support show that our unease is justified. As has been made clear, a very large part of import support is used for imports of consumer goods which are mainly demanded in urban areas. A small and disappearing part has gone to industry, agriculture and the social sectors. One argument for import support is that it gives rise to a counter-value, which in turn allows increased volumes of credits. The problem with this is that the credits are used in general terms in the form of so-called short credits (90 days) for internal trade and go to a very small extent to productive invest-ments (Sharpley, 1993). As far as we have been able to ascertain, no studies have been carried out to analyse the extent to which this high turnover rate affects the rate of inflation (which is calculated to amount to just over 50 per cent for

1992). Increased productive investments with a lower turnover rate of capital would probably provide scope for both an increased volume of credit and a lower rate of inflation.

259. As a rule political leaders (also from Frelimo) from the northern and central areas of the country never fail to point out in private conversations that all Frelimo's presidents, Mondlane, Machel and Chissano, were born in Gaza province, in villages which can be found within a circle with a radius of about 50 km.

260. World Bank, 1993c.

261. Government of Mozambique, 1991 and 1993a.

262. World Bank, 1985, 1987 and 1992.

9. Democracy and Civil Society

263. Republica Popular de Moçambique, 1988, Projecto de revisão da constituição da República Popular de Moçambique, Maputo.

264. The debate during the People's Assembly is summarised in *Mozambique File*, November 1990, No. 172.

265. AIM Report, 1983, April, Maputo.

266. Published, *inter alia*, in *Noticias*, 26 January 1991.

267. See Acordo Geral da Paz, III.

268. Boletin da República; I Serie – Número 2; 12 de Janeiro 1994.

269. There is an extensive and protracted discussion about how a nation-state should be defined. Most of those who have been involved in this question appear to agree that people's own personal perception of their own national, and ethnic, affiliation must be a central element of a definition. Regardless of which observable indicators are used to define an ethnic group or a nation – origin, language, culture, history, geographical affiliation, etc. – the decisive question appears to be the individual person's perception of their and other's affiliation. If two people recognise each other as members of the same nation or ethnic group, it is a safer criterion than any other indicator visible to those outside. This means that questions involving nations and ethnic groups cannot only be dealt with using supposedly objective criteria. Political expressions of nationalism and ethnicity build principally on the interpretations of the situation of the people involved. A discussion on this subject could be found in note 154.

270. There is much to indicate that we are today in a historical period where the attempts of the last thirty years to create nation-states on the European model are proving to have severe consequences. It is not hard to find current examples of state formations which are having difficulties in holding together: Somalia, Sudan, Liberia and Rwanda. Even if these states differ in their history and in the underlying causes for their disintegration, the state-building project has failed in as much as the state is no longer a legitimate institution in the whole territory. If the nation-state crisis in Africa has any connection with the difficulties people have in rapidly developing a national consciousness on command, instead of a geographically limited system of loyalties within families, generations, ethnic groups or nations, intra-state and international border adjustments ought to be a remedy. International border adjustments, however, have hitherto been taboo in Africa. A very early decision in the OAU (Organisation

of African Unity) established that the colonial border demarcations should not be modified. Even if the African political élites also wish to maintain this principle in future, developments may be such that the world around may feel called upon to force ethnically determined border adjustments in Africa. This may eventually offer the only possibility for preventing local conflicts from spreading or causing extensive intra- or inter-continental migrations. The UN operation in Somalia may prove to have been one of the last attempts to save a torn-apart state-building process. The new leadership in Ethiopia has taken a step in this direction by adjusting the country's administrative divisions according to traditional ethnic boundaries.

271. Babtista-Lundin, 1992. There is cause to stop for a moment and look at the expression of the rural population's 'return to traditional society'. A more correct term for the circumstances referred to would perhaps be to employ some societal procedures which in spite of modernisation efforts still prevail. Instead of traditional society it may be more relevant to talk about Mozambican national society. The use of the concept of 'national society' is rendered difficult as the society referred to varied over the period in its content between different population groups and areas of the country. When we therefore choose to use the term 'traditional', it should also be pointed out that this is not based in any way on a static view of a society's development or on the perception that some parts of a society were isolated from other parts of that society. A societal movement may incorrectly be perceived as being limited in two directions – forwards and backwards. Backwards movement is thus implicitly negative. The word 'traditional' can lead our thoughts in that direction. According to our point of view traditional society and the content of the circumstances we are describing were developed over time. When a traditional society again acquires a greater significance for people's supplies and social confidence it reflects the fact that the society has been developed to contain a set of concepts which fulfil an important function in the reality characterising the Mozambican rural population. The 'failure' of modernisation has contributed to 'traditional' society being allowed to redevelop its social and economic capacity sufficiently to again represent functional elements in people's lives.

272. By alternative élites we mean all the élites, with different origins and social bases, who are outside political and economic influence.

273. Gramsci, 1971.

274. We do not intend to enter into a theoretical discussion about the concept of a civil society. However, it should be noted that our use of the concept of a civil society is inspired by our interpretation of Gramsci. In this interpretation we have also been assisted by Cox, 1983 and Gill, 1992. A more 'mainstream' way of looking at civil society in Africa is that it actually lacks organisational forms which can fill a perceived void between the state and the individual citizen. This point of view means that one disregards the genuine African organisational forms stemming from family, clan or ethnic identity. Because these forms are not always easy to discover, it is concluded that no organisational form exists. A natural next step is thus to recommend that organisations must be created which can fill the empty spaces in African politics. Our intention in making a distinction between traditional society and civil society is to question the attitude existing in aid donor circles, that a quantitative increase in the number of domestic

voluntary (or non-governmental) organisations would automatically be a sign of growing strength of civil society and thus contribute to resolving the problem of legitimacy, which many African states suffer from. Our hypothesis is that principles creating legitimacy differ between the civil society and the traditional. Therefore we cannot presuppose that imported forms of organisation from European or American civil societies will immediately come to be considered to be legitimate and thus contribute to increasing stability in African societies on the way to disintegration.

275. Polanyi, 1944.

276. Traditional society in Africa most closely resembles the society that the French economic historian Fernand Braudel calls a material civilisation, i.e. the forms of subsistence agriculture and barter that characterised people's organisation of their survival before the market economy penetrated through to local level (Braudel, 1979).

10. Transition in Turmoil

277. UNDP, 1992b and Odén, 1993.

278. UNDP, 1992b.

279. At SADCC's annual meeting of heads of state in the Namibian capital of Windhoek in August 1992, the organisation was renamed the 'Southern Africa Development Community' (SADC). Agreements were also reached on several important changes regarding the organisation's goals and legal status. The changes reflect the importance which the member countries place on the organisation's future. While SADCC functioned more as a project coordination organisation, SADC, in accordance with its new statutes, will strive for more substantial regional integration, where supranationality is not precluded. Apart from regional economic development, security and economic policy cooperation are also included in SADC's goals. SADCC's earlier goals of reducing dependency have been removed completely.

280. A photocopy of a document which was retrieved from a captured Renamo base in the Maringue district in March 1991. *MIO News Review*, No. 221, 16 April 1992.

281. It is the irony of history that one of the effects of the negotiations in Rome and the subsequent peace accord is that Remamo has been supplied with both an army it never had (through the training for the new army) and a political programme and organisation it never managed to develop during the war. All this was done at the expense of the donors.

11. Searching for a Way Out

282. For this reason the South African social researcher, Abdul Minty, for example, prefers to talk of 'neo-apartheid' instead of 'post-apartheid'.

283. See, for example, Judge Goldstone's investigation into the participation of the police in the organisation of acts of violence in the townships, described in, *inter alia*, *Weekly Mail*, 8 May 1992.

284. By fanonist violence we mean a spontaneous violence which grows out of desperation in an impossible life situation. In Fanon's opinion this violence is

legitimate in the sense that it grows from the anger of the oppressed. Fanon, 1961.

285. Cawthra, 1986, Grundy, 1988, pp. 71–6.

286. In Davidson, 1992, a description is given of this development which emphasises how the African development process towards state-building was disrupted through the slave trade and the long colonial period. When the state-building process was resumed in the middle of the 1950s this was done on a different basis, namely the European model for nation-states. The two countries which have probably been most successful in Southern Africa are Botswana and Tanzania. However, they are each in an extreme situation with regard to ethnic homogeneity. Botswana has a mainly homogenous population with one language. Tanzania, on the other hand, has an abundance of smaller ethnic groups, none of which have been strong enough to be able to dominate the others.

287. Magode and Kahn, 1992.

288. By alternative élites we mean all élites, with different origins and social bases, who stand outside political and economic influence.

289. There is some doubt, however, about federal or regionalised solutions for the restructuring of the Mozambican state. Both could lead to a 'territorialisation' of ethnicity, which today is not politicised. Territorialisation refers to the administrative division of the country being changed in a direction towards it largely corresponding with the areas of different ethnic groups. An attempt at this has been implemented by the government in Ethiopia. A territorialisation of ethnicity in Mozambique could become a political claim from certain regional or provincial élites who are attempting to broaden their social base. A restructuring which means that political representation *must* be based on ethnic affiliation will come to increase the need for ethnic mobilisation and may also lead to an 'ethnic cleansing', as in Yugoslavia, in order to homogenise the population within established regions. It should be noted in this context that all parties in the recent elections used the campaigning strategy to fill their lists for the eleven electoral circles (coinciding with provinces) with people from the respective province, whether or not they had lived there during their adult lives.

290. Several researchers in the Third World who can observe nation-building from within feel that it is not nation-building that is going on, but nation-destruction. In order to build up a new nation it is consequently required that an unspecified number of other nations are disrupted. The Indian sociologist, Partha N. Mukherji, considers that it is not possible to base the nation concept on an ethnic and cultural identity and at the same time see the nation as a stable base for the state. The definition of the nation must instead emphasise citizens as the most important component in state-building, which allows it to develop a comprehensive 'civil' culture, which in turn makes it possible for a multiplicity of cultural expressions to coexist. Citizens must be superior to other categories such as race, sex, caste or class as a deciding concept for the nation. Such questioning of the Western nation concept does not mean, for Mukherji, that ethnic and cultural groups can henceforth also seek their own political organisational forms, including independence. The expectations behind such a redefinition would be that all citizens will find a place for their need for their own identity within a nation guided by an all-embracing and generous cultural view. It will thus be possible to begin to introduce the concept of a multi-nation

state as a replacement for a nation-state, with regard to state organisation in multi-ethnic societies. See Mukherji, 1992, pp. 27ff.

291. See Chapter 1.

292. *Anuário Estatístico*, 1992.

293. The lack of concentration on rural development is illustrated by the fact that in many areas there is still a shortage of hoes in Mozambique. During 1993 the peasant farmers' need for seed and hoes could only be satisfied by 25 per cent and 75 per cent respectively. In connection with the population in the town of Milange, in Zambezia province, plundering a food store in the middle of March 1993, they did not satisfy themselves with carrying away the food found in the store, but also took 7,500 hoes with them (*Mozambiquefile*, March 1993). An inquiry from the Angonia district at the turn of the year 1993/1994 shows that the peasants had on average two hoes per family. This means that for the majority they were restricted in making use of the labour force within the family.

294. The study carried out by Sveriges Lantbruksuniversitet [Sweden's University for Agriculture] in Ulltuna, in cooperation with Mozambican authorities under the leadership of Lars Erik Birgegård, in 1990, has made us aware of this problem. See Carrilho et al., 1990.

295. World Bank, 1993c.

296. World Bank, 1993a.

297. Government of Mozambique, 1993.

298. A financing gap consists of the difference between a country's import requirement (imports, debt servicing and arrears) and its financial resources (export and service revenues, aid and loans). Different reports published by the Bretton Woods institutions record different financing gaps, depending on which calculation bases are used. The majority of the IMF's and the World Bank's calculations show that the financing gap will almost be closed around the year 2000, on the assumption that a 5 per cent annual production increase will take place, that revenues from exports and services will develop as calculated, that debt relief is granted and that the flow of aid continues to increase. World Bank, 1992a and IMF, 1991.

299. IMF, 1991 and 1993. The prognoses for coal exports constitute a clear example of completely unrealistic assumptions. Mozambique's coal stocks are located in Tete province, which is 500 km from the nearest export port. The railway line which previously carried coal to Beira has been destroyed by the war and non-existent maintenance over the last ten years. The existing coal terminus in Beira port is completely inadequate for the estimated export quantities. A South African/Brazilian coal consortium has calculated the future potential of coal exports. The IMF's prognosis up to the year 2000 regarding the possibilities for closing the financial gap is partly based on revenues from these increased coal exports. While 30 per cent of export revenues in the year 2000 are expected to come from the mineral sector, coal exports are expected, according to the prognoses, to account for 15 per cent or around 3 million tonnes (IMF 1991). The previous maximum export of coal amounted to 236,000 tons per year. The IMF's prognosis greatly exceeds the pace of the private coal consortium's extraction plans. At the same time the Fund underestimates the necessary investments for extraction, transportation and handling. According to the consortium's plans, the total cost of necessary new investments is calculated

at 1.3 billion dollars over a four-year period (according to the consortium's calculations). According to the IMF's prognoses, total private foreign investments for all sectors in the whole country amount to a maximum of $450 million. This corresponds to only 30 per cent of what is required in order to bring about profitable coal-mining. The question of who is expected to finance the remaining costs has not been answered. The Mozambican government's plan for public investments during the period 1991–93 anticipates no public inputs to support the plans for increased coal exports (PTIP, 1991–93).

300. Our interpretation of the IMF's over-optimistic prognoses is that these can hardly be explained by the Fund's lack of access to an economic analysis capacity. The Fund's prognoses should, according to our interpretation, be regarded more as an attempt to make the structural adjustment programmes credible, thereby facilitating the mobilisation of the international creditors' and aid donors' financing of their implementation. This interpretation is also supported (even though implicitly) in personal conversations with Mozambican decision-makers who consider that there was reason for our doubts but that we must understand that the whole prognosis exercise was rather a matter of 'political and accounting technique'. In this also lies, according to our interpretation, the reason that the Fund, in the name of its board, has chosen to present such a defective risk analysis as they have, where the war is hardly mentioned as an obstructing factor. The IMF's task is above all political. Against the background of the political situation that prevailed in Southern Africa at the time of Mozambique's membership of the Bretton Woods institutions, the Reagan administration was clearly interested in a Mozambican rapprochement with the West. At the same time it was hard for the Reagan administration to convince Congress of the importance of more extensive American financial support. In order for a Mozambican rapprochement with the West to be possible, not only would the country's economy and policy, not least its foreign policy, therefore need to be changed but also wider international financial preconditions would need to be created which would also make it possible to implement these domestic political system changes in practice. The only possible way for the Americans to mobilise such financing was through the IMF. Our point is not the financial mobilisation as such. It is that, for political reasons in Washington, an incorrect diagnosis of the Mozambican economic situation was presented, giving rise to the design and implementation of an unsuitable remedy.

301. See World Bank, 1992a.

302. SIDA, 1992.

Select Bibliography

Abrahamsson, Hans, 1989, *Transport Structures and Dependency Relations in Southern Africa: The Need for a Reorientation of Nordic Aid*, Nordic Africa Institute, Uppsala.

Abrahamsson, Hans and Nilsson, Anders, 1992, *Power and Powerlessness in a Starving Mozambique*, report to SIDA, mimeo.

— 1993, *Education and Society in Mozambique*, report to SIDA, mimeo.

Accelerated Development in Sub-Saharan Africa, (The Berg Report), Washington, 1981.

Adam, Yussuf, 1987, *Cooperativização agrícola e modificação das relações de produção no período colonial em Moçambique*, Teses de licenciatura, Centro de Estudos Africanos, Universidade Eduardo Mondlane, Maputo.

Adam, Yussuf and Gentili, Ana Maria, 1983, 'O Movimento dos Liguilanilu no Planalto de Mueda 1957–1962', *Estudos Moçambicanos*, No. 4.

Adam, Yussuf and Cruz e Silva, Teresa, 1989, *Mercados e Preços nas Zonas Rurais*, CEA, UEM, Maputo.

Amin, Samir, Chitala Derrick and Mandaza, Ibo, 1987, *SADCC–Prospects for Disengagement and Development in Southern Africa*, Zed Books, London.

Anderson, Benedict, 1983, *Imagined Communities*, Verso, London.

Anuário Estatístico, 1990, 1991, 1992, Commissão Nacional do Plano, Maputo.

Atlas Geográfico, Vol. I, Esselte, Stockholm.

Babtista-Lundin, Iraê, 1992, *Modelos Sócio Culturais*, paper presented at the seminar 'Moçambique no Pós Guerra – Desafios e Realidades', organised by the Higher Institute for International Relations (ISRI) in Maputo 14–18 December 1992.

Bender, Gerald et al., 1985, *African Crisis Areas and U.S. Foreign Policy*, University of California Press, Berkeley, CA.

Berger, Lewis, 1988, *Evaluation of OFDA and FFP Grants to Care International in Mozambique*, Washington.

Bernis de, Destanne, 1970, 'L'Économie Algérienne depuis l'Indépendance', *L'Annuaire de l'Afrique du Nord*, ANN, CNRS, Paris.

Blomström, Magnus and Hettne, Björn, 1984, *Development theory in transition. The dependency debate and beyond – Third World responses*, Zed Books, London.

Boletin da República, 1994, 12 January.

Bratton, Michael, 1989, 'Beyond the State: Civil Society and Associational Life in Africa', *World Politics*, Volume XLI, No. 3, April 1989, pp. 407–30.

Braudel, Fernand, 1979, *Les structures du quotidien: le possible et l'impossible*, Librairie Armand Colin, Paris.

Brennan, Tom and Lockwood, Richard, 1985, *Evaluation of OFDA Grant ASB-OOOO-G-SS-4108 to Care/Mozambique to establish an emergency assistance logistical unit*, OFDA, Washington.

Brochmann, Grete and Ofstad, Arve, 1990, *Mozambique, Norwegian Assistance in a Context of Crisis*, Chr. Michelsen Institute, Bergen.

Brzezinski, Zbigniew, 1963, *Africa and the Communist World*, Stanford University Press, Stanford, CA.

— 1983, *Power and Principle*, Weidenfeld and Nicholson, London.

Burton, John, 1990, *Conflict: Resolution and Prevention*, Macmillan, Houndmill.

Bushin, Vladimir, 1989, *Social Democracy and Southern Africa*, Progress Publishers, Moscow.

Buzan, Barry, 1991, *People, States and Fear*, Harvester Wheatsheaf, London.

Cahen, Michael, 1992, *The Unitary State and the Pluralist State/Social Stability*, paper presented during the seminar 'Moçambique no Pós Guerra – Desafios e Realidades', organised by the Higher Institute for International Relations (ISRI) in Maputo, 14–18 December 1992.

Cardoso, Fernando Jorge, 1992, 'SADCC e interdependência na Africa Austral – Realidades a perspectivas', *Estudos Moçambicanos*, CEA, No. 10, Maputo.

Carrilho, João, et al., 1990, *An Alternative Strategy for Agricultural Development*, Maputo.

Cassen, Robert (ed.), 1985, *Soviet Interests in the Third World*, Royal Institute of International Affairs, London.

Cawthra, Gavin, 1986, *Brutal Force, The Apartheid War Machine*, IDAF, London.

CEA, 1980, 'A Transformacão na Agricultura Familiar na Província de Nampula', *Relatório* No. 80/3, CEA, Maputo.

CEA, 1982, *Agricultural Marketing in the District of Alto Molocue, Zambezia Province*, CEA, Maputo.

CEA, 1985, *South African Capital and the Process of Containerisation*, Report No. 84/3, EUM, Maputo.

Chabal, Patrick, 1992, *Power in Africa*, Macmillan, London.

Clarence-Smith, Gervase, 1989, 'The Roots of the Mozambican Counter-Revolution', *Southern African Review of Books*, April/May.

Cline, Sibyl W., 1989, *Renamo em Defesa da Democracia em Moçambique*, Conselho de Estratégia Global dos Estados Unidos, Washinton, DC.

Cohen, Abner, (ed.), 1974, *Urban Ethnicity*, Tavistock Publications, London,

Cole, Barnara, 1984, *The elite. The Story of the Rhodesian Special Air Service*, The Three Knights, Transkei.

— 1986, *The elite. Rhodesian Special Air Service. Pictorial*, The Three Knights, Amanzimtoti, South Africa.

Cox, Robert W., 1983, 'Gramsci, Hegemony and International relations: An Essay in Method', *Millenium*, 1983, No. 2, pp. 162–75.

Crocker, Chester, A., 1992, *High noon in Southern Africa – making peace in a rough neighbourhood*, W.W. Norton, New York.

Cronje, S., Ling, M. and Cronje, G., 1976, *Lonrho. Portrait of a Multinational*, Penguin, Suffolk.

Darch, Colin, 1983, 'Notas Sobre Fontes Estatísticas Oficiais Refrentes Á Economia Colonial Moçambicana: Uma Crítica Geral', *Estudos Moçambicanos*, No. 4.

Davidson, Basil, 1992, *The Black Man's Burden*, James Currey, London.

Defender a legalidade para fortalecer o estado e consolidar a democracia, Informaçãoda procuradoria-geral da República à 4: a sessão ordinária da Assembleia da República, 1992, Imprensa Nacional de Moçambique, Maputo.

Divisão administrativa de Moçambique por regedorias, Direcção provincial dos servoços de planeamento e integração económica da província de Moçambique, 1970.

Dutton, J.R., 1978, 'Military Aspects of National Security', in Louw, H.H., *National Security: A Modern Approach*, Institute for Strategic Studies, University of Pretoria, Pretoria.

Eduards, Krister, et al., 1990, *Market intervention and Price Policies for Agricultural Marketing in Mozambique*, Report to the Agriculture Bureau, SIDA, Stockholm.

Fanon, Frantz, 1961, *The Wretched of the Earth*, Grove Press, New York.

Fauvet, Paul, 1984, 'The Roots of Counter-Revolution: The Mozambique National Resistance', in *Review of African Political Economy*, No. 29.

— 1985, *Who are these people anyway?*, Mozambique News Agency Feature, No. AF0185E.

Fauvet, Paul and Gomes, Alves, 1979, 'The Mozambique National Resistance', Supplement to *AIM Bulletin* No. 69.

Fernandes, Rosário, 1992, *The Manufacture Industry: A Strategy for Economic Recovery*, paper presented at the seminar 'Moçambique no Pós Guerra – Desafios e Realidades', organised by the Higher Institute for International Relations (ISRI) in Maputo, 14–18 December 1992.

First, Ruth and Davies, Robert, 1980, *Migrant Labour to South Africa: A Sanctions Programme?*, International University Exchange Fund, Geneva.

Flower, Ken, 1987, *Serving Secretly*, John Murray, London.

Frelimo, 1977, *Relatório do Comité Central ao 3 Congresso*, Frelimo, Maputo.

— 1977, *Directivas Económicas e Sociais*, Frelimo, Maputo.

— 1983, *Relatório do Comité Central ao 4 Congresso*, Frelimo, Maputo.

— 1983, *Directivas Económicas e Sociais*, Frelimo, Maputo.

— 1983, *Intervenções dos Delegados 4 Congresso*, Frelimo, Maputo.

Gebauer, Herman, 1991, *The subsidized food distribution system in Mozambique and its socio-economic impact*, mimeo, Maputo.

Geffray, Christian, 1991, *A Causa das Armas*, Edições Afrontamento, Porto.

Geffray, Christian and Pedersen, Mogens, 1985, Transformação da Organização Social e do Sistema Agrário do Campesinato no Distrito do Errati: Process de Socialização do Campo e Diferenciação Social (Departamento de Arqueologia e Antropologia Universidade Eduardo Mondlane, Departamento de Desenvolvimento Rural Ministério de Agricultura, mimeo, Maputo)

— 1986, Sobre a Guerra na província de Nampula. Elementos de análise e hipóteses sobre as determinações sócio-económicas locais, in Revista Internacional de Estudos Africanos nr 4–5, January–December 1986.

Geldenhuys, Dean, 1984, *The Diplomacy of Isolation – South African Policy Making*, Macmillan, Johannesburg.

Gellner, Ernst, 1983, *Nations and Nationalism*, Basil Blackwell, Oxford.

Gersony, Robert, 1988, *Summary of Mozambican Refugee Accounts of Principally Conflict-related Experience in Mozambique*, report submitted to Ambassador Jonathan Moore, Director, Bureau for Refugee Programs, and Dr Chester Crocker, Assistant Secretary of State for African Affairs, April.

Gill, Stephen, 1992, 'Historical Materialism, Gramsci and IPE', in Murphy, Craig N., and Tooze, Roger, eds.

Gilpin, Robert, 1987, *The Political Economy of International Relations*, Princeton University Press, Princeton, NJ.

Gorongosa documents. A selection of handwritten notes, transmitted and received radio messages of the MNR, Ministry of Information, Maputo.

Government of Mozambique, 1987, *Policy Framework Paper 1987–89*, Maputo.

Government of Mozambique, 1990, *Priority District Programme*, mimeo, Maputo.

Government of Mozambique, 1991a, *Policy Framework Paper 1991–1993*, Maputo.

Government of Mozambique, 1991b, *Strategy and Programme for Economic and Social development 1992–94*, mimeo, Maputo.

Government of Mozambique, 1993a, *Policy Framework Paper 1994–1996*, Maputo.

Government of Mozambique, 1993b, *Strategy for the transition from emergency to reconstruction – priority needs for 1994–1995*, Maputo.

Gramsci, Antonio, 1971, *Selections from Prison Notebooks*, International Publishers, New York.

Griffin, K., 1989, *Alternative Strategies for Development*, Macmillan, London.

Grundy, Kenneth W., 1988, *The Militarization of South African Politics*, Oxford University Press, Oxford.

Guerra, João Paulo, 1988, *As Flechas atacam de novo*, Nosso Mundo/Caminho, Lisbon.

Hancock, Graham, 1989, *Lords of Poverty*, Macmillan, London.

Hanlon, Joseph, 1984, *Mozambique: The revolution under fire*, Zed Books, London.

— 1986, *Apartheid's Second Front. South Africa's war against Its Neighbours*, Penguin Books, Harmondsworth.

— 1986b, *Beggar your Neighbours*, Catholic Institute for International Relations, London.

— 1991, *Mozambique – Who calls the shots?*, James Currey, London.

Henriksen, T.H., 1979, *Mozambique: A History*, Rex Collins, London.

Hermele, Kenneth, 1988a, *Country Report – Mozambique*, Report to the Planning Secretariat, SIDA, Stockholm.

— 1988b, *Land Struggles and Social Differentiation in Southern Mozambique*, Scandinavian Institute for African Studies, Uppsala.

— 1989, 'Structural adjustment and political alliances in Angola, Guinea-Bissau and Mozambique', *AKUT* No. 41, Uppsala.

Hettne, Björn, 1990, *Development Theory and the Three Worlds*, Longman, Harlow.

— 1992, *Economic Development and Ethnic Conflicts*, Padrigu, Gothenburg.

História de Moçambique, Volume 1, Cadernos TEMPO, Maputo.

História de Moçambique, Volume 2, Cadernos TEMPO, Maputo.

Hoile, David, 1989, *Mozambique: a Nation in Crisis*, Claridge Press, London.

Hydén Göran, 1983, *No shortcuts to progress*, University of California Press, Los Angeles.

IMF (International Monetary Fund), 1991, *Republic of Mozambique – Request for Second Annual Arrangement under the Enhanced Structural Adjustment Facility* (report EBS/91/136).

— 1993, *Mozambique – Recent Economic Developments* (report SM/93/161).

Informação Estatística, 1975–84, 1985, 1986, 1987, 1988, 1989, Comissão Nacional do Plano, Maputo.

Isaacman, Allen F., 1976, *The Tradition of Resistance in Mozambique*, Heinemann, London.

Isaacman, Allen and Isaacman, Barbara, 1983, *Mozambique. From Colonialism to Revolution*, Zimbabwe Publishing House, Harare.

Jardim, Jorge, 1976, *Terra Queimada*, Editorial Intervenção, Lisbon.

Johnson, Phyllis and Martin, David, eds, 1986, *Destructive Engagement*, Zimbabwe Publishing House, Harare.

Karlström, Bo, 1991, 'Korruptionens anatomi', *Debatt Sida*, No. 2/91.

Kitson, Frank, 1969, *Gangs and Countergangs*, Barie & Rockcliff, London.

— 1971, *Low Intensity Operations*, Faber & Faber, London.

Klare, Michael T., 1981, *Beyond the Vietnam Syndrome. US Interventionism in the 1980s*, Institute for Policy Studies, Washington.

Körner, Peter et al., 1987, *The IMF and the debt crisis*, Zed Books, London.

Leys, Roger and Tostenson, Arne, 1982, 'Regional Cooperation in Southern Africa: The SADCC', *Review of African Political Economy*, No. 23: 52–82.

Lisegang, Gerhard, 1986, *Vassalagem ou Tratado de Amizade? História do Acto de Vassalagem de Ngungunyane nas Relações externas de Gaza*, Arquivo Históroco, Maputo.

Lindholm, Helena, ed., 1992, *International Political Economy*, Padrigu Papers, Gothenburg.

Logistic Support Unit (LSU), 1991, *1990 Annual Report*, mimeo, Maputo.

Low, Allan, 1986, *Agricultural Development in Southern Africa*, James Currey, London.

Machel, Moisés, Samora, 1974, *The People's Democratic Revolutionary Process in Mozambique – The Mozambican Revolution in the World revolutionary Process*. Written in February 1974 for the Soviet Academy of Sciences and published in Moscow in 1975. The text is reproduced in its entirety in Munslow, 1985, pp. 34ff.

— 1975, *A Nossa Luta*, Imprensa Nacional, Maputo.

Mackintosh, Maureen, 1983, 'Comércio e Acumulação: A Comercialização do Milho na Alta Zambezia', *Estudos Moçambicanos* No. 4.

— 1986, 'O capital privado e o estado no sistema de transportes da África Austral', *Estudos Moçambicanos*, No. 5/6, Maputo.

Magaia, Lina, 1986, *Dumba Nengue*, Cadernos Tempo, Maputo.

Magode, José, Mário and Khan, Ângela, 1992, *The Unitary State and the National Question*, paper presented at the seminar 'Moçambique no Pós Guerra – Desafios e Realidades', organised by the Higher Institute for International Relations (ISRI) in Maputo, 14–18 December 1992.

Manghezi, Alpheus, 1983, 'Khu Thekela: Strategies for Survival against Famine in Southern Mozambique', *Estudos Moçambicanos*, No. 4.

Matthew, Martin, 1993, *Macroeconomic Evaluation of Import Support Programmes to Mozambique*, mimeo, Maputo.

O Mineiro Moçambicano. Um Estudo sobre Exportaçãde Mão de Obra, second edn 1988, Centro de Estudos Africanos, Universidade de Eduardo Mondlane, Maputo.

Minter, William, 1989, 'The Mozambican National Resistance (Renamo) as Described by Ex-Participants', *Development Dialogue* 1989: 1.

Mondlane, Eduardo, 1969, *The Struggle for Mozambique*, Zed Books, London.

Munslow, Barry, ed., 1983, *Mozambique: The Revolution and its Origins*, Longman, London.

— 1985, *Samora Machel, An African Revolutionary. Selected Speeches and Writings*, Zed Books, London.

Mukherji, Partha, 1992, 'Class and Ethnic Movements in India', in Rudebeck, Lars, ed., 1992, *When democracy makes sense*, Akut, Uppsala.

Murphy, Craig N. and Tooze, Roger (eds), 1991, *New International Political Economy*, Lynne Riener, Boulder, CO.

Nilsson, Anders, 1990, *Unmasking the bandits. The True Face of the MNR. European Involvement with Apartheid's Tool of Terror*, ECASAAMA, Dublin.

— 1991, 'From Pseudoterrorism to Brigandage', paper presented at the workshop on Security and Cooperation in Post-apartheid Southern Africa, Maputo, 2–6 September, 1991. Revised version in *Review of African Political Economy*, No. 57 and 58/1993.

— 1991b, *Low Intensity Warfare in Mozambique. The creation and development of the Mozambique National Resistance*, mimeo, Padrigu, Gothenburg.

Nogueira da Costa, Inês, 1986, *Contribuição para o estudo do colonial-fascismo em Moçambique*, Arquivo Histórico, Universidade Eduardo Mondlane, Maputo.

Odén, Bertil, 1993, 'Factors Affecting the Flows of External capital to Post-Apartheid Southern Africa', in Odén, Bertil, ed., *Southern Africa after apartheid*, Seminar Proceedings No. 28, Scandinavian Institute of African Studies, Uppsala.

Odén, Bertil and Othman, Haroub, 1989, *Regional Cooperation in Southern Africa*, Scandinavian Institute of African Studies, Uddevalla.

Østergaard, Tom, 1989, 'Aiming Beyond Conventional Development Assistance: An analysis of Nordic Aid in the SADCC region', in Odén, Bertil and Othman, Haroub, *Regional Cooperation in Southern Africa – a post-apartheid perspective*, North Africa Institute, Uppsala.

Paul, John, 1975, *Memories of a Revolution*, Penguin, Harmondsworth.

Payer, Cheryl, 1991, *Lent and Lost, Foreign Credit and Third World Development*, Zed Books, London.

Pereira Leite, Joana, 1990, 'La Reproduction du Résau Imperial Portugais: Quelques Précisions sur la formation du circuit d'or Mozambique/Portugal 1959–1973', *Estudos de Economia*, Vol. X, No. 3, April–June.

Plano Económico e Social, 1993, Comissão Nacional do Plano, Maputo.

Plano Trienal de Investimento Público, various years, Comissão do Plano, Maputo.

Polanyi, Karl, 1944, *The Great Transformation*, Beacon Press, Boston, MA.

Projecto de Revisão da Constituição, 1988, Assemblea Popular, Maputo.

Ratilal, Prakash, 1990, *Emergency in Mozambique – Using Aid to End the Emergency*, UNDP, Maputo.

1 Recenseamento geral da População, 1983, Conselho Coordenador de Recenseamento, Maputo.

Reid-Daly, Ron, 1983, *Selous Scouts. Top Secret War*, Galago, Alberton, South Africa.

Republica Popular de Moçambique, 1984, *Address to the creditors of the People's Republic of Mozambique*, mimeo, Maputo.

Rudebeck, Lars, 1990, 'Conditions of People's Development in Post-Colonial Africa', *AKUT* No. 43 Unit of Development Studies, Uppsala University, Uppsala.

Saul, John, 1985, *A Difficult Road: The Transition to Socialism in Mozambique*, Monthly Review Press, New York.

Serra, Carlos, 1986, *Como a penetração estrangeira transformou o modo de produção dos camponeses moçambicanos*, Vol. 1–2, Universidade Eduardo Mondlane, Maputo.

Sharpley, Jennifer, 1991, *Macroeconomic Evaluation of Sweden's Import Support to Mozambique*, Report to the Planning Secretariat, SIDA, Stockholm.

— 1993, *Supply Oriented Sequencing of Adjustment Politics*, Report of the Commission of the European Community.

SIDA, 1992, *A way out of the debt trap*, SIDA, Stockholm.

Sklar, Molly, ed., 1980, *Trilateralism – The Trilateral Commission and Elite Planning for World Management*, Black Rose Books, Montreal.

South Africa: Time Running Out. The Report of the Study Commission on U.S. Policy Toward Southern Africa, University of California Press, Berkeley and Los Angeles.

Spero, Joan, 1990, *The Politics of International Economic Relations*, Unwin Hyman, London.

Steele, Jonathan, 1985, *Soviet Relations with Angola and Mozambique*, in Cassen, 1985.

Stephens, Jeanne, 1991, *The Political Economy of Transport in Mozambique: Implications for Regional development*, University of Sussex, IDS, Brighton.

Swift, Kerry, 1975, *Mozambique and the Future*, Robert Hale and Company, London.

Sørenson, Georg, 1991, *Democracy, Dictatorship and Development. Economic Development in Selected regimes of the Third World*, Macmillan, London.

— 1992, *Democracy and the Developmental State*, Institute of Political Science, Aarhus.

Tajú, Gulamo, 1990, *O projecto do engenheiro Jorge Jardim 1971–74*, Thesis, Instituto Superior Pedagógico, Departamento de História, Maputo.

— 1992, *Processos inconclusos, pendentes e presentes. Três gerações de desmobilizados a reintegrar na sociedade civil*, paper presented at the seminar 'Moçambique no Pós Guerra – Desafios a Realidades' organised by the Higher Institute for International Relations (ISRI) in Maputo 14–18 December 1992.

Tickner, Vincent, 1985, *The Agricultural Marketing System in Mozambique*, Report to SIDA, Stockholm.

Torp, Jens Erik, 1979, *Industrial Planning and Development in Mozambique*, Scandinavian Institute of African Studies, Uppsala.

UNICEF, 1988, *Children in the Frontline: The impact of apartheid, destabilization and warfare on children in Southern and South Africa*, UNICEF, New York.

Vail, L., and White, L., 1981, *Capitalism and Colonialism in Mozambique*, Heinemann, London.

Valkenier, Elisabeth, 1986, 'Revolutionary Change in the Third World: Recent Soviet Reassessments', *World Politics*, Vol. XXXVIII, No. 3, April.

Vylder de, Stefan, 1993, *Why Deficits Grow – A critical discussion of the impact of structural adjustment leaning on the external account in low-income countries*, mimeo, Stockholm.

Vines, Alex, 1991, *Renamo. Terrorism in Mozambique*, Centre for African Studies, University of York, James Currey, London.

World Bank, 1985, *Report and recommendation on a proposed IDA credit* (Report P-4100-Moz).

World Bank, 1987, *Report and recommendation on a proposed IDA credit* (Report P-4608-Moz).

World Bank, 1988, *Mozambique – Agricultural Sector Survey*, (Report 7094-Moz).

World Bank, 1989, *Report and recommendation on a proposed IDA credit* (Report P-5303-Moz).

World Bank, 1990a, *Mozambique – Restoring Rural Production and Trade, Volume I and II* (Report 8370-Moz).

World Bank, 1990b, *Economic Policy Framework 1990–92*.

World Bank, 1990c, *Poverty Reduction Framework Paper*.

World Bank, 1990d, *Mozambique – Population, Health and Nutrition Sector Report* (Report 7422-Moz).

World Bank, 1991a, *Policy Framework Paper 1991–93*.

World Bank, 1991b, *Capacity Building Policy Framework Paper*.

World Bank, 1992a, *Report and recommendation on a proposed development credit* (Report P-5775-Moz).

World Bank, 1992b, *Mozambique Counterpart Funds Management*.

World Bank, 1992c, *Status report for Mozambique*.

World Bank, 1993a, *Transition from Emergency to Sustainable Growth*.

World Bank, 1993b, *Aid – Improving its effectiveness*.

World Bank, 1993c, *From emergency to sustainable development*.

Wuyts, Marc, 1978, *Peasants and Rural Economy in Moçambique*, Centro de Estudos Africanos, Maputo.

— 1989, *Money and Planning for Socialist Transition*, Gower, Aldershot.

Zacarias, Agostinho, ed., 1991, *Repensando Sobre Moçambique e Africa Austral*, Instituto Superior de Relações Internacionais, Maputo.

Index

Southern Africa, 42; subsidised oil
from, 135
United Nations, 39, 43, 66, 110, 131;
agencies, 99, 108, 145; Children's
Fund (UNICEF), 66, 128, 133;
Development Programme
(UNDP), 132–3; first development
decade, 34–5; Security Council,
109; World Food Programme, 100
United States of America (USA):
black civil rights, 44; cancelled
aid, 45; Congress, 33, 42, 44, 99,
107–8; denial of emergency aid,
99–100; food aid, 102, 140; interest
rates, 105; isolationist groups, 32;
nuclear technology, guidance to
South Africa, 109; State
Department, 101; transnational
companies, 38; ultra-conservative
circles, 63
USAID, 141

vaccination programme, 48
Vietnam, American defeat, 37–8, 225
Vilanculos, Artur, 62
Vorster, John, 8, 42, 44, 108, 225,
228; detente policy, 39–41

wages, 54
warlords, 189
water: access, 219; provision, 36, 129,
118
Wells, Melissa, 107
western capitalism, 28
white colonisers, flight from
Mozambique, 27, 52
'Wild West' capitalism, 156, 158
World Bank, 33, 101, 106, 110–13,
128, 131, 133–5, 138–40, 148, 150,
160, 162–3, 211, 215–17, 231;

Young, Andrew, 38

Zambezia province, 25, 66, 194
Zambia, 72
ZANZA House, 62
Zimbabwe, 15, 38, 72, 120, 195, 228;
independence, 45, 59, 102–3
Zimbabwe African National Union
(ZANU), 1, 43, 45, 59, 227
Zimbabwe African People's Union
(ZAPU), 1
Zimbabwean National Liberation
Union (ZANLA), 60, 95–6

DATE DUE

DEC 2 3 2004 · APR 2 8 2006